FIRST AN

"Donald A. Wollheim was first in the field and he still manages to beat his competitors to the draw each year. As usual, his pick of the best makes for a satisfying anthology."

So wrote one reviewer and in very similar words so wrote dozens of other reviewers in newspapers and magazines all over the world.

The 1977 Annual upholds their confidence.

Here are the stories that will spark the imagination as no others . . . tales that span all space and all time, by:

BRIAN W. ALDISS

BARRINGTON J. BAYLEY

LESTER DEL REY

JOHN VARLEY

ISAAC ASIMOV

and more. . . .

Anthologies from DAW

THE 1977 ANNUAL WORLD'S BEST SF

Edited by

DONALD A. WOLLHEIM

with Arthur W. Saha

DAW BOOKS, INC.

DONALD A. WOLLHEIM, PUBLISHER

1301 Avenue of the Americas
New York, N. Y.   10019

Table of Contents

INTRODUCTION

By all acounts, 1976 must be considered a good year for science fiction—in fact a boom year. Optimists consider that this state of affairs may well be permanent, with 1977 and the years following proving that science fiction has at last achieved its rightful place as a branch of the world stream of literature. Fantastic projections, imaginary voyages, and science-fiction-based adventures have always been elements in human storytelling; why then should this not be taken for granted?

Certainly the past year saw most major paperback publishers and a few hardbound ones adding sf books as regular items in their lists. In fact, reports of astonishingly high bidding for certain novels and evidence of advances paid to authors far in excess of previous records give verification to the belief in science fiction held by publishers and editors not previously well acquainted with the field.

This all sounds very encouraging, but it bears closer scrutiny. Lester Del Rey, writing in *Analog*'s January 1977 issue, warns of a "boom and bust" cycle, such as has happened before in the sf field—particularly where magazines were concerned. As he points out there is a great amount of activity, new magazines are projected, increases are in prospect for publishers' lists, and "a lot of the activity is being shown by people who haven't the faintest idea of what science fiction is all about."

Del Rey then points out that if all these projects fail to make good the finance and labor behind them, then the blame is not put on the fact that the selections were unwise or the amounts paid economically unsound; the blame is put on the genre itself. Consequently publishers pull out, cut their losses, announce that science fiction was "just a fad" and they should have ignored it. Other publishers, actually doing profitably, hear this, and, being only human, panic and reduce their buying themselves—and the bust is on.

How probable is all this? Well, we are forced to say that there is evidence that points both ways. Science fiction has been good for publishers so far; it should continue profitably if nobody overdoes it, if the market is not flooded beyond the real purchasing and reading capacity of its audience, if not too much avant-garde junk is overpraised and not too much simplistic trash is overproduced.

If we examine the situation of the science fiction magazines, we may be able to obtain some meaningful data. *Analog*, the strongest and bestselling sf monthly, has had approximately the same circulation figures for over a decade. It sells about 110,000 copies a month, give or take a few thousand, and it has *not* climbed with the alleged "boom." Now the magazine has had to announce a raise in its price to cover inflated printing and paper costs (as has been true of all publishing). Its one-time closest competitor, *Galaxy*, is not doing well, is hanging on virtually on an issue to issue basis and has not reflected any "boom." *Amazing* and *Fantastic* continue to survive by the skin of their teeth. *Fantasy and Science Fiction* remains, like *Analog*, just where it has been in sales figures for years—and it also faces rising costs.

A new magazine, *Odyssey*, died after two issues, blaming poor distribution. Another magazine, *Galileo*, is trying to survive on subscriptions alone. The British *Science Fiction Monthly* discontinued in 1976 and has not been replaced. It was an odd sort of periodical but the reports of its first year's sales were quite encouraging. Yet 1977 is to see at least two major efforts to produce viable new sf periodicals, both edited and published by people who ought to know what it is all about. One wonders at the contradictions here—if existing magazines are in a holding pattern, why should new magazines find any demand? Yet publishing is not an exact science—they may ride in on a boom whose existence is yet unproven.

A very well financed effort to produce a line of paperback books catering to those with no previous knowledge of science fiction and seeking to stylize the field in a manner successful in the light romantic category has finally shut down. The failure can be attributed to a complete misunderstanding of the special appeal of science fiction and the nature of its addictive readers. Nobody "in the know" ever believed this venture would succeed. Nonetheless this sort of news can have a cautionary and even panicky effect on observers, booksellers, and disinterested publishers. In spite of Del Ray's wise words of caution, yet another attempt has been announced for 1977 to flood the field and take advantage of the alleged "boom." Only this time the imprint will utilize books from a major of publisher's backlist augmented with new titles by capable writers.

So it would seem that the "boom" continues. . . .

As far as fan and reader activity is concerned, there are no doubts. Conventions are being held on almost a weekly basis. The major ones are still getting record crowds and though admission costs are high, attendees are not deterred. In the field of fan publishing, more and more semi-professionals are producing limited hardbound editions with beautiful color plates, charging very high prices, and getting them.

Abroad, the situation is mixed. In England, many publishers are becoming cautious. In France there is still a strong market. In Germany hardbound sf is now almost non-existent, but paperbacks and magazine-type publications still thrive. In Italy there is a rising tide, with many companies vying for what appears to be a growing market.

The first international sf convention held on the other side of the "Wall" came off in Poland in August and is accounted successful, although pedantic, The first special conference of professionals—writers and editors, translators and publishers—was held in Dublin with the promise of more to come. A world organization of sf professionals has been projected and should come into existence soon.

Beside the prolific number of conventions there is a great increase in the number of awards being presented for "bests." Along with the Hugo and Nebula awards, there may now be a dozen or more such given by various conventions and committees.

So we enter 1977 with both optimism and pessimism. As for this anthology, we think that it is a good one—and the only trend we can note is that towards nostalgia. There's a certain amount of mood feeling as to how we got that way, where we were, and why we continue to feed our imaginations on fantasy and speculation.

Donald A. Wollheim

APPEARANCE OF LIFE

by Brian W. Aldiss

For the past few years Brian W. Aldiss has been writing exquisite short stories which baffle the comprehension. He seems to have been interested in utilizing his own high talent for experimental ventures in literary coloration and poetic theme along the margins of the sf sphere. It was therefore a really pleasant surprise to find that he has turned out a story which is clearly and truly science fiction, which has quite an original premise, and which nevertheless continues to display his great stylistic skill.

Something very large, something very small: a galactic museum, a dead love affair. They came together under my gaze.

The museum is very large. Less than a thousand light years from Earth, countless worlds bear constructions which are formidably ancient and inscrutable in purpose. The museum on Norma is such a construction.

We suppose that the museum was created by a species which once lorded it over the galaxy, the Korlevalulaw. The spectre of the Korlevalulaw has become part of the consciousness of the human race as it spreads from star-system to star-system. Sometimes the Korlevalulaw are pictured as demons, hiding somewhere in a dark nebula, awaiting the moment when they swoop down on mankind and wipe every last one of us out, in reprisal for having dared to invade their territory. Sometimes the Korlevalulaw are pictured as gods, riding with the awfulness and loneliness of gods through the deserts of space, potent and wise beyond our imagining.

These two opposed images of the Korlevalulaw are of course images emerging from the deepest pools of the human mind. The demon and the god remain with us still.

But there were Korlevalulaw, and there are facts we know about them. We know that they abandoned the written word by the time they reached their galactic-building phase. Their very name comes down to us from the single example of their alphabet we have, a sign emblazoned across the façade of a construction on Lacarja. We know that they were inhuman. Not only does the scale of their constructions imply as much; they built always on planets inimical to man.

What we do not know is what became of the Korlevalulaw. They must have reigned so long, they must have been so invincible to all but Time.

Where knowledge cannot go, imagination ventures. Men have supposed that the Korlevalulaw committed some kind of racial suicide. Or that they became a race divided, and totally annihilated themselves in a region of space beyond our galaxy, beyond the reach of mankind's starships.

And there are more metaphysical speculations concerning the fate of the Korlevalulaw. Moved by evolutionary necessity, they may have grown beyond the organic; in which case, it may be that they still inhabit their ancient constructions, undetected by man. There is a stranger theory which places emphasis on Mind identifiable with Cosmos, and supposes that once a species begins to place credence in the idea of occupying the galaxy, then so it is bound to do, this is what mankind has done, virtually imagining its illustrious predecessors out of existence.

Well, there are many theories, but I was intending to talk about the museum on Norma.

Like everything else, Norma possesses its riddles.

The museum demarcates Norma's equator. The construction takes the form of a colossal belt girdling the planet, some sixteen thousand kilometres in length. The belt varies curiously in thickness, from twelve kilometres to over twenty-two.

The chief riddle about Norma is this: is its topographical conformation what it always was, or are its peculiarities due to the meddling of the Korlevalulaw? For the construction neatly divides the planet into a northern land hemisphere and a southern oceanic hemisphere. On one side lies an endless territory of cratered plain, scoured by winds and bluish snow. On the other side writhes a formidable ocean of ammonia, unbroken by islands, inhabited by firefish and other mysterious denizens.

On one of the widest sections of the Korlevalulaw construction stands an incongruous huddle of buildings. Coming in from space, you are glad to see the huddle. Your ship takes you down, you catch your elevator, you emerge on the roof of the construction itself, and you rejoice that—in the midst of the inscrutable symmetrical universe (of which the Korlevalulaw formed a not inconsiderable part)—mankind has established an untidy foothold.

For a moment I paused by the ship, taking in the immensity about me. A purple sun was rising amid cloud, making shadows race across the infinite-seeming plane on which I stood. The distant sea pounded and moaned, lost to my vision. It was a solitary spot, but I was accustomed to solitude—on the planet I called home, I hardly met with another human from one year's end to the next, except on my visits to the Breeding Centre.

The human-formed buildings on Norma stand over one of the enormous entrances to the museum. They consist of a hotel for visitors, various office blocks, cargo-handling equipment, and gigantic transmitters—the walls of the museum are impervious to the electromagnetic spectrum, so that any information from inside the construction comes by cable through the entrance, and is then transmitted by second-space to other parts of the galaxy.

'Seeker, you are expected. Welcome to the Norma Museum.'

So said the android who showed me into the airlock and guided me through into the hotel. Here as elsewhere, androids occupied all menial posts. I glanced at the calendar clock in the foyer, punching my wrisputer like all arriving travellers to discover where in time Earth might be now.

Gently sedated by alpha-music, I slept away my light-lag, and descended next day to the museum itself.

The museum was run by twenty human staff, all female. The Director gave me all the information that a Seeker might need, helped me to select a viewing vehicle, and left me to move off into the museum on my own.

Although we had many ways of growing unimolecular metals, the Korlevalulaw construction on Norma was of an incomprehensible material. It had no joint or seam in its entire length. More, it somehow imprisoned or emanated light, so that no artificial light was needed within.

Beyond that, it was empty. The entire place was equatorially empty. Only mankind, taking it over a thousand years before, had turned it into a museum and started to fill it with galactic lumber.

As I moved forward in my vehicle, I was not overcome by the idea of infinity, as I had expected. A tendency towards infinity has presumably dwelt in the minds of mankind ever since our early ancestors counted up to ten on their fingers. The habitation of the void has increased that tendency. The happiness which we experience as a species is of recent origin, achieved since our maturity; it also contributes to a disposition to neglect any worries in the present in order to concentrate on distant goals. But I believe—this is a personal opinion—that this same tendency towards infinity in all its forms has militated against close relationships between individuals. We do not even love as our planet-bound ancestors did; we live apart as they did not.

In the summer, a quality of the light mitigated any intimations of infinity. I knew I was in an immense enclosed space; but, since the light absolved me from any sensations of clausagrophobia, I will not attempt to describe that vastness.

Over the previous ten centuries, several thousand hectares had been occupied with human accretions. Androids worked perpetually, arranging exhibits. The exhibits were scanned by electronic means, so that anyone on any civilised planet, dialing the museum, might obtain by second-space a three-dimensional image of the required object in his room.

I travelled almost at random through the displays.

To qualify as a Seeker, it was necessary to show a high serendipity factor. In my experimental behaviour pool as a child, I had exhibited such a factor, and had been selected for special training forthwith. I had taken additional courses in Philosophical, Alpha-humerals, Incidental Tetrachotomy, Apunctual Synchonicity, Homoontogenesis, and other subjects, ultimately qualifying as a Prime Esemplastic Seeker. In other words, I put two and two together in situations where

other people were not thinking about addition. I connected. I
made wholes greater than parts.

Mine was an invaluable profession in a cosmos increasingly full of parts.

I had come to the museum with a sheaf of assignments
from numerous institutions, universities, and individuals all
over the galaxy. Every assignment required my special talent—a capacity beyond holography. Let me give one example. The Audile Academy of the University of Paddin on the
planet Rufadote was working on an hypothesis that, over the
millennia, human voices were gradually generating fewer
phons or, in other words, becoming quieter. Any evidence I
could collect in the museum concerning this hypothesis would
be welcome. The Academy could scan the whole museum by
remote holography; yet only to a rare physical visitor like me
was a gestalt view of the contents possible; and only to a
Seeker would a significant juxtapositioning be noted.

My car took me slowly through the exhibits. There were
nourishment machines at intervals throughout the museum, so
that I did not need to leave the establishment. I slept in my
vehicle; it was comfortably provided with bunks.

On the second day, I spoke idly to a nearby android before
beginning my morning drive.

'Do you enjoy ordering the exhibits here?'

'I could never tire of it.' She smiled pleasantly at me.

'You find it interesting?'

'It's endlessly interesting. The quest for pattern is a basic
instinct.'

'Do you always work in this section?'

'No. But this is one of my favourite sections. As you have
probably observed, here we classify extinct diseases—or diseases which would be extinct if they were not preserved in
the museum. I find the micro-organism beautiful.'

'You are kept busy?'

'Certainly. New exhibits arrive every month. From the
largest to the smallest, everything can be stored here. May I
show you anything?'

'Not at present. How long before the entire museum if
filled?'

'In fifteen and a half millennia, at current rate of intake.'

'Have you entered the empty part of the museum?'

'I have stood on the fringes of emptiness. It is an alarming
sensation. I prefer to occupy myself with the works of man.'

'That is only proper.'

I drove away, meditating on the limitations of android thinking. Those limitations had been carefully imposed by mankind; the androids were not aware of them. To an android, the android umwelt or conceptual universe is apparently limitless. It makes for their happiness, just as our umwelt makes for our happiness.

As the days passed, I came across many juxtapositions and objects which would assist clients. I noted them all in my wrisputer.

On the fifth day, I was examining the section devoted to ships and objects preserved from the earliest days of galactic travel.

Many of the items touched me with emotion—an emotion chiefly composed of nosthedony, the pleasure of returning to the past. For in many of the items I saw reflected a time when human life was different, perhaps less secure, certainly less austere.

That First Galactic Era, when men—often accompanied by 'wives' and 'mistresses', to use the old terms for love-partners—had ventured distantly in primitive machines, marked the beginning of the time when the human pair-bond weakened and humanity rose towards maturity.

I stepped into an early spaceship, built before second-space had been discovered. Its scale was diminutive. With shoulders bent, I moved along its brief corridors into what had been a relaxation room for the five-person crew. The metal was old-fashioned refined; it might almost have been wood. The furniture, such as it was, seemed scarcely designed for human frames. The mode aimed at an illusionary functionalism. And yet, still preserved in the air, were attributes I recognised as human: perseverance, courage, hope. The five people who had once lived here were kin with me.

The ship had died in vacuum of a defective recycling plant—their micro-encapsulation techniques had not included the implantation of oxygen in the corpuscles of the blood never mind the genetosurgery needed to make that implantation hereditary. All the equipment and furnishings lay as they had done aeons before, when the defect occurred.

Rifling through some personal lockers, I discovered a thin band made of the antique metal, gold. On the inside of it was a small but clumsily executed inscription in ancient script. I balanced it on the tip of my thumb and considered its function. Was it an early contraceptive device?

At my shoulder was a museum eye. Activating it, I requested the official catalogue to describe the object I held.

The reply was immediate. 'You are holding a ring which slipped on to the finger of a human being when our species was of smaller stature than today,' said the catalogue. 'Like the spaceship, the ring dates from the First Galactic Era, but is thought to be somewhat older than the ship. The dating tallies with what we know of the function—largely symbolic— of the ring. It was worn to indicate married status in a woman or man. This particular ring may have been an hereditary possession. In those days, marriages were expected to last until progeny were born, or even until death. The human biomass was then divided fifty-fifty between males and females, in dramatic contrast to the ten-to-one preponderance of females in our stellar societies. Hence the idea of coupling for life was not so illogical as it sounds. However, the ring itself must be regarded as a harmless illogic, designed merely to express a bondage or linkage—'

I broke the connection.

A wedding ring . . . It represented symbolic communication. As such, it would be of value to a professor studying the metamorphoses of nonverbality who was employing my services.

A wedding ring . . . A closed circuit of love and thought.

I wondered if this particular marriage had ended for both the partners on this ship. The items preserved did not answer my question. But I found a flat photograph, encased in plastic windows, of a man and a woman together in outdoor surroundings. They smiled at the apparatus recording them. Their eyes were flat, betokening their undeveloped cranial reserves, yet they were not attractive. I observed that they stood closer together than we would normally care to do.

Could that be something to do with the limitations of the apparatus photographing them? Or had there been a change in the social convention of closeness? Was there a connection here with the decibel-output of the human voice which might interest my clients of the Audile Academy? Possibly our auditory equipment was more subtle than that of our ancestors when they were confined to one planet under heavy atmospheric pressure. I filed the details away for future reference.

A fellow-Seeker had told me jokingly that the secret of the

universe was locked away in the museum if only I could find it.

'We'll stand a better chance of that when the museum is complete,' I told her.

'No,' she said. 'The secret will then be too deeply buried. We shall merely have transferred the outside universe to inside the Korlevalulaw construction. You'd better find it now or never.'

'The idea that there may be a secret or key to the universe is in any case a construct of the human mind.'

'Or of the mind that built the human mind,' she said.

That night, I slept in the section of early galactic travel and continued my researches there on the sixth day.

I felt a curious excitement, over and above nosthedony and simply antiquarian interest. My senses were alert.

I drove among twenty great ships belonging to the Second Galactic Era. The longest was over five kilometres in length and had housed many scores of woman and men in its day. This had been the epoch when our kind had attempted to establish empires in space and extend primitive national or territorial obsessions across many light-years. The facts of relativity had doomed such efforts from the start; under the immensities of space-time, they were put away as childish things. It was no paradox to say that, among interstellar distances, mankind had become more at home with itself.

Although I did not enter these behemoths, I remained among them, sampling the brutal way in which militaristic technologies expressed themselves in metal. Such excesses would never recur.

Beyond the behemoths, androids were arranging fresh exhibits. The exhibits slid along in transporters far overhead, conveyed silently from the museum entrance, to be lowered where needed. Drawing closer to where the new arrivals were being unloaded, I passed among an array of shelves.

On the shelves lay items retrieved from colonial homes or ships of the quasi-imperial days. I marvelled at the collection. As people had proliferated, so had objects. A concern with possession had been a priority during the immaturity of the species. These long-dead people had seemingly thought of little else but possession in one form or another; yet like androids in similar circumstances, they could not have recognised the limitations of their own umwelt.

Among the muddle, a featureless cube caught my eye. Its sides were smooth and silvered. I picked it up and turned it over. On one side was a small depression. I touched the depression with my finger.

Slowly, the sides of the cube clarified and a young woman's head appeared three-dimensionally inside them. The head was upside down. The eyes regarded me.

'You are not Chris Mailer,' she said. 'I talk only to my husband. Switch off and set me right way up.'

'Your "husband" died sixty-five thousand years ago,' I said. But I set her cube down on the shelf, not unmoved by being addressed by an image from the remote past. That it possessed environmental reflexion made it all the more impressive.

I asked the museum catalogue about the item.

'In the jargon of the time, it is a "holocap",' said the catalogue. 'Its is a hologrammed image of a real woman, with a facsimile of her brain implanted on a collapsed germanium-alloy core. It generates an appearance of life. Do you require the technical specifics?'

'No. I want its provenance.'

'It was taken from a small armed spaceship, a scout, built in the two hundred and first year of the Second Era. The scout was partially destroyed by a bomb from the planet Scundra. All aboard were killed but the ship went into orbit about Scundra. Do you require details of the engagement?'

'No. Do we know who the woman is?'

'These shelves are recent acquisitions and have only just been catalogued. Other Scundra acquisitions are still arriving. We may find more data at a later date. The cube itself has not been properly examined. It was sensitised to respond only to the cerebral emissions of the woman's husband. Such holocaps were popular with the Second Era woman and men on stellar flights. They provided life-mimicking mementoes of partners elsewhere in the cosmos. For further details you may—'

'That's sufficient.'

I worked my way forward, but with increasing lack of attention to the objects around me. When I came to where the unloading was taking place, I halted my vehicle.

As the carrier-platforms sailed down from the roof, unwearying androids unloaded them, putting the goods in their translucent wraps into nearby lockers. Larger items were handled by crane.

'This material is from Scundra?' I asked the catalogue.

'Correct. You wish to know the history of the planet?'

'It is an agricultural planet, isn't it?'

'Correct. Entirely agricultural, entirely automated. No humans go down to the surface. It was claimed originally by Soviet India and its colonists were mainly, although not entirely, of Indian stock. A war broke out with the nearby planets of the Pan-Slav Union. Are these nationalist terms familiar to you?'

'How did this foolish "war" end?'

'The Union sent a battleship to Scundra. Once in orbit, it demanded certain concessions which the Indians were unable or unwilling to make. The battleship sent a scoutship down to the planet to negotiate a settlement. The settlement was reached but, as the scout ship re-entered space and was about to enter its mother-ship, it blew up. A party of Scundran extremists had planted a bomb in it. You examined an item preserved from the scoutship yesterday, and today you drove past the battleship concerned.

'In retaliation for the bomb, the Pan-Slavs dusted the planet with Panthrax K, a disease which wiped out all human life on the planet in a matter of weeks. The bacillus of Panthrax K was notoriously difficult to contain, and the battleship itself became infected. The entire crew died. Scout, ship, and planet remained incommunicado for many centuries. Needless to say, there is no danger of infection now. All precautions have been taken.'

The catalogue's brief history plunged me into mediation.

I thought about the Scundra incident, now so unimportant. The wiping out of a whole world full of people—evidence again of that lust for possession which had by now relinquished its grip on the human soul. Or was the museum itself an indication that traces of the lust remained, now intellectualised into a wish to possess, not merely objects, but the entire past of mankind and, indeed, what my friend had jokingly referred to as 'the secret of the universe'? I told myself then that cause and effect operated only arbitrarily on the level of the psyche; that lust to possess could itself create a secret to be found, as a hunt provides its own quarry. And if once found? Then the whole complex of human affairs might be unravelled beneath the spell of one gigantic simplification, until motivation was so lowered that life would lose its purport; whereupon our species would wither and die, all tasks fulfilled. Such indeed could have happened to the unassailable Korlevalulaw.

To what extent the inorganic and the organic universe were unity could not be determined until ultimate heat-death brought parity. But it was feasible to suppose that each existed for the other, albeit hierarchically. Organic systems with intelligence might achieve unity—union—with the encompassing universe through knowledge, through the possession of that 'secret' of which my friend joked. That union would represent a peak, a flowering. Beyond it lay only decline, a metaphysical correspondence to the second law of thermodynamics!

Breaking from this chain of reasoning, I realised two things immediately: firstly, that I was well into my serendipitous Seeker phase, and, secondly, that I was about to take from an android's hands an item he was unloading from the carrier-platform.

As I unwrapped it from its translucent covering, the catalogue said, 'The object you hold was retrieved from the capital city of Scundra. It was found in the apartment of a married couple named Jean and Lan Gopal. Other objects are arriving from the same source. Do not misplace it or our assistants will be confused.'

It was a 'holocap' like the one I had examined the day before. Perhaps it was a more sophisticated example. The casing was better turned, the button so well concealed that I found it almost by accident. Moreover, the cube lit immediately, and the illusion that I was holding a man's head in my hands was strong.

The man looked about, caught my eye, and said, 'This holocap is intended only for my ex-wife, Jean Gopal. I have no business with you. Switch off and be good enough to return me to Jean. This is Chris Mailer.'

The image died. I held only a cube in my hands.

In my mind questions flowered.

Sixty-five thousand years ago . . .

I pressed the switch again. Eyeing me straight, he said in unchanged tones, 'This holocap is intended only for my ex-wife, Jean Gopal. I have no business with you. Switch off and be good enough to return me to Jean. This is Chris Mailer.'

Certainly it was all that was left of Chris Mailer. His face made a powerful impression. His features were generous, with high forehead, long nose, powerful chin. His grey eyes were wide-set, his mouth ample but firm. He had a neat beard, brown and streaked with grey. About the temples his hair also carried streaks of grey. His face was unlined and generally alert, although not without melancholy. I resurrected him up from the electronic distances and made him go through his piece again.

'Now I shall unite you with your ex-wife,' I said.

As I loaded the holocap into my vehicle and headed back towards the cache of the day before, I knew that my trained talent was with me, leading me.

There was a coincidence and a contradiction here—or seemed to be, for both coincidences and contradictions are more apparent than real. It was no very strange thing that I should come upon the woman's holocap one day and the man's the next. Both were being unloaded from the same planetary area, brought to the museum in the same operation. The contradiction was more interesting. The woman had said that she spoke only to her husband, the man that he spoke only to his ex-wife; was there a second woman involved?

I recalled that the woman, Jean, had seemed young, whereas the man, Mailer, was past the flush of youth. The woman had been on the planet, Scundra, whereas Mailer had been in the scoutship. They had been on opposing sides in that 'war' which ended in death for all.

How the situation had arisen appeared inexplicable after six hundred and fifty centuries. Yet as long as there remained power in the submolecular structure of the holocap cells, the chance existed that this insignificant fragment of the past could be reconstructed.

Not that I knew whether two holocaps could converse together.

I stood the two cubes on the same shelf, a metre apart. I switched them on.

The images of two heads were reborn. They looked about them as if alive.

Mailer spoke first staring intensely across the shelf at the female head.

'Jean, my darling, it's Chris, speaking to you after all this long time. I hardly know whether I ought to, but I must. Do you recognise me?'

Although Jean's image was of a woman considerably

younger than his, it was less brilliant, more grainy, captured by an inferior piece of holocapry.

'Chris, I'm your wife, your little Jean. This is for you wherever you are. I know we have our troubles but ... I was never able to say this when we were together, Chris, but I do love our marriage—it means a lot to me, and I want it to go on. I send you love wherever you are. I think about you a lot. You said—well, you know what you said, but I hope you still care. I want you to care, because I do care for you.'

'It's over a dozen years since we parted, my darling Jean,' Mailer said. 'I know I broke up the marriage in the end, but I was younger then, and foolish. Even at the time, a part of me warned that I was making a mistake. I pretended that I knew you didn't care for me. You cared all the time, didn't you?'

'Not only do I care, but I will try to show more of my inner feelings in future. Perhaps I understand you better now. I know I've not been as responsive as I might be, in several ways.'

I stood fascinated and baffled by this dialogue, which carried all sorts of overtones beyond my comprehension. I was listening to the conversation of primitive beings. The image of her face had vivacity; indeed, apart from the flat eyes and an excess of hair she passed for pretty, with a voluptuous mouth and wide eyes—but to think she took it for granted that she might have a man for her own possession, while he acted under similar assumptions! Whereas Mailer's mode of speech was slow and thoughtful, but without hesitation, Jean talked fast, moving her head about, hesitating and interrupting herself as she spoke.

He said, 'You don't know what it is like to live with regret. At least, I hope you don't, my dear. You never understood regret and all its ramifications as I do. I remember I called you superficial once, just before we broke up. That was because you were content to live in the present; the past or the future meant nothing to you. It was something I could not comprehend at the time, simply because for me both past and future are always with me. You never made reference to things past, whether happy or sad, and I couldn't stand that. Fancy, I let such a little matter come between our love! There was your affair with Gopal, too. That hurt me and, forgive me, that fact that he was black added salt in my wound. But even there I should have taken more of the blame. I was more arrogant then than I am now, Jean.'

'I'm not much good at going over what has been, as you know,' she said. 'I live each day as it comes. But the entanglement with Lan Gopal—well, I admit I was attracted to him—you know he went for me and I couldn't resist—not that I'm exactly blaming Lan . . . He was very sweet, but I want you to know that that's all over now, really over. I'm happy again. We belong to each other.'

'I still feel what I always did, Jean. You must have been married to Gopal for ten years now. Perhaps you've forgotten me, perhaps this holocap won't be welcome.'

As I stood there, compelled to listen, the two images stared raptly at each other, conversing without communicating.

'We think differently—in different ways, I mean,' Jean said, glancing downwards. 'You can explain better—you were always the intellectual. I know you despise me because I'm not clever, don't you? You used to say we had non-verbal communication . . . I don't quite know what to say. Except that I was sad to see you leave on another trip, going off hurt and angry, and I wished—oh well, as you see, your poor wife is trying to make up for her deficiencies by sending you this holocap. It comes with love, dear Chris, hoping—oh, everything—that you'll come back here to me on Earth, and that things will be as they used to be between us. We do belong to each other and I haven't forgotten.'

During this speech, she became increasingly agitated.

'I know you don't want me back, Jean,' Mailer said. 'Nobody can turn back time. But I had to get in touch with you when the chance came. You gave me a holocap fifteen years ago and I've had it with me on my travels ever since. When our divorce came through, I joined a fleet of space-mercenaries. Now we're fighting for the Pan-Slavs. I've just learnt that we're coming to Scundra, although not with the best of motives. So I'm having this holocap made, trusting there'll be a chance to deliver it to you. The message is simple really— I forgive anything you may think there is to forgive. After all these years, you still mean a lot to me, Jean, though I'm less than nothing to you.'

'Chris, I'm your wife, your little Jean. This is for you wherever you are. I know we have our troubles but ... I was never able to say this when we were together, Chris, but I do love our marriage—it means a lot to me, and I want it to go on.'

'It's a strange thing that I come as an enemy to what is

now, I suppose, your home planet since you married Gopal. I always knew that bastard was no good, worming his way in between us. Tell him I bear him no malice, as long as he's taking care of you, whatever else he does.'

She said: 'I sent you love wherever you are. I think about you a lot . . .'

'I hope he's made you forget all about me. He owes me that. You and I were once all in all to each other, and life's never been as happy for me again, whatever I pretend to others.'

'You said—well, you know what you said, but I hope you still care. I want you to care, because I do care for you . . . Not only do I care, but I will try to show more of my inner feelings in future. Perhaps I understand you better now.'

'Jean, my darling, it's Chris, speaking to you after all this long time. I hardly know whether I ought to, but I must.'

I turned away. At least I understood. Only the imcomprehensible things of which the images spoke had concealed the truth from me for so long.

/ The images could converse, triggered by pauses in each other's monologues. But what they had to say had been programmed before they met. Each had a role to play and was unable to transcend it by a hairbreadth. No matter what the other image might say, they could not reach beyond what was predetermined. The female, with less to say than the male, had run out of talk first and simply begun her chatter over again.

Jean's holocap had been made some fifteen years before Mailer's. She was talking from a time when they were still married, he from a time some years after their divorce. Their images spoke completely at odds—there had never been a dialogue between them . . .

These trivial resolutions passed through my mind and were gone.

Greater things occupied me.

Second Era man had passed, with all his bustling possessive affairs.

The godly Korlevalulaw too had passed away. Or so we thought. We were surrounded by their creations, but of the Korlevalulaw themselves there was not a sign.

We could no more see a sign of them than Jean and

Mailer could see a sign of me, although they had responded in their own way . . .

My function as a Prime Emplastic Seeker was more than fulfilled. I had made an ultimate whole greater than the parts. I had found what my joking friend called 'the secret of the universe'.

Like the images I had observed, the galactic human race was merely a projection. The Korlevalulaw had created us— not as a genuine creation with free will, but as some sort of a reproduction.

There would never be proof of that, only intuition. I had learned to trust my intuition. As with those imprisoned images, the human species was gradually growing fainter, less able to hear the programmed responses. As with those imprisoned images, we were all drifting further apart, losing definition. As with those imprisoned images, we were doomed to root through the debris of the past, because copies can have no creative future.

Here was my one gigantic simplification, here my union with the encompassing universe! This was the flowering before the decline.

No, my idea was nonsense! A fit had seized me! My deductions were utterly unfounded. I knew there was no ultimate 'secret of the universe'—and in any case, supposing humanity to be merely a construct of the Korlevalulaw: who then 'constructed' the Korlevalulaw? The prime question was merely set back one step.

But for every level of existence there is a key to its central enigma. Those keys enable life-forms to ascend the scale of life or to reach an impasse—to flourish or to become extinct.

I had found a key which would cause the human species to wither and die. Ours was merely an umwelt, not a universe.

I left the museum. I flew my ship away from Norma. I did not head back to my home world. I went instead to a desolate world on which I now intend to end my days, communicating with no one. Let them assume that I caught a personal blight instead of detecting a universal one. If I communicate, the chance is that the dissolution I feel within me will spread.

And spread for ever.

Such was my mental agony that only when I reached this

barren habitation did I recall what I neglected to do in the museum. I forgot to switch off the holocaps.

There they may remain, conducting their endless conversation, until power dies. Only then will the two talking heads sink into blessed nothingness and be gone.

Sound will fade, images die, silence remain.

OVERDRAWN AT THE MEMORY BANK

by John Varley

The author of this one is the fastest rising star of the new batch of magazine sf writers. And, as this story of the computerized future shows, he packs originality and skill into his tales.

It was schoolday at the Kenya disneyland. Five nine-year-olds were being shown around the medico section where Fingal lay on the recording table, the top of his skull removed, looking up into a mirror. Fingal was in a bad mood (hence the trip to the disneyland) and could have done without the children. Their teacher was doing his best, but who can control five nine-year-olds?

"What's the big green wire do, teacher?" asked a little girl, reaching out one grubby hand and touching Fingal's brain where the main recording wire clamped to the built-in terminal.

"Lupus, I told you you weren't to touch anything. And look at you, you didn't wash your hands." The teacher took the child's hand and pulled it away.

"But what does it matter? You told us yesterday that the reason no one cares about dirt like they used to is dirt isn't dirty anymore."

"I'm sure I didn't tell you exactly *that*. What I said was that when humans were forced off Earth, we took the golden opportunity to wipe out all harmful germs. When there were

28

only three thousand people alive on the moon after the Occupation it was easy for us to sterilize everything. So the medico doesn't need to wear gloves like surgeons used to, or even wash her hands. There's no danger of infection. But it isn't polite. We don't want this man to think we're being impolite to him, just because his nervous system is disconnected and he can't do anything about it, do we?"

"No, teacher."

"What's a surgeon?"

"What's 'infection'?"

Fingal wished the little perishers had chosen another day for their lessons, but like the teacher had said, there was very little he could do. The medico had turned his motor control over to the computer while she took the reading. He was paralyzed. He eyed the little boy carrying the carved stick, and hoped he didn't get a notion to poke him in the cerebrum with it. Fingal was insured, but who needs the trouble?

"All of you stand back a little so the medico can do her work. That's better. Now, who can tell me what the big green wire is? Destry?"

Destry allowed as how he didn't know, didn't care, and wished he could get out of here and play spat ball. The teacher dismissed him and went on with the others.

"The green wire is the main sounding electrode," the teacher said. "It's attached to a series of very fine wires in the man's head, like the ones you have, which are implanted at birth. Can anyone tell me how the recording is made?"

The little girl with the dirty hands spoke up.

"By tying knots in string."

The teacher laughed, but the medico didn't. She had heard it all before. So had the teacher, of course, but that was why he was a teacher. He had the patience to deal with children, a rare quality now that there were so few of them.

"No, that was just an analogy. Can you all say analogy?"

"*Analogy*," they chorused.

"Fine. What I told you is that the chains of FPNA are very much *like* strings with knots tied in them. If you make up a code with every millimeter and every knot having a meaning, you could write words in string by tying knots in it. That's what the machine does with the FPNA. Now ... can anyone tell me what FPNA stands for?"

"Ferro-Photo-Nucleic Acid," said the girl, who seemed to be the star pupil.

"That's right, Lupus. It's a variant on DNA, and it can be knotted by magnetic fields and light, and made to go through chemical changes. What the medico is doing now is threading long strings of FPNA into the tiny tubes that are in the man's brain. When she's done, she'll switch on the machine and the current will start tying knots. And what happens then?"

"All his memories go into the memory cube," said Lupus.

"That's right. But it's a little more complicated than that. You remember what I told you about a divided cipher? The kind that has two parts, neither of which is any good without the other? Imagine two of the strings, each with a lot of knots in them. Well, you try to read one of them with your decoder, and you find out that it doesn't make sense. That's because whoever wrote it used two strings, with knots tied in different places. They only make sense when you put them side-by-side and read them that way. That's how this decoder works, but the medico uses twenty-five strings. When they're all knotted the right way and put into the right openings in that cube over there," he pointed to the pink cube in the medico's bench, "they'll contain all this man's memories and personality. In a way, he'll be in the cube, but he won't know it, because he's going to be an african lion today."

This excited the children, who would much rather be stalking the Kenya savanna than listening to how a multi-holo was taken. When they quieted down the teacher went on, using analogies that got more strained by the minute.

"When the strings are in ... class, pay attention. When they're in the cube, a current sets them in place. What we have then is a multi-holo. Can anyone tell me why we can't just take a tape-recording of what's going on in this man's brain, and use that?"

One of the boys answered, for once.

"Because memory isn't ... what's that word?"

"Sequential?"

"Yeah, that's it. His memories are stashed all over his brain and there's no way to sort them out. So this recorder takes a picture of the whole thing at once, like a hologram. Does that mean you can cut the cube in half and have two people?"

"No, but that's a good question. This isn't that sort of hologram. This is something like ... like when you press your hand into clay, but in four dimensions. If you chip off a part of the information, right? Well, this is sort of like that. You can't see the imprint because it's too small, but everything the man ever did and saw and heard and thought will be in the cube."

"Would you move back a little?" asked the medico. The children in the mirror over Fingal's head shuffled back and became more than just heads with shoulders sticking out. The medico adjusted the last strand of FPNA suspended in his cortex to the close tolerances specified by the computer.

"I'd like to be a medico when I grow up," said one boy.

"I thought you wanted to go to college and study to be a scientist."

"Well, maybe. But my friend is teaching me to be a medico. It looks a lot easier."

"You should stay in school, Destry. I'm sure your parent will want you to make something of yourself." The medico fumed silently. She knew better than to speak up—education was a serious business and interference with the duties of a teacher carried a stiff fine. But she was obviously pleased when the class thanked her and went out the door, leaving dirty footprints behind them.

She viciously flipped a switch, and Fingal found he could breath and move the muscles in his head.

"Lousy conceited college graduate," she said. "What the hell's wrong with getting your hands dirty, I ask you?" She wiped the blood from her hands onto her blue smock.

"Teachers are the worst," Fingal said.

"Ain't it the truth? Well, being a medico is nothing to be ashamed of. So I didn't go to college, so what? I can do my job, and I can see what I've done when I'm through. I always did like working with my hands. Did you know that being a medico used to be one of the most respected professions there was?"

"Really?"

"Fact. They had to go to college for years and years, and they made a hell of a lot of money, let me tell you."

Fingal said nothing, thinking she must be exaggerating. What was so tough about medicine? Just a little mechanical sense and a steady hand, that was all you needed. Fingal did a lot of maintenance on his body himself, going to the shop only for major work. And a good thing, at the prices they charged. It was not the sort of thing one discussed while lying helpless on the table, however.

"Okay, that's done." She pulled out the modules that contained the invisible FPNA and set them in the developing solution. She fastened Fingal's skull back on and tightened the recessed screws set into the bone. She turned his motor control back over to him while she sealed his scalp back into place. He stretched and yawned. He always grew sleepy in the medico's shop; he didn't know why.

"Will that be all for today, sir? We've got a special on blood changes, and since you'll just be lying there while you're out doppling in the park, you might as well . . ."

"No, thanks. I had it changed a year ago. Didn't you read my history?"

She picked up the card and glanced at it. "So you did. Fine. You can get up now, Mr. Fingal." She made a note on the card and set it down on the table. The door opened and a small face peered in.

"I left my stick," said the boy. He came in and started looking under things, to the annoyance of the medico. She attempted to ignore the boy as she took down the rest of the information she needed.

"And are you going to experience this holiday now, or wait until your double has finished and play it back then?"

"Huh? Oh, you mean . . . yes. I see. No, I'll go right into the animal. My psychist advised me to come out here for my nerves, so it wouldn't do me much good to wait it out, would it?"

"No, I suppose it wouldn't. So you'll be sleeping here while you dopple in the park. Hey!" She turned to confront the little boy, who was poking his nose into things he should stay away from. She grabbed him and pulled him away.

"You either find what you're looking for in one minute or you get out of here, you see?" He went back to his search, giggling behind his hand and looking for more interesting things to fool around with.

The medico made a check on the card, glanced at the glowing numbers on her thumbnail and discovered her shift was almost over. She connected the memory cube through a machine to a terminal in the back of his head.

"You've never done this before, right? We do this to avoid blank spots, which can be confusing sometimes. The cube is almost set, but now I'll add the last ten minutes to the record at the same time as I put you to sleep. That way you'll experience no disorientation, you'll move through a dream state to full awareness of being in the body of a lion. Your body will be removed and taken to one of our slumber rooms while you're gone. There's nothing to worry about."

Fingal wasn't worried, just tired and tense. He wished she would go on and do it and stop talking about it. And he wished the little boy would stop pounding his stick against the table leg. He wondered if his headache would be transferred to the lion.

She turned him off.

They hauled his body away and took his memory cube to the installation room. The medico chased the boy into the corridor and hosed down the recording room. Then she was off to a date she was already late for.

The employees of Kenya disneyland installed the cube into a metal box set into the skull of a full-grown African lioness. The social structure of lions being what it was, the proprietors charged a premium for the use of a male body, but Fingal didn't care one way or the other.

A short ride in an underground railroad with the sedated body of the Fingal-lioness, and he was deposited beneath the blazing sun of the Kenya savanna. He awoke, sniffed the air, and felt better immediately.

The Kenya disneyland was a total environment buried twenty kilometers beneath Mare Moscoviense on the farside of Luna. It was roughly circular with a radius of two hundred kilometers. From the ground to the "sky" was two kilometers except over the full-sized replica of Kilimanjaro, where it bulged to allow clouds to form in a realistic manner over the snowcap.

The illusion was flawless. The ground curved away consistent with the curvature of the Earth, so that the horizon was much more distant than anything Fingal was used to. The trees were real, and so were all the animals. At night an astronomer would have needed a spectroscope to distinguish the stars from the real thing.

Fingal certainly couldn't spot anything wrong. Not that he wanted to. The colors were strange but that was from the limitations of feline optics. Sounds were much more vivid, as were smells. If he'd thought about it, he would have realized the gravity was much too weak for Kenya. But he wasn't thinking; he'd come here to avoid that necessity.

It was hot and glorious. The dry grass made no sound as

he walked over it on broad pads. He smelled antelope, wilde-beest, and . . . was that baboon? He felt pangs of hunger but he really didn't want to hunt. But he found the lioness body starting on a stalk anyway.

Fingal was in an odd position. He was in control of the lioness, but only more or less. He could guide her where he wanted to go, but he had no say at all over instinctive behav-iors. He was as much a pawn to these as the lioness was. In one sense, he *was* the lioness; when he wished to raise a paw or turn around, he simply did it. The motor control was com-plete. It felt great to walk on all fours, and it came as easily as breathing. But the scent of the antelope went on a direct route from the nostrils to the lower brain, made a connection with the rumblings of hunger, and started him on the stalk.

The guidebook said to surrender to it. Fighting it wouldn't do anyone any good, and could frustrate you. If you were paying to be a lion, read the chapter on "Things to Do," you might as well *be* one, not just wear the body and see the sights.

Fingal wasn't sure he liked this as he came up downwind and crouched behind a withered clump of scrub. He pon-dered it while he sized up the dozen or so antelope grazing just a few meters from him, picking out the small, the weak, and the young with a predator's eye. Maybe he should back out now and go on his way. These beautiful creatures were not harming him. The Fingal part of him wished mostly to admire them, not eat them.

Before he quite knew what had happened, he was standing triumphant over the bloody body of a small antelope. The others were just dusty trails in the distance.

It had been incredible!

The lioness was fast, but might as well have been moving in slow-motion compared to the antelope. Her only advantage lay in surprise, confusion, and quick, all-out attack. There had been the lifting of a head, ears had flicked toward the bush he was hiding in, and he had exploded. Ten seconds of furi-ous exertion and he bit down on a soft throat, felt the blood gush and the dying kicks of the hind legs under his paws. He was breathing hard and the blood coursed through his veins. There was only one way to release the tension.

He threw his head back and roared his bloodlust.

He'd had it with lions at the end of the weekend. It wasn't

worth it for the few minutes of exhilaration at the kill. It was a life of endless stalking, countless failures, then a pitiful struggle to get a few bites for yourself from the kill you had made. He found to his chagrin that his lioness was very low in the dominance-order. When he got his kill back to the pride—he didn't know why he had dragged it back but the lioness seemed to know—it was promptly stolen from him. He/she sat back helplessly and watched the dominant male take his share, followed by the rest of the pride. He was left with a dried haunch four hours later, and had to contest even that with vultures and hyenas. He saw what the premium payment was for. That male had it *easy*.

But he had to admit that it had been worth it. He felt better; his psychist had been right. It did one good to leave the insatiable computers at his office for a weekend of simple living. There were no complicated choices to be made out here. If he was in doubt, he listened to his instincts. It was just that the next time, he'd go as an elephant. He'd been watching them. All the other animals pretty much left them alone, and he could see why. To be a solitary bull, free to wander where he wished with food as close as the nearest tree branch . . .

He was still thinking about it when the collection crew came for him.

He awoke with the vague feeling that something was wrong. He sat up in bed and looked around him. Nothing seemed to be out of place. There was no one in the room with him. He shook his head to clear it.

It didn't do any good. There was still something wrong. He tried to remember how he had gotten there, and laughed at himself. His own bedroom! What was so remarkable about that?

But hadn't there been a vacation, a week-end trip? He remembered being a lion, eating raw antelope meat, being pushed around within the pride, fighting it out with the other females and losing and retiring to rumble to him/herself.

Certainly he should have come back to human consciousness in the disneyland medical section. He couldn't remember it. He reached for his phone, not knowing who he wished to call. His psychist, perhaps, or the Kenya office.

"I'm sorry, Mr. Fingal," the phone told him. "This line is no longer available for outgoing calls. If you'll . . ."

"Why not?" he asked, irritated and confused. "I paid my bill."

"That is of no concern to this department, Mr. Fingal. And please do not interrupt. It's hard enough to reach you. I'm fading, but the message will be continued if you look to your right." The voice and the power hum behind it faded. The phone was dead.

Fingal looked to his right and jerked in surprise. There was a hand, a woman's hand, writing on his wall. The hand faded out at the wrist.

"Mene, Mene . . ." it wrote, in thin letters of fire. Then the hand waved in irritation and erased that with its thumb. The wall was smudged with soot where the words had been.

"You're projecting, Mr. Fingal." the hand wrote, quickly etching out the words with a manicured nail. "That's what you expected to see." The hand underlined the word "expected" three times. "Please cooperate, clear your mind, and see what is *there,* or we're not going to get anywhere. Damn, I've about exhausted this medium."

And indeed it had. The writing had filled the wall and the hand was now down near the floor. The apparition wrote smaller and smaller in an effort to get it all in.

Fingal had an excellent grasp on reality, according to his psychist. He held tightly onto that evaluation like a talisman as he leaned closer to the wall to read the last sentence.

"Look on your bookshelf," the hand wrote. "The title is *Orientation in Your Fantasy World.*"

Fingal knew he had no such book, but could think of nothing better to do.

His phone didn't work, and if he was going through a psychotic episode he didn't think it wise to enter the public corridor until he had some idea of what was going on. The hand faded out, but the writing continued to smoulder.

He found the book easily enough. It was a pamphlet, actually, with a gaudy cover. It was the sort of thing he had seen in the outer office of the Kenya disneyland, a promotional booklet. At the bottom it said, "Published under the auspices of the Kenya computer; A. Joachim, operator." He opened it and began to read.

CHAPTER ONE
"Where Am I?"

You're probably wondering by now where you are. This is an entirely healthy and normal reaction, Mr. Fingal. Anyone would wonder, when beset by what seem to be paranormal manifestations, if his grasp on reality had weakened. Or, in simple language, "Am I nuts, or what?"

No. Mr. Fingal, you are not nuts. But you are not, as you probably think, sitting on your bed, reading a book. It's all in your mind. You are still in the Kenya disneyland. More specifically, you are contained in the memory cube we took of you before your weekend on the savanna. You see, there's been a big goof-up.

CHAPTER TWO
"What Happened?"

We'd like to know that, too, Mr. Fingal. But here's what we do know. Your body has been misplaced. Now, there's nothing to worry about, we're doing all we can to locate it and find out how it happened but it will take some time. Maybe it's small consolation, but this has never happened before in the seventy-five years we've been operating, and as soon as we find out how it happened this time, you can be sure we'll be careful not to let it happen again. We're pursuing several leads at this time, and you can rest easy that your body will be returned to you intact just as soon as we locate it.

You are awake and aware right now because we have incorporated your memory cube into the workings of our H-210 computer, one of the finest holo-memory systems available to modern business. You see, there are a few problems.

CHAPTER THREE
"What Problems?"

It's kind of hard to put in terms you'd understand, but let's take a crack at it, shall we?

The medium we use to record your memoires isn't the one you've probably used yourself as insurance against accidental death. As you must know, that system will store your memories for up to twenty years with no degradation or loss of information, and is quite expensive. The system we use is a temporary one, good for two, five, fourteen, or twenty-eight days, depending on the length of your stay. Your memories are put in the cube, where you might expect them to remain static and unchanging, like they do in your insurance-recording. If you thought that, you would be wrong, Mr. Fingal. Think about it. If you die, your bank will immediately start a clone from the plasm you stored along with the memory cube. In six months your memories would be played back into the clone and you would awaken, missing the memories that were accumulated in your body from the time of your last recording. Perhaps this has happened to you. If it has, you know the shock of wakening from the recording process to be told that it is three or four years later, and that you died in that time.

In any case, the process we use is an *ongoing* one, or it would be worthless to you. The cube we install in the African animal of your choice is capable of adding the memories of your stay in Kenya to the memory cube. When your visit is over, these memories are played back into your brain and you leave the disneyland with the exciting, educational, and refreshing experiences you had as an animal, though your body never left our slumber room. This is known as "doppling," from the German *doppelganger*.

Now, to the problems we talked about. Thought we'd *never* get around to them, didn't you?

First, since you registered for a week-end stay, the medico naturally used one of the two-day cubes as part of our budget-excursion fare. These cubes have a safety factor, but aren't much good beyond three days at best. At the end of that time the cube would start to deteriorate. Of course, we fully expect to have you installed in your own body before then. Additionally, there is the problem of storage. Since these ongoing memory cubes are intended to be in use all the time your memories are stored in them, it presents certain problems when we find ourselves in the spot we are now in. Are you following me, Mr. Fingal? While the cube has already passed its potency for use in co-existing with a live host, like the lioness you just left, it *must* be kept in constant activation at all times or loss of information results. I'm sure you wouldn't want that to happen, would you? Of course not. So what we have done is to "plug you in" to our computer, which will keep you aware and healthy and guard against the randomizing of your memory nexi. I won't go into that; let it stand that randomizing is not the sort of thing you'd like to have happen to you.

CHAPTER FOUR
"So What Gives, Huh?"

I'm glad you asked that. (Because you *did* ask that, Mr. Fingal. This booklet is part of the analogizing process that I'll explain further down the page.)

Life in a computer is not the sort of thing you could just jump into and hope to retain the world-picture-compatibility so necessary for sane functioning in this complex society. This has been tried, so take our word for it. Or, rather, my word. Did I introduce myself? I'm Apollonia Joachim, First Class Operative for the Data-Safe computer trouble-shooting firm. You've probably never heard of us, even though you do work with computers.

Since you can't just come aware in the baffling, on-and-off world that passes for reality in a data system, your mind, in cooperation with an analogizing program I've given the computer, interprets things in ways that seem safe and comfortable to it. The world you see around you is a figment of your imagination. Of course, it looks real to you because it comes from the same part of the mind that you normally use to interpret reality. If we wanted to get philosophical about it, we could probably argue all day about what constitutes reality and why the one you are perceiving now is any less real than the one you are used to. But let's not get into that, all right?

The world will likely continue to function in ways you are accustomed for it to function. It won't be exactly the same. Nightmares, for instance. Mr. Fingal, I hope you aren't the nervous type, because your nightmares can come to life where you are. They'll seem quite real. You should avoid them if you can, because they can do you real harm. I'll say more about this later if I need to. For now, there's no need to worry.

CHAPTER FIVE
"What Do I Do Now?"

I'd advise you to continue with your normal activities. Don't be alarmed at anything unusual. For one thing, I can only communicate with you by means of paranormal phenomena. You see, when a message from me is fed into the computer it reaches you in a way your brain is not capable of dealing with. Naturally, your brain classifies this as an unusual event and fleshes the communication out in unusual fashion. Most of the weird things you see, if you stay calm and don't let your own fears out of the closet to persecute you, will be me. Otherwise, I anticipate that your world should look, feel, taste, sound, and smell pretty normal. I've talked to your psychist. He assures me that your world-grasp is strong. So sit tight. We'll be working hard to get you out of there.

CHAPTER SIX
"Help!"

Yes, we'll help you. This is a truly unfortunate thing to have happened, and of course we will refund all your money promptly. In addition, the lawyer for Kenya wants me to ask you if a lump sum settlement against all future damages is a topic worthy of discussion. You can think about it, there's no hurry.

In the meantime, I'll find ways to answer your questions. It might become unwieldy the harder your mind struggles to normalize my communications into things you are familiar with. That is both your greatest strength—the ability of your mind to bend the computer world it doesn't wish to see into media you are familiar with—and my biggest handicap. Look for me in tea-leaves, on billboards, on holovision; anywhere! It could be exciting if you get into it.

Meanwhile, if you have received this message you can talk to me by filling in the attached coupon and dropping it in the mailtube. Your reply will probably be waiting for you at the office. Good luck!

Yes! I received your message, and am interested in the excit-

ing opportunities in the field of *computer living!* Please send
me, without cost or obligation, your exciting catalog telling
me how I can *move up* to the big, wonderful world outside!
NAME ....
ADDRESS ....
I.D. ....

Fingal fought the urge to pinch himself. If what this booklet said was true—and he might as well believe it—it would
hurt and he would *not* wake up. He pinched himself anyway.
It hurt.

If he understood this right, everything around him was the
product of his imagination. Somewhere, a woman was sitting
at a computer input and talking to him in normal language,
which came to his brain in the form of electron pulses it
could not cope with and so edited into forms he was conversant with. He was analogizing like mad. He wondered if he
had caught it from the teacher, if analogies were contagious.

"What the hell's wrong with a simple voice from the air?"
he wondered aloud. He got no response, and was rather glad.
He'd had enough mysteriousness for now. And on second
thought, a voice from the air would probably scare the pants
off him.

He decided his brain must know what it was doing. After
all, the hand startled him but he hadn't panicked. He could
see it, and he trusted his visual sense more than he did voices
from the air, a classical sign of insanity if ever there was one.

He got up and went to the wall. The letters of fire were
gone, but the black smudge of the erasure was still there. He
sniffed it: carbon. He fingered the rough paper of the pamphlet, tore off a corner, put it in his mouth and chewed it. It
tasted like paper.

He sat down and filled out the coupon and tossed it to the
mailtube.

Fingal didn't get angry about it until he was at the office.
He was an easy-going person, slow to boil. But he finally
reached a point where he had to say something.

Everything had been so normal he wanted to laugh. All his
friends and acquaintances were there, doing exactly what he
would have expected them to be doing. What amazed and bemused him was the number and variety of spear-carriers, mi-

nor players in this internal soap-opera. The extras that his mind had cooked up to people the crowded corridors; like the man he didn't know who had bumped into him on the tube to work, apologized, and disappeared, presumably back into the bowels of his imagination.

There was nothing he could do to vent his anger but test the whole absurd set-up. There was doubt lingering in his mind that the whole morning had been a fugue, a temporary lapse into dreamland. Maybe he'd never gone to Kenya, after all, and his mind was playing tricks on him. To get him there, or keep him away? He didn't know, but he could worry about that if the test failed.

He stood up at his desk-terminal, which was in the third column of the fifteenth row of other identical desks, each with its diligent worker. He held up his hands and whistled. Everyone looked up.

"I don't believe in you," he screeched. He picked up a stack of tapes on his desk and hurled them at Felicia Nahum at the desk next to his. Felicia was a good friend of his, and she registered the proper shock until the tapes hit her. Then she melted. He looked around the room and saw that everything had stopped like a freeze-frame in a motion picture.

He sat down and drummed his fingers on his desk top. His heart was pounding and his face was flushed. For an awful moment he had thought he was wrong. He began to calm down, glancing up every few seconds to be sure the world really *had* stopped.

In three minutes he was in a cold sweat. What the hell had he *proved*? That this morning had been real, or that he really was crazy? It dawned on him that he would never be able to test the assumptions under which he lived. A line of print flashed across his terminal.

"But when could you ever do so, Mr. Fingal?"

"Ms. Joachim?" he shouted, looking around him. "Where are you? I'm afraid."

"You mustn't be," the terminal printed. "Calm yourself. You have a strong sense of reality, remember? Think about this: even before today, how could you be sure the world you saw was not the result of catatonic delusions? Do you see what I mean? The question 'What is reality?' is, in the end, unanswerable. We all must accept at some point what we see and are told, and live by a set of untested and untestable assumptions. I ask you to accept the set I gave you this morning because, sitting here in the computer room where you cannot see me, my world-picture tells me that they are the true set. On the other hand, you could believe that I'm deluding myself, that there's nothing in the pink cube I see and that you're a spear-carrier in *my* dream. Does that make you more comfortable?"

"No," he mumbled, ashamed of himself. "I see what you mean. Even if I am crazy, it would be more comfortable to go along with it than to keep fighting it."

"Perfect, Mr. Fingal. If you need further illustrations you could imagine yourself locked in a strait-jacket. Perhaps there are technicians laboring right now to correct your condition, and they are putting you through this psycho-drama as a first step. Is that any more attractive?"

"No, I guess it isn't."

"The point is that it's as reasonable an assumption as the set of facts I gave you this morning. But the main point is that you should behave the same if either set is true. Do you see? To fight it in the one case will only cause you trouble, and in the other, would impede the treatment. I realize I'm asking you to accept me on faith. And that's all I can give you."

"I believe in you," he said. "Now, can you start everything going again?"

"I told you I'm not in control of your world. In fact, it's a considerable obstacle to me, seeing as I have to talk to you in these awkward ways. But things should get going on their own as soon as you let them. Look up."

He did, and saw the normal hum and bustle of the office. Felicia was there at her desk, as though nothing had happened. Nothing had. Yes, something had, after all. The tapes were scattered on the floor near his desk, where they had fallen. They had unreeled in an unruly mess.

He started to pick them up, then saw they weren't as messy as he had thought. They spelled out a message in coils of tape.

"You're back on the track," it said.

For three weeks Fingal was a very good boy. His co-workers, had they been real people, might have noticed a certain standoffishness in him, and his social life at home was drastically curtailed. Otherwise, he behaved exactly as if everything around him were real.

But his patience had limits. This had already dragged on far beyond what he had expected of it. He began to fidget at his desk, let his mind wander. Feeding information into a computer can be frustrating, unrewarding, and eventually stultifying. He had been feeling it even before his trip to Kenya; it had been the *cause* of his trip to Kenya. He was sixty-eight years old, with centuries ahead of him, and stuck in a ferro-magnetic rut. Longlife could be a mixed blessing when you felt boredom creeping up on you.

What was getting to him was the growing disgust with his job. It was bad enough when he merely sat in a real office with two hundred real people shoveling slightly unreal data into a much-less-than-real-to-his senses computer. How much worse now, when he knew that the data he handled had no meaning to anyone but himself, was nothing but occupational therapy created by his mind and a computer program to keep him busy while Joachim searched for his body?

For the first time in his life he began punching some buttons for himself. Under slightly less stress he would have gone to see his psychist, the approved and perfectly normal thing to do. Here, he knew he would only be talking to himself. He failed to perceive the advantages of such an idealized psychoanalytic process; he'd never really believed that a psychist did little but listen in the first place.

He began to change his own life when he became irritated with his boss. She pointed out to him that his error-index was on the rise, and suggested that he shape up or begin looking for another source of employment.

This enraged him. He'd been a good worker for twenty-five years. Why should she take that attitude when he was just not feeling himself for a week or two?

Then he was angrier than ever when he thought about her being merely a projection of his own mind. Why should he let *her* push him around?

"I don't want to hear it," he said. "Leave me alone. Better yet, give me a raise in salary."

"Fingal," she said promptly, "you've been a credit to your section these last weeks. I'm going to give you a raise."

"Thank you. Go away." She did, by dissolving into thin air. This really made his day. He leaned back in his chair and thought about his situation for the first time since he was young.

He didn't like what he saw.

In the middle of his ruminations, his computer screen lit up again.

"Watch it, Fingal," it read. "That way lies catatonia."

He took the warning seriously, but didn't intend to abuse the newfound power. He didn't see why judicious use of it now and then would hurt anything. He stretched, and yawned broadly. He looked around, suddenly hated the office with its rows of workers indistinguishable from their desks. Why not take the day off?

On impulse, he got up and walked the few steps to Felicia's desk.

"Why don't we go to my house and make love?" he asked her.

She looked at him in astonishment, and he grinned. She was almost as surprised as when he had hurled the tapes at her.

"Is this a joke? In the middle of the day? You have a job to do, you know. You want to get us fired?"

He shook his head slowly. "That's not an acceptable answer."

She stopped, and rewound from that point. He heard her repeat her last sentences backwards, then she smiled.

"Sure, why not?" she said.

Felicia left afterwards in the same, slightly disconcerting way his boss had left earlier; by melting into the air. Fingal sat quietly in his bed, wondering what to do with himself. He felt he was getting off to a bad start if he intended to edit his world with care.

His telephone rang.

"You're damn right," said a woman's voice, obviously irritated with him. He sat up straight.

"Apollonia?"

"Ms. Joachim to you, Fingal. I can't talk long, this is quite a strain on me. But listen to me, and listen hard. Your navel is very deep, Fingal. From where you're standing, it's a pit I can't even see the bottom of. If you fall into it I can't guarantee to pull you out."

"But do I have to take *everything* as it is? Aren't I allowed some self-improvement?"

"Don't kid yourself. That wasn't self-improvement. That

was sheer laziness. It was nothing but masturbation, and while there's nothing wrong with that, if you do it to the exclusion of all else your mind will grow in on itself. You're in grave danger of excluding the external universe from your reality."

"But I thought there was no external universe for me here."

"Almost right. But I'm feeding you external stimuli to keep you going. Besides, it's the attitude that counts. You've never had trouble finding sexual partners; why do you feel compelled to alter the odds now?"

"I don't know," he admitted. "Like you said, laziness, I guess."

"That's right. If you want to quit your job, feel free. If you're serious about self-improvement, there are opportunities available to you there. Search them out. Look around you, explore. But don't try to meddle in things you don't understand. I've got to go now. I'll write you a letter if I can, and explain more."

"Wait! What about my body? Have they made any progress?"

"Yes, they've found out how it happened. It seems . . ." her voice faded out, and he switched off the phone.

The next day he received a letter explaining what was known so far. It seemed that the mix-up had resulted from the visit of the teacher to the medico section on the day of his recording. More specifically, the return of the little boy after the others had left. They were sure now that he had tampered with the routine card that told the attendants what to do with Fingal's body. Instead of moving it to the slumber room, which was a green card, they had sent it somewhere—no one knew where yet—for a sex change, which was a blue card. The medico, in her haste to get home for her date, had not noticed the switch. Now the body could be in any of several thousand medico shops in Luna. They were looking for it, and for the boy.

Fingal put the letter down and did some hard thinking.

Joachim had said there were opportunities for him in the memory banks. She had also said that not everything he saw was his own projections. He was receiving, was capable of receiving, external stimuli. Why was that? Because he would tend to randomize without them, or some other reason? He wished the letter had gone into that.

In the meantime, what did he do?

Suddenly he had it. He wanted to learn about computers. He wanted to know what made them tick, to feel a sense of power over them. It was particularly strong when he thought about being a virtual prisoner inside one. He was like a worker on an assembly line. All day long he labors, taking small parts off a moving belt and installing them on larger assemblies. One day, he happens to wonder who puts the parts on the belt? Where do they come from? How are they made? What happens after he installs them?

He wondered why he hadn't thought of it before.

The admissions office of the Lunar People's Technical School was crowded. He was handed a form and told to fill it out. It looked bleak. The spaces for "previous experience" and "aptitude scores" were almost blank when he was through with them. All in all, not a very promising application. He went to the desk and handed the form to the man sitting at the terminal.

The man fed it into the computer, which promptly decided Fingal had no talent for being a computer repairperson. He started to turn away, when his eye was caught by a large poster behind the man. It had been there on the wall when he came in, but he hadn't read it.

LUNA NEEDS
COMPUTER TECHNICIANS
THIS MEANS YOU
MR. FINGAL!

Are you dissatisfied with your present employment? Do you feel you were cut out for better things? Then today may be your lucky day. You've come to the right place, and if you grasp this golden opportunity you will find doors opening that were closed to you.

Act, Mr. Fingal. This is the time. Who's to check up on you? Just take that stylus and fill it in any old way you want. Be grandiose, be daring! The fix is in, and you're on your way to

BIG MONEY!

The secretary saw nothing unusual about Fingal coming to

the desk a second time, and didn't even blink when the computer decided he was eligible for the accelerated course.

It wasn't easy at first. He really did have little aptitude for electronics, but aptitude is a slippery thing. His personality matrix was as flexible now as it would ever be. A little effort at the right time would go a long way toward self-improvement. What he kept telling himself was that everything that made him what he was was etched in that tiny cube wired in to the computer, and if he was careful he could edit it.

Not radically, Joachim told him in a long, helpful letter later in the week. That way led to complete disruption of the FPNA matrix and catatonia, which in this case would be distinguishable from death only to a hair-splitter.

He thought a lot about death as he dug into the books. He was in a strange position. The being known as Fingal would not die in any conceivable outcome of this adventure. For one thing, his body was going toward a sex change and it was hard to imagine what could happen to it that would kill it. Whoever had custody of it now would be taking care of it just as well as the medicos in the slumber room would have. If Joachim was unsuccessful in her attempt to keep him aware and sane in the memory bank, he would merely awake and remember nothing from the time he fell asleep on the table.

If, by some compounded unlikelihood, his body *was* allowed to die, he had an insurance recording safe in the vault of his bank. The recording was three years old. He would awaken in the newly-grown clone body knowing nothing of the last three years, and would have a fantastic story to listen to as he was brought up to date.

But none of that mattered to *him*. Humans are a time-binding species, existing in an eternal *now*. The future flows through them and becomes the past, but it is always the present that counts. The Fingal of three years ago was *not* the Fingal in the memory bank. The simple fact about immortality by memory recording was that it was a poor solution. The three-dimensional cross-section that was the Fingal of now must always behave as if his life depended on his actions, for he would feel the pain of death if it happened to him. It was small consolation to a dying man to know that he would go on, several years younger and less wise. If Fingal lost out here, he would *die*, because with memory recording he was three people: the one who lived now, the one lost somewhere on Luna, and the one potential person in the bank vault. They were really no more than close relatives.

Everyone knew this, but it was so much better than the alternative that few people rejected it. They tried not to think about it and were generally successful. They had recordings made as often as they could afford them. They heaved a sigh of relief as they got onto the table to have another recording taken, knowing that another chunk of their lives was safe for all time. But they awaited the awakening nervously, dreading being told that it was now twenty years later because they had died sometime after the recording and had to start all over. A lot can happen in twenty years. The person in the new clone body might have to cope with a child he or she had never seen, a new spouse, or the shattering news that his or her employment was now the function of a machine.

So Fingal took Joachim's warnings seriously. Death was death, and though he could cheat it, death still had the last laugh. Instead of taking your whole life from you death now only claimed a percentage, but in many ways it was the most important percentage.

He enrolled in classes. Whenever possible he took the ones that were available over the phone lines so he needn't stir from his room. He ordered his food and supplies by phone and paid his bills by looking at them and willing them out of existence. It could have been intensely boring, or it could have been wildly interesting. After all, it was a dream-world, and who doesn't think of retiring into fantasy from time to time? Fingal certainly did, but firmly suppressed the idea when it came. He intended to get out of this dream.

For one thing, he missed the company of other people. He waited for the weekly letters from Apollonia (she now allowed him to call her by her first name) with a consuming passion and devoured every word. His file of such letters bulged. At lonely moments he would pull one out at random and read it again and again.

On her advice, he left the apartment regularly and stirred around more or less at random. During these outings he had wild adventures. Literally. Apollonia hurled the external stimuli at him during these times and they could be anything from The Mummy's Curse to Custer's Last Stand with the original cast. It beat hell out of the movies. He would just walk down the public corridors and open a door at random.

Behind it might be King Solomon's mines or the sultan's harem. He endured them all stoically. He was unable to get any pleasure from sex. He knew it was a one-handed exercise, and it took all the excitement away.

His only pleasure came in his studies. He read everything he could about computer science and came to stand at the head of his class. And as he learned, it began to occur to him to apply his knowledge to his own situation.

He began seeing things around him that had been veiled before. Patterns. The reality was starting to seep through his illusions. Every so often he would look up and see the faintest shadow of the real world of electron flow and fluttering circuits he inhabited. It scared him at first. He asked Apollonia about it on one of his dream journeys, this time to Coney Island in the mid-twentieth century. He liked it there. He could lay on the sand and talk to the surf. Overhead, a skywriter's plane spelled out the answers to his questions. He studiously ignored the brontosaurus rampaging through the roller coaster off to his right.

"What does it mean, O Goddess of Transistoria, when I begin to see circuit diagrams on the walls of my apartment? Overwork?"

"It means the illusion is beginning to wear thin," the plane spelled out over the next half-hour. "You're adapting to the reality you have been denying. It could be trouble, but we're hot on the trail of your body. We should have it soon and get you out of there." This had been too much for the plane. The sun was going down now, the brontosaurus vanished, and the plane ran out of gas. It spiraled into the ocean and the crowds surged closer to the water to watch the rescue. Fingal got up and went back to the boardwalk.

There was a huge billboard. He laced his fingers behind his back and read it.

"Sorry for the delay. As I was saying, we're almost there. Give us another few months. One of our agents thinks he will be at the right medico shop in about one week's time. From there it should go quickly. For now, avoid those places where you see the circuits showing through. They're no good for you, take my word for it."

Fingal avoided the circuits as long as he could. He finished his first courses in computer science and enrolled in the intermediate section. Six months rolled by.

His studies got easier and easier. His reading speed was increasing phenomenally. He found that it was more advantageous for him to see the library as composed of books instead of tapes. He could take a book from the shelf, flip through it rapidly, and know everything that was in it. He knew enough now to realize that he was acquiring a facility to interface directly with the stored knowledge in the computer, bypassing his senses entirely. The books he held in his hands were merely the sensual analogs of the proper terminals to touch. Apollonia was nervous about it, but let him go on. He breezed through the intermediate and graduated into the advanced classes.

But he was surrounded by wires. Everywhere he turned, in the patterns of veins beneath the surface of a man's face, in a plate of french fries he ordered for lunch, in his palmprints, overlaying the apparent disorder of a head of blonde hair on the pillow beside him.

The wires were analogs of analogs. There was little in a modern computer that consisted of wiring. Most of it was made of molecular circuits that were either embedded in a crystal lattice or photographically reproduced on a chip of silicon. Visually, they were hard to imagine, so his mind was making up these complex circuit diagrams that served the same purpose but could be experienced directly.

One day he could resist it no longer. He was in the bathroom, on the traditional place for the pondering of the imponderable. His mind wandered, speculating on the necessity of moving his bowels, wondering if he might safely eliminate the need to eliminate. His toe idly traced out the pathways of a circuit board incorporated in the pattern of tiles on the floor.

The toilet began to overflow, not with water, but with coins. Bells were ringing happily. He jumped up and watched in bemusement as his bathroom filled with money.

He became aware of a subtle alteration in the tone of the bells. They changed from the merry clang of jackpot to the tolling of a death knell. He hastily looked around for a manifestation. He knew that Apollonia would be angry.

She was. Her hand appeared and began to write on the wall. This time the writing was in his blood. It dripped menacingly from the words.

"What are you doing?" the hand wrote, and having writ, moved on. "I told you to leave the wires alone. Do you know what you've done? You may have wiped the financial records for Kenya. It could take *months* to straighten them out."

"Well what do I care?" he exploded. "What have they done for me lately? It's *incredible* that they haven't located my body by now. It's been a full *year*."

The hand was bunched up in a fist. Then it grabbed him around the throat and squeezed hard enough to make his eyes bulge out. It slowly relaxed. When Fingal could see straight, he backed warily away from it.

The hand fidgeted nervously, drummed its fingers on the floor. It went to the wall again.

"Sorry," it wrote, "I guess I'm getting tired. Hold on."

He waited, more shaken than he remembered being since his odyssey began. There's nothing like a dose of pain, he reflected, to make you realize that it *can* happen to you.

The wall with the words of blood slowly dissolved into a heavenly panorama. As he watched, clouds streamed by his vantage point and mixed beautifully with golden rays of sunshine. He heard organ music from pipes the size of sequoias.

He wanted to applaud. It was so overdone, and yet so convincing. In the center of the whirling mass of white mist an angel faded in. She had wings and a halo, but lacked the traditional white robe. She was nude, and hair floated around her as if she were underwater.

She levitated to him, walking on the billowing clouds, and handed him two stone tablets. He tore his eyes away from the apparition and glanced down at the tablets:

> Thou shalt not screw around with
> things you do not understand.

"All right, I promise I won't," he told the angel. "Apollonia, is that you? Really you, I mean?"

"Read the Commandments, Fingal. This is hard on me."

He looked back at the tablets.

Thou shalt not meddle in the hardware systems of the Kenya
    Corporation, for Kenya shall not hold him indemnifiable
    who taketh freedoms with its property.
Thou shalt not explore the limits of thy prison. Trust in the
    Kenya Corporation to extract thee.
Thou shalt not program.
Thou shalt not worry about the location of thy body, for it

has been located, help is on the way, the cavalry has arrived, and all is in hand.

Thou shalt meet a tall, handsome stranger who will guide thee from thy current plight.

Thou shalt stay tuned for further developments.

He looked up and was happy to see that the angel was still there.

"I won't, I promise. But where is my body, and why has it taken so long to find it? Can you . . ."

"Know thee that appearing like this is a great taxation upon me, Mr. Fingal. I am undergoing strains the nature of which I have not time to reveal to thee. Hold thy horses, wait it out, and thou shalt soon see the light at the end of the tunnel."

"Wait, don't go." She was already starting to fade out.

"I cannot tarry."

"But . . . Apollonia, this is charming, but why do you appear to me in these crazy ways? Why all the pomp and circumstance? What's wrong with letters?"

She looked around her at the clouds, the sunbeams, the tablets in his hand, and at her body, as if seeing them for the first time. She threw her head back and laughed like a symphony orchestra. It was almost too beautiful for Fingal to bear.

"Me?" she said, dropping the angelic bearing. "Me? I don't pick 'em, Fingal. I told you, it's *your* head, and I'm just passing through." She arched her eyebrows at him. "And really, sir, I had no idea you felt this way about me. Is it puppy love?" And she was gone, except for the grin.

The grin haunted him for days. He was disgusted with himself about it. He hated to see a metaphor overworked so. He decided his mind was just an inept analogizer.

But everything had its purpose. The grin forced himself to look at his feelings. He was in love; hopelessly, ridiculously, just like a teenager. He got out all his old letters from her and read through them again, searching for the magic words that could have inflicted this on him. Because it was *silly*. He'd never met her except under highly figurative circumstances. The one time he saw her, most of what he saw was the product of his own mind.

There were no clues in the letters. Most of them were as impersonal as a textbook, though they tended to be rather chatty. Friendly, yes; but intimate, poetic, insightful, revealing? No. He failed utterly to put them together in any way that should add up to love, or even a teenage crush.

He attacked his studies with renewed vigor, awaiting the next communication. Weeks dragged by with no word. He called the post office several times, placed personal advertisements in every periodical he could think of, took to scrawling messages on public buildings, sealed notes in bottles and flushed them down the disposal, rented billboards, bought television time. He screamed at the empty walls of his apartment, buttonholed strangers, tapped Morse Code on the water pipes, started rumors in skid row taprooms, had leaflets published and distributed all over the solar system. He tried every medium he could think of, and could not contact her. He was alone.

He considered the possibility that he had died. In his present situation, it might be hard to tell for sure. He abandoned it as untestable. That line was hazy enough already without his efforts to determine which side of the life/death dichotomy he inhabited. Besides, the more he thought about existing as nothing more than kinks in a set of macromolecules plugged into a data system, the more it frightened him. He'd survived this long by avoiding such thoughts.

His nightmares moved in on him, set up housekeeping in his apartment. They were a severe disappointment, and confirmed his conclusion that his imagination was not as vivid as it might be. They were infantile boogeyman, the sort that might scare him when glimpsed hazily through the fog of a nightmare, but were almost laughable when exposed to the full light of consciousness. There was a large, talkative snake that was crudely put together, fashioned from the incomplete picture a child might have of a serpent. A toy company could have done a better job. There was a werewolf whose chief claim to dread was a tendency to shed all over Fingal's rugs. There was a woman who consisted mostly of breasts and genitals, left over from his adolescence, he suspected. He groaned in embarrassment every time he looked at her. If he had ever been that infantile he would rather have left the dirty traces of it buried forever.

He kept booting them into the corridor but they drifted in at night like poor relations. They talked incessantly, and always about him. The things they knew! They seemed to have a very low opinion of him. The snake often expressed the opinion that Fingal would never amount to anything because he had so docilely accepted the results of the aptitude tests he took as a child. That hurt, but the best salve for the wound was further study.

Finally a letter came. He winced as soon as he got it open. The salutation was enough to tell him he wasn't going to like it.

Dear Mr. Fingal,

I won't apologize for the delay this time. It seems that most of my manifestations have included an apology and I feel I deserved a rest this time. I can't be always on call. I have a life of my own.

I understand that you have behaved in an exemplary manner since I last talked with you. You have ignored the inner workings of the computer just as I told you to do. I haven't been completely frank with you, and I will explain my reasons.

The hook-up between you and the computer is, and always has been, two-way. Our greatest fear at this end had been that you would begin interfering with the workings of the computer, to the great discomfort of everyone. Or that you would go mad and run amuck, perhaps wrecking the entire data system. We installed you in the computer as a humane necessity, because you would have died if we had not done so, though it would have cost you only two days of memories. But Kenya is in the business of selling memories, and holds them to be a sacred trust. It was a mix-up on the part of the Kenya Corporation that got you here in the first place, so we decided we should do everything we could for you.

But it was at great hazard to our operations at this end.

Once, about six months ago, you got tangled in the weather-control sector of the computer and set off a storm over Kilimanjaro that is still not fully under control. Several animals were lost.

I have had to fight the Board of Directors to keep you on-line, and several times the program was almost terminated. You know what that means.

Now, I've leveled with you. I wanted to from the start, but the people who own things around here were worried that you might start fooling around out of a spirit of vindictiveness if you knew these facts, so they were kept from you. You could still do a great deal of damage before we could shut you off. I'm laying it on the line now, with Directors chewing their nails over my shoulder. *Please* stay out of trouble.

On to the other matter.

I was afraid from the outset that what has happened might happen. For over a year I've been your only contact with the world outside. I've been the only other person in your universe. I would have to be an extremely cold, hateful, awful person—which I am not—for you *not* to feel affection for me under those circumstances. You are suffering from intense sensory-deprivation and it's well-known that someone in that state becomes pliable, suggestible, and lonely. You've attached your feelings to me as the only thing around worth caring for.

I've tried to avoid intimacy with you for that reason, to keep things firmly on the last-name basis. But I relented during one of your periods of despair. And you read into my letters some things that were not there. Remember, even in the printed medium it is your mind that controls what you see. You censor has let through what it wanted to see and maybe even added some things of its own. I'm at your mercy. For all I know, you may be reading this letter as a passionate affirmation of love. I've added every reinforcement I know of to make sure the message comes through on a priority channel and is not garbled. I'm sorry to hear that you love me. I do not, repeat not, love you in return. You'll understand why, at least in part, when we get you out of there.

It will never work, Mr. Fingal. Give up.

                                         Apollonia Joachim

Fingal graduated first in his class. He had finished the required courses for his degree during the last long week after his letter from Apollonia. It was a bitter victory for him, marching up to the stage to accept the sheepskin, but he clutched it to him fiercely. At least he had made the most of his situation, at least he had not meekly let the wheels of the machine chew him up like a good worker.

He reached out to grasp the hand of the college president and saw it transformed. He looked up and saw the bearded,

robed figure flow and and writhe and become a tall, uniformed woman. With a surge of joy, he knew who it was.
Then the joy became ashes in his mouth, which he hurriedly
spit out.

"I always knew you'd choke on a figure of speech," she
said, laughing tiredly.

"You're here," he said. He could not quite believe it. He
stared dully at her, grasping her hand and the diploma with
equal tenacity. She was tall, as the prophecy had said, and
handsome. Her hair was cropped short over a capable face,
and the body beneath the uniform was muscular. The uniform was open at the throat, and wrinkled. There were
circles under her eyes, and the eyes were bloodshot. She
swayed slightly on her feet.

"I'm here, all right. Are you ready to go back?" She turned
to the assembled students. "How about it, gang? Do you
think he deserves to go back?"

The crowd went wild, cheering and tossing mortarboards
into the air. Fingal turned dazedly to look at them, with a
dawning realization. He looked down at the diploma.

"I don't know," he said. "I don't know. Back to work at
the data room?"

She clapped him on the back.

"No. I promise you that."

"But how could it be different? I've come to think of this
piece of paper as something . . . real. Real! How could I have
deluded myself like that? Why did I accept it?"

"I helped you along," she said. "But it wasn't all a game.
You really did learn all the things you learned. It won't go
away when you return. That thing in your hand is imaginary,
for sure, but who do you think prints the real ones? You're
registered where it counts—in the computer—as having
passed all the courses. You'll get a real diploma when you return."

Fingal wavered. There was a tempting vision in his head.
He'd been here for over a year and had never really exploited
the nature of the place. Maybe that business about dying in
the memory bank was all a shuck, another lie invented to
keep him in his place. In that case, he could remain here and
satisfy his wildest desires, become king of the universe with
no opposition, wallow in pleasure no emperor ever imagined.
Anything he wanted here he could have, anything at all.

And he really felt he might pull it off. He'd noticed many

things about this place, and now had the knowledge of computer technology to back him up. He could squirm around and evade their attempts to erase him, even survive if they removed his cube by programming himself into other parts of the computer. He could do it.

With a sudden insight he realized that he had no desires wild enough to keep him here in his navel. He had only one major desire right now, and she was slowly fading out. A lap-dissolve was replacing her with the old college president.

"Coming? she asked.

"Yes." It was as simple as that. The stage, president, students, and auditorium faded out and the computer room at Kenya faded in. Only Apollonia remained constant. He held onto her hand until everything stabilized.

"Whew," she said, and reached around behind her head. She pulled out a wire from her occipital plug and collapsed into a chair. Someone pulled a similar wire from Fingal's head, and he was finally free of the computer.

Apollonia reached out for a steaming cup of coffee, on a table littered with empty cups.

"You were a tough nut," she said. "For a minute I thought you'd stay. It happened once. You're not the first to have this happen to you, but you're no more than the twentieth. It's an unexplored area. Dangerous."

"Really?" he said. "You weren't just saying that?"

"No," she laughed. "Now the truth can be told. It *is* dangerous. No one had ever survived more than three hours in that kind of cube, hooked into a computer. You went for six. You *do* have a strong world-picture."

She was watching him to see how he reacted to this. She was not surprised to see him accept it readily.

"I should have known that," he said. "I should have thought of it. It was only six hours out here, and more than a year for me. Computers think faster. Why didn't I see that?"

"I helped you not see it," she admitted. "Like the push I gave you not to question why you were studying so hard. Those two orders worked a lot better than some of the orders I gave you."

She yawned again, and it seemed to go on forever.

"See, it was pretty hard for me to interface with you for six hours straight. No one's ever done it before, it can get to be quite a strain. So we've both got something to be proud of."

She smiled at him but it faded when he did not return it.

"Don't look so hurt, Fingal . . . what *is* your first name? I knew it, but erased it early in the game."

"Does it matter?"

"I don't know. Surely you must see why I haven't fallen in love with you, though you may be a perfectly lovable person. I haven't had *time*. It's been a very long six hours, but it was still only six hours. What can I do?"

Fingal's face was going through awkward changes as he absorbed that. Things were not so bleak after all.

"You could go to dinner with me."

"I'm already emotionally involved with someone else, I should warn you of that."

"You could still go to dinner. You haven't been exposed to my new determination. I'm going to really make a case."

She laughed warmly and got up. She took his hand.

"You know, it's possible that you might succeed. Just don't put wings on me again, all right? You'll never get anywhere like that."

"I promise. I'm through with visions—for the rest of my life."

THOSE GOOD OLD DAYS
OF LIQUID FUEL

by Michael G. Coney

These are the great days of nostalgia, when the collection of everything old, from railroad memorabilia, old lead soldiers, and yellowed pulp magazines, is experiencing an unprecedented peak of popularity. What will the collectors and nostalgia addicts of the next century want? Here Coney strikes an achingly familiar note to anyone who has ever watched freight trains in order to spot the colors and insignia of some obscure and faraway line turning up in the midst of a string of empties.

Early that damp December morning I drove to the northernmost tip of the Peninsula where the ferry leaves for the short journey across the Strait. Despite the hour, the queue was long, and I was forced to park on the highway outside the ferry entrance. I was scanning my Newspocket to pass away the time, when my interest was suddenly caught by a news item.

The derelict ships at Pacific Northwest had been sold. A wrecking team was arriving today to start work, and before long a notable landmark—some say an eyesore—would be lost. Other news items followed, flicking across the portovee screen as I sat waiting and the rain slanted against the windows, but I don't recollect them. I was thinking about those ships, and my youth, and how it is that we keep losing little bits of our life without realizing they are gone.

In due course, the ferry arrived, and the long line of ground-effect vehicles stirred like an awakening snake and inched their way into the protective belly of a hoverferry big enough to ride the choppy waves of the Strait. As I sat in the coffee lounge watching the distant mountains while the ferry weaved through the archipelago of islets, a huge silver anti-grav vehicle slid silently by at an altitude of about a thousand feet and reminded me that even this ship on which I rode would shortly be phased out—like the shuttle ships at Pacific Northwest. The lounge was crowded and the customers as grey and apathetic as travelers always are at this hour. I wondered what they thought I looked like.

I imagine I looked as well as could be expected, for a man who had just seen a ghost on his portovee . . .

The weather was clearing by the time we docked at the mainland, and the clouds were lifting from the nearer mountains, although still shrouding the gaunt thousand-mile-long escarpment which marks forever the line of the Western Seaboard Slide. My consignment at Sentry Down was not due to arrive until midafternoon, and so I had time to kill; I had taken the early ferry to make sure of getting a place, and now, as had happened before, I was regretting it. There was not much of interest in this part of the country for a man with a few hours to spare.

As I waited in line in the dim hold of the hoverferry, I debated whether to drive straight to Sentry Down and spend the rest of the morning in the observation lounge watching the arrivals and departures. There had been definite signs of blue sky in that direction, and the terminal would be busy and therefore interesting—or lonely, according to the mood I was in. Then I recalled that Sentry Down was *always* busy; the antigrav shuttles could descend from the orbiting starships at any speed they chose, hovering in crowded columns of traffic, reversing direction if necessary, inching down through the heaviest cloud.

Unlike the obsolete liquid-fuel ships at Pacific Northwest, doomed and now destined for the breaker's yard . . .

Some year ago the development of the first commercially viable antigrav orbit-shuttle had burst upon the space-transport world like a nova. Boeing-Toyota had been first in the field with the Stratolift; you can still see a number of these machines about today as a tribute to sound design in a rapidly developing field. The shuttle business was immediately revolutionized; these new machines were virtually silent and almost infinitely controllable; they could therefore be used in close proximity to the large centers of population.

So the old-style roaring spaceport miles from the nearest city became unnecessary and obsolete, replaced by a thousand small fields such as Sentry Down, quiet and sedate and safe ... and soulless. Pacific Northwest was closed down although not entirely deserted, because many of the larger operators such as the Hetherington Organization had mothballed their liquid-fuel shuttle ships there, leaving behind a skeleton maintenance staff to keep the vandals away—God knows why.

And now at last, all those old ships had been sold and would shortly fall to the wrecker's lasers.

Pacific Northwest is two hundred miles from the ferry terminal, away in the mountain foothills. Two hours drive, then two hours back. I glanced at my watch. I could drive there, spend an hour or two looking around, and still have time to get to Sentry Down, pick up my consignment of breeding slithes from Coprahedra IV, and catch the last ferry home.

It would be good to see Pacific Northwest again.

I suppose it was natural that I should think of Charlesworth as I drove north through the undulating foothills. Charlesworth and my childhood and Pacific Northwest seemed to go together, an indivisible trinity forever fixed in my memory. Charlesworth and the rockets and that girl of his—what was her name?—Annette. Charlesworth's first love, and possibly his last.

I wondered what Charlesworth was doing now; at high school he, like me, had studied Galactic languages and geography—subjects singularly useless in everyday life, as I have since found out. I now rear slithes for their skins at an impoverished farm on the coast of the Peninsula. I recollect reading once that Charlesworth had gone into the titanium business down the coast, but again I'm not sure. Whatever it was, you can be sure that it bore no connection with languages or geography. It's odd how a man can lose touch with people; as a youth of fifteen I would never have believed the day would come when I didn't know Charlesworth's address.

As I topped a rise, the land before me lay low and smooth, a vast bowl rimmed by hills and, to the east, snow-capped mountains. The road eased downhill directly into the center of this bowl, where stood huge blocks of grey glass and concrete buildings, dull and damp and abandoned; even from this distance I fancied I could see grass growing in the geometric streets. As though to suit my mood, the rain had begun again, drifting across the landscape as the rise of the mountains squeezed wetness from the west wind.

I drove through the straight main street, and the empty windows gaped at me in blind astonishment; then I turned left and the abandoned stores and office blocks petered out almost immediately. To my right stood the shell of the college; at some time in the past a fire had shattered the windows and stained the walls in dead black streaks; yet the general outline of the place was still capable of evoking nostagia. I remembered the anxiety of my parents when they found that the college was so close to the spaceport; the principal assured them that the place was totally soundproofed, but for weeks afterward I dared not ask my mother to repeat any remark she made, for fear she would conclude I was going deaf.

"I can't think why we had to come and live here," she said to my father one evening as we sat around the 3-V alcove and the rockets were a mere rumble in the distance.

"What's that you say?" My father cupped a hand to his ear—a habit of his, born of his job as maintenance supervisor at Pacific Northwest. "I can't hear you for this damned 3-V."

If my mother had known just how I spent my leisure hours, she would have had genuine cause for worry.

It was at the college that I met Charlesworth; he was my age—fourteen at that time. I had noticed him but never actually spoken to him; boys can be like that. One day I was involved in a brawl and had hit a girl—not entirely by accident—who had fallen to the ground screaming. Annette La-Rouge was a popular figure, and I suddenly found myself the center of mass antagonism. I withdrew rapidly to a distant washroom where I met Charlesworth staunching the flow of blood from his nose; in mutual sympathy we struck up a friendship which lasted through college.

I debated whether to stop and look around the wrecked buildings but decided against it; my memories there were not happy ones. In common with most people, my schooldays had been haunted by fear. Fear of retribution for the incomplete assignment, fear of the strong boy with small eyes and big fists, fear of finding myself in a class of total strangers listening to a subject of total incomprehensibility. Fear, in such a case, of finding I was in the wrong room—or worse still, the right room.

The good times had been after school hours, in the summer evenings and throughout the long weekends when time passed so much more slowly than it does now. These had been the times when Charlesworth and I gained illegal entry to the spaceport and stood watching from close range as the shuttles came in. These were the times I was thinking about as I drove the last mile across the open scrubland and though the huge archway, past the terminal buildings and onto the vast concrete field where the old ships stood, some squat like crabs, some taller than the buildings themselves—and all of them beautiful.

After twenty years, I had come back to Pacific Northwest.

Charlesworth was a leader. It was he who had found the way under the tall wire fence at the point where there was an underground shelter.

"In case a ship blows up," he explained with relish. There were two entrances to the shelter, one from outside the wire, one inside. We merely walked down the steps, through the concrete corridor, and up the steps at the far end. Then, there we were—and my stomach always heaved with glory at this point—standing on the landing area itself, about a half mile from the terminal buildings. All around stood the shuttle ships, large and small, passenger and freight, some bearing the insignia of International Space Service. These we despised. Most of the craft, however, were privately owned by corporations with flamboyant livery and evocative names such as Rendezvous, Inc., Orbitry, Circular Spaceways, First Step, Black Midnight Meetings, and the more prosaic Sid's Shuttles, whose craft always looked in need of maintenance.

Then there were the deep-space pinnaces, those glamorous vessels owned by the giant Galactic corporations so wealthy that they could afford to operate—and more important carry through space—their own shuttle craft. These ships were rare birds of passage, and we would constantly be scanning the bulletins for news of their arrival, then hurrying to the spaceport after school to feast our young eyes on the craft which had come from many light-years away; some of them, in fact, had not even been built on Earth. The pinnaces would belong to such corporations as the Hetherington Organization and Cosmic Enterprises and would be carried in the bellies of the giant starships across the reaches of deep space, bearing witness to the wealth of their owners at every planetfall across the Galaxy.

Charlesworth and I were enthralled by all these, both equally eager to spend every spare moment watching their arrival and departure, equally grudging of every moment wasted in school—yet we differed in our attitude towards the ships in a very fundamental way.

"I mean, Sagar," he said to me one day, as we had flinched to the thunderous touchdown of *Leviathan*, shuttle ship number 11 of the oddly named Up and Down Under, Pty., "just where do you get your kicks? Like, you watched that tub as though you'd never seen it before."

"Today was the first time I've seen Old Legs land," I said carefully. We had our own names for regular visitors. There was no way I could explain to Charlesworth that I enjoyed watching Number Eleven touch down equally as much as the rarest pinnace from the furthest outpost.

That was the difference between us.

Charles was a collector. He carried with him a little book—it was almost as though it had been published with him in mind—listing every conceivable ship which might land at any Earth spaceport. It was prepared in co-operation with all the larger operators and most of the smaller ones, and was intended for official use only. Charlesworth, however, had obtained a contraband copy, and whenever he saw a ship, he consulted his book. If he had never seen that particular vessel before, he checked it off neatly in green ink and was deliriously happy. I got a kick out of watching him. He would regard the blasting jets of a descending ship raptly—as did I—but as soon as he was able to identify it, his interest was transferred to the printed page. His ratlike face intent, he would scrutinize his list. In the majority of cases he would then frown with disgust, shutting the book with a snap and kicking moodily at a rock, or belching loudly. Charlesworth's was a dead-end passion. The moments of happiness grew fewer as the check marks in his book multiplied like algae, and as I looked over his shoulder, I could estimate to within a few months when he would quit the hobby, or maybe shoot himself.

The area around the underground shelter developed its own history; Charlesworth and I were not the only enthusiasts who would gather there at weekends, and after a while it became possible for talk to grow nostalgic, as we reminisced about the rocky landing of the First Step *Victory*, last September, or the exploits of Stagg, who was no longer with us, having kicked the habit.

Stagg's period of ascendancy had been brief but memorable—he had bequeathed to us Stagg's Tower. This was a steel structure beside the shelter; to the uninitiated it might appear as a prosaic water tower, but to us it was Stagg's Tower, and always will be.

A steel ladder climbed from the base of the tower to the tank some forty feet above. In the later afternoons when the novelty of the ships began to wane, we used to compete against one another on the ladder. We would see who could jump from the greatest altitude. I imagine the record, held by Charlesworth who had nerves of titanium, was in the region of fifteen feet. Nobody ever thought to climb any higher than that, let alone jump; such a feat was only attained by the godlike astronautic maintenance men of Pacific Northwest.

But Stagg did not like Charlesworth and was determined to wrest the record from his enemy. In order to achieve this he first got drunk—but mildly, so that we wouldn't notice and therefore disqualify him. In fact, Stagg's inebriation did not come to light until the next day, when the principal made his famous "Shun the Shuttles" speech at the college.

It was a Sunday afternoon when Stagg appeared, greeted us, and with no further notice of intent turned to the ladder and began steadily to climb.

I have found since that drink can play tricks on the memory. So I assume that Stagg, who was gazing upwards as he went, lost track of just how high he was. He reached the really difficult part where the ladder takes a slight overhang before climbing the side of the tank itself, before he stopped and turned, all set to jump. Then he found he was thirty feet up, and froze. We shouted encouragement and Charlesworth even hurled a few stones which clanged off the tank next to his head, but there was no way we could help Stagg. His nerve had gone.

His moment of glory was yet to come, however. After some discussion it was agreed we send for help, and our smallest member, named Wilkins, was dispatched to notify the authorities. Wilkins, however, went straight home. The following day, when the principal in the course of his address called for the members of our group to step forward and identify themselves, Wilkins stood motionless and treacherous. Nobody else moved either—but the point is that Wilkins didn't. Two wrongs, as my mother used to say with distressing frequency, do not make a right.

We waited for an hour while the white face of Stagg peered down at us from the sky, and every so often the ground and the tower would shudder as a shuttle lifted off. Then, unexpectedly, a scarlet maintenance vehicle swayed toward us, and within seconds we were through the tunnel and outside the wire. Uniformed men glanced at us, held a muttered discussion; then one of them began to climb, calling encouragement to Stagg. The man sounded enormously sympathetic and reasonable about the whole affair. Stagg wasn't to worry. Stagg wasn't to look down. Stagg had only to hold on for just one second more; then his new friend would be beside him, and everything would be all right.

Stagg's reply was simple and graphic. As the uniformed official reached up, hand outstretched to Stagg's ankle, smiling, comforting and assuring that the whole thing would be forgotten just as soon as they were down, Stagg vomited . . .

It was a cold December midmorning as I walked across the abandoned concrete towards my memories; although the surface was pitted and grass oozed from the cracks like gangrene, the water tower still stood. Standing also were the ships. I walked under the squat shape of *Rendezvous III*, and the rusting brown belly dripped chill water over me. Further on, the tall figure of *Vulcan* stood a little apart from the others; I glanced up into the powerful mystery of the tail pipes, then moved on, turning once to admire that sleek classic shape which had never ceased to thrill my boyhood emotions.

No doubt we were sublimating our adolescent urges in those days, but in our innocence we thought we were watching the spaceships.

Our urges did not go entirely sublimated, however. There was a day in June when Charlesworth and I were the only people in the spotting spot, as we called it; the ferry from Intertrade *Crusader* had just touched down in a storm of flame and din and sweet indescribable stench of exhaust. Charlesworth ignored the ferry; he had seen it before, many times. He was telling me about Hetherington pinnace number 4, which was the only craft owned by that Galactic corporation as yet unchecked in his little book. Having never seen the ship, I was not especially interested, but Charlesworth lived for the day when Hetherington Number 4 would touch down.

We were alone, and I was happy just to see and breathe spaceships, but Charlesworth was discontented. I think even he was beginning to get an inkling of the blind alley into which his enthusiasms were leading him—or maybe he had reached a certain age. I remember thinking that day, that maybe a guy grew out of spaceships—that the day would eventually come when, inconceivably, the sight of a liftoff would leave him unmoved. In which case, I concluded, he would truly have joined the ranks of the adults, with their lukewarm hobbies and obsession with work, with success, with women, with all the dull colors of boredom.

So it could be said that the thought of women crossed my mind, that June afternoon.

Charlesworth's earnest voice droned on as he anticipated in fullest detail the orgasm of delight which would be his when Number Four touched down. I was standing on the fifth rung of Stagg's Tower, and my gaze had inexplicably strayed from the perfect contours of Intertrade *Crusader II* across the rough pasture outside the wire; to my disgust I saw two girls approaching, a large black animal bounding around them. Even at this distance I recognized the queen of grade 9, Annette LaRouge with her courtier Rita Coggins. They had seen me and were threading their way through the tussocks in the direction of the tunnel under the wire.

"LaRouge is coming," I interrupted Charlesworth. "And Bunny."

"What for?"

"How the hell should I know?"

"Let's hide, Sagar, for Christ's sake."

"They've seen me."

"So bloody what? We can't have girls here. It's ... not right. They'd be in the way."

I sympathized with his view; it is the outlook which, later in life, I encounter in men's clubs everywhere. It implies nothing personal, not even a generalized male chauvinism; it is merely that a certain type of person must be excluded from activities which do not concern them and would not interest them. It is coincidental that the type of person excluded is of the opposite sex.

While we were discussing the problem, the huge black

paracat came bounding from the darkness of the tunnel and
jumped Charlesworth. I climbed two rungs higher, well out of
the reach of even this agile beast.

"For Christ's sake, call him off!" howled Charlesworth, his
thin face contorted with fear. The paracat had its paws on his
shoulders and was peering seriously into his eyes, as though it
had something important to tell him.

In fact paracats are reputed to be telepathic, but only
among their own species. The natives of their home planet
train them for hunting, but on Earth they are pets and, if
truth be known, conversation pieces. For several years they
were a popular status symbol, and people even organized
shows and laid stress on physical characteristics by which
they could tell, so they said, whether or not an animal was of
the stuff that champions were made—but in recent years they
have almost died out. Far more interesting pets can be
wrought from life already existing here on Earth, with a little
ingenuity—as witness the recent popularity of land sharks.

"Bagheera!" Annette LaRouge climbed the last few steps
out of the tunnel and stepped sedately into the sunshine,
somehow managing to ignore Charlesworth's presence as her
pet returned to her side. She settled herself carefully on the
grass bank at the side of the tunnel entrance, flanked on one
side by her rabbit-faced friend Rita, on the other side by the
still-slavering paracat. She whispered something to Rita, who
giggled, then the two girls looked long and poisedly at the
nearest rocket, while the awkward silence between Charlesworth and I lengthened.

I climbed down the ladder and stood beside him, drawing
confidence from his nearness. Behind us, the cool voice
spoke.

"Some people waste ā lot of time when they ought to be
doing something useful, don't they, Rita?"

Rita's reply was inaudible and accompanied by a giggle.

"It's childish," Annette resumed, "collecting numbers of
spaceships and writing them down in little books. My brother
does it. He's eight. It's kid's stuff."

Rita's whispered reply drew a peal of musical laughter
from the grade 9 queen, and I glanced at Charlesworth involuntarily. His face was scarlet.

I whirled round to face the smiling girl. "Look," I spluttered. "Nobody asked you to come here, making remarks. We
don't need you. Get back through the tunnel."

She was the same age as Charlesworth and I, but she had the knack of making a guy feel young and immature. She was self-contained, as though she had no need of the admiration of friendship of her fellows. She made us feel dependent and inadequate. I know better now. Looking back from the standpoint of adulthood, I can now realize that Annette LaRouge needed reassurance more than any of us, but at the time it seemed that she was a young woman, whereas Charlesworth and I were kids.

She pretended to ignore my outburst and addressed the pathetic Rita. "Some people ought to learn their manners," she said. She opened a small stylish purse and examined her face in a tiny mirror. "But you can't expect any better from a coward who beats up girls," she added.

I moved closer, feeling a desire violently to destroy her complacency but unsure how to accomplish it. I tried the reasonable approach, matching her calm tones. "Knocking you down doesn't make a coward. If I'd let *you* knock *me* down, and *I'd* run screaming to the teacher—then I'd be a coward."

"Some people are always making excuses for themselves," she informed Rita, who nodded wisely. To my amazed indignation, I heard Charlesworth chuckle appreciatively, as though the girl had made a telling point.

The one-sided argument was interrupted by the far-off thunder of an arrival from above. We watched as a tiny cloud formed white and drifting as the still-invisible ship descended through its own exhaust gases. Even now, I can still relive the thrill of those touchdowns; the active delight in the vision of power accompanied by the speculative delight of conjecture: Where has it come from? What ship is it, and to which corporation does it belong? And, in Charlesworth's case, have I seen it before?

Darting flames were fingering toward us, seemingly straight at us, and the air was a pandemonium of noise and scattering debris. It was a big ship, three-legged and dart-shaped; therefore a fairly old ship. Chances were, I guessed as the flames drew nearer, that it was one of the local shuttles. I glanced at Annette and my heart thumped in unholy joy; her eyes were wide with fear and her mouth open in a drowned scream as she visualized the machine squatting directly onto our position. She clung to the paracat; its ears were laid back and its upper lip curled in a terrified snarl.

Charlesworth and I had slipped on our goggles and

watched unconcernedly as the blown dust, stones and waste paper whirled about our heads and the girls snatched at their skirts. The paracat broke free and, tail tucked protectively around its genitals, fled into the tunnel. The ground was trembling now, a fast dull drumming as the throbbing exhaust gases pounded the unyielding concrete with ultrasonics.

The giant legs stepped towards us gingerly, reaching to straddle the circular void of the exhaust pit; and I remembered, as always, the time *Orbiter VIII* had missed its footing, planting two legs firmly on the concrete while the third hung rigid and nervous over the pit; I could hear the acceleration of the engines and imagine the frantic whirring of the gyroscopes as the pilot realized his error, fought to maintain balance and, at last, lifted laboriously off for another try—which, disappointingly for us youthful ghouls, was successful . . . Such incidents are the foundation blocks of childhood memories.

The present touchdown afforded no such excitement, however. Charlesworth suddenly lost interest as it became apparent that the ship was old *Leviathan,* the din decreased as the exhaust jetted directly into the pit, and quiet fountains of smoke arose at the perimeter of the field, ducted there by the stygian system of exhaust tunnels linking the pits to the perimeter vents.

A recurrent juvenile nightmare of mine concerned being trapped in those tunnels and hearing an approaching ship . . .

Leviathan rocked on her legs and was still. Charlesworth and I removed our goggles, and as our ears began to recover, we became aware of Annette screaming, having for once lost her cool.

"My mom and dad'll kill me if I lose Bagheera!"

It seemed to me that this was her problem, but Charlesworth thought otherwise. "Come on, Sagar!" he shouted. "He can't have gone far!"

"So bloody what?" I muttered.

"Come on," he repeated, with a sideways glance at Annette. "Have some decency. It won't hurt you to help someone else for once!"

As I look back to that afternoon, I can now realize that, for Charlesworth and I, it represented a milestone. Neither of us was quite the same afterwards; neither was our relationship the same. We gained knowledge and we lost innocence. Charlesworth learned the meaning of love; I learned the meaning of treachery. Thereby we lost simple pleasure, and the relationship between him, me and the ships became more complex. I think we lost trust.

The trio of Charlesworth, Annette and the paracat became a familiar sight around the streets of Pacific Northwest during the next weeks as school finished and the long summer vacation stretched gloriously ahead. I know adults got a kick out of seeing them together and would nudge one another and point them out with sentimental smiles; they thought the sight was innocent and sweet. In fact the adults were the innocent parties; I alone knew—because Charlesworth had confided in me—how he spent sleepless nights sweating with lust as the vision of Annette swayed through his imagination.

All in vain, of course; he wasn't getting anything from her—except permission to trot at her heels in tandem with the paracat and register a devotion which the animal had too much self-respect to emulate. Charlesworth made a complete idiot of himself, that summer.

Occasionally he would show up at the spotting spot, grinning sheepishly. I assumed those were the days when Annette had her hair done. He would punch me on the biceps and call me "man" and try to behave as though nothing had happened—as did I—but as the hours wore on, he would become restless, and I would catch his gaze straying across the scrubland in the direction of town. He was hoping Annette would come along, but she seldom did. The appalling din of a touchdown at close quarters was too raw for her sensitive nerves.

During those weeks his attitude changed in another way, too. At first he was proud of what he imagined to be his conquest—that was when he made the revelation concerning his lascivious nights—but after a couple of weeks even he realized that Annette was the conqueror, and he began to get a haunted, hangdog look like a kid caught misbehaving.

As Charlesworth went downhill, so Annette LaRouge thrived, like a vampire. With school over for the summer she was permitted to assume a more individualistic style of dress, and she took full advantage of this, with strutting high heels, padded bra, no-skirt skirts, and a jeweled collar for the paracat. Even I had to admit that she looked pretty good—but there was no envy of Charlesworth in this private confession. I was scared of her power, scared of what she was doing to Charlesworth and glad that I was well out of it.

Rita Coggin's rabbit features could occasionally be seen in the coffee bar; invariably she would be alone, staring disconsolately into the depths of a cola. She had been dropped because she was a mere hanger-on—unlike Charlesworth who was a genuine sexual conquest, and possibly Annette's first.

Pacific Northwest was a maelstrom of adolescent emotions, that summer.

The tunnel was still there, although smaller than I remembered it; but as I began to descend the steps, I was brought up short by an expanse of black water stretching from the third step across the sloping roof. I had hoped to examine the walls beneath to see if the graffiti were still there, but perhaps it was fortunate that this was impossible. Outside again, I regarded the grassy banks now overgrown with scrub, the tall wire fence rusted and broken down, in some places missing entirely. Stagg's Tower was still intact, although I wouldn't have liked to try an ascent of those decayed wire-thin rungs.

I was vaguely dissatisfied with the place. The memories were there, somewhere, but they would not come to life. They were lost in decay and growth and the strange indescribable way a landscape will rot, when not frequently revisited. Every change seems to be a change for the worse. I should have come here more often, and I should have looked up Charlesworth and brought him along too, and between us we could have coaxed things to life.

I turned and looked at the landing field again, testing my memories on the nearest ship. It was badly stained with dirt and weather but still possessed that economical racy look which characterized the pinnace in the days of liquid fuel, before antigravity stripped shuttles of their soul. The lettering was patchy and faded but legible, and the crest above the name was instantly recognizable; the stylized diagonal spaceship with parallel lightning flash. The words below read HETHERINGTON ORGANIZATION.

There was a number further down; I could barely read it. It was the number 4.

That was when my memories really came alive.

One day in late July, I met Charlesworth, for once alone, in the main street. I glanced at him and made to pass by; it seemed he hardly knew me these days, and he hadn't been near the spaceport for weeks. Something about his manner made me look again, however, and mutter a greeting.

"Sagar," he cried, clutching my sleeve, his face more animated than I had seen it for a long time. "Have you heard the news?"

"You've got her pregnant," I said sarcastically, knowing this to be the least likely thing imaginable.

He ignored this. "Are you coming to the spotting spot this afternoon?"

"I thought you'd given all that up."

"Nonsense, man. Nonsense. I've been busy, that's all."

"Wasting your time, I guess."

"It was her father put me onto it," he said meaninglessly. "He said it was about time Bagheera had a mate. He said it was unkind to keep the bastard all alone, but I can tell you, Sagar, the man wants to make money out of it. Paracats cost a fortune, and he means to breed them."

"So he's shipping a female in this afternoon?" I was beginning to see the connection.

"You're quick, Sagar, you're quick. But I'll bet you don't know what else."

"What the hell are you talking about?" His manner was irritating me. Talking to him for the first time in days, I suddenly knew that his manner had always irritated me. There was something unstable about Charlesworth. No man in his right mind could prefer Annette LaRouge to spaceships for example.

"The paracat's coming in Number Four! I was looking at the bill of lading, and I noticed she was coming via Hetherington *Endeavor,* and for the hop down Earthside they're using pinnace number four! Christ!" He waited for me to share his joy.

"That was the ship you wanted to see, was it? One of the last ones on your list?"

His eyes held the old fanaticism. "The *last* number on the list, Sagar. When I've seen Number Four, I've seen them all. Every goddamned one. Every goddamned ship that ever visits the planet Earth, I've seen them all. By Christ. I've waited all my life for this!" His young face peered at me; he looked thinner than ever, intense, with acne erupting all over, which shows what the Annette LaRouges of this world will do to a man's health.

"Charlesworth," I said, trying to keep a straight face, "you won't have anything left to live for, afterwards."

He eyed me oddly. "You'll never understand, will you. Let me tell you this, Sagar, I hate those bloody ships and all those bloody hours I've wasted watching them and checking them off in that stupid little book. Annette says it's kid's stuff and she's right, by God. This is the last time you'll ever see me at that place. Just this one last time . . ."

His voice dropped so suddenly that he almost whispered, and an unhealthy tingle passed down my spine. I was in the presence of something I didn't understand. Maybe I do now, but at the age of fifteen I couldn't see how anyone could fail to love and venerate anything so big, so powerful, so virile as a shuttleship. I couldn't understand why Charlesworth should want to *beat* the things in this oblique way, or why he seemed to consider a complete list of numbers as a victory.

"I'll see you at the spotting spot," I said unhappily. Even at my young age, Charlesworth had become a part of my life, and the spaceport would not be the same without him, for all his faults. So many others were losing interest too: Stagg played around with girls all the time; Simpson had left the district; Walker was talking about some nebulous future career . . . After today, I would be the only one. No matter how much you may dislike your friends, the day will always come when you wish you still had them around.

I was the first to arrive at the spotting spot. The spaceport was quiet, that bright July afternoon, with a quietness that to my juvenile imagination suggested ominous pauses, the lull before the storm, any one of many adult cliches to describe the benefits of hindsight. It just so happened, I told myself determinedly, that the schedules had conspired to desert Pacific Northwest at this particular hour, on this particular day. It was nothing to do with the fact that Charlesworth would soon be here and I was uncertain about his reactions, his motives, or indeed about himself.

When at last I saw him picking his way through the thornbushes, across the long yellowing grass of midsummer, I felt a sudden thud of dismay in my stomach because Annette LaRouge was with him, head high, chest out, paracat frolicking at her heels. This was the ultimate in treachery, for Charlesworth to bring the unspeakable Annette with him on this afternoon of all afternoons.

When they stepped from the tunnel, she ignored me, but

Charlesworth greeted me with quiet sheepishness, avoiding my eye as he buckled the leash onto the paracat's bejeweled collar at Annette's command.

"These horrible ships frighten him," she informed Charlesworth. "I can't think why you wanted to come."

"Well, I thought we ought to be here . . . what with your father having another animal coming . . ."

"Nonsense, Roger," she said firmly. Charlesworth had always professed a hatred for his Christian name. "You just wanted to watch the ships again, that's what you wanted to do." There was an edge to her voice.

These exchanges had cheered me up considerably. It seemed that Charlesworth had, unbelievably, succeeded in imposing his will upon Annette. I addressed him. "It's all confirmed about Number Four, then?"

He stared at me blankly, as though surprised to see me. "What are you talking about, Sagar?"

"You know . . . you said, this morning . . ." I stammered, put off by his cold look.

"I don't remember saying anything this morning." And he turned away, turned his damned back on me and began to converse with Annette LaRouge in a pseudoadult fashion which made me want to smash his face in.

It was no good. I should have realized before. Charlesworth and I were through, and had been through for weeks. I moved away a few paces; there is nothing more lonely than standing too close to people who ignore you. I watched them as they chatted like a grown-up couple; Annette with her haughty look and undeniably classic features standing like a posing model. God, how I hated her. At fifteen years old, I found classic features singularly unattractive, preferring plump cheeks and ripe lips, bright eyes and big tits.

And as an adult, my preferences have not changed one iota. Which proves that I was pretty damned mature at the age of fifteen, maybe.

Charlesworth was spoiling the effect somewhat as he struggled to control the fractious paracat, thin sinews standing out on his puny wrists while his rodent face was turned attentively and gravely towards Annette and they discussed Orwell's *1984*, the year's set book, with every appearance of absorption.

At last the pretentious scene was interrupted by the familiar, simple and wonderful thunder from the sky. I looked up and saw the tiny cloud, and from the corner of my eye I saw Charlesworth watching too, and for a moment it was possible to believe that the old times were back. Life is so full at that age that a man can become nostalgic about the happenings of last month.

But Annette was still determinedly talking.

Charlesworth missed his cue and earned a sharp look and an enquiry as to the state of his hearing.

I could make out the tiny black dot now, and the little spark was visible even on this bright summer day.

Annette prattled on, and Charlesworth answered with desperate interest.

A light wind was trailing the smoke across the sky like a comet's tail. Charlesworth jerked suddenly as the paracat tugged at the leash.

"But of course, the exaggerated problems met by Winston Smith were inspired by the fears of the age in which Orwell lived."

Maybe she was right, but so what? So what on a summer's afternoon when a rocket is squatting towards you on scarlet tailfeathers?

"Yeah, I'm sure," muttered Charlesworth, looking up.

And now it was clearly in view, gleaming silver through the smoke and flame, tall and sharp and beautiful, strong talons downhung like a stooping hawk, roaring with power so that the Earth shook.

I watched it with love, Charlesworth watched it.

"Roger! I'm speaking to you!"

No doubt she had more to say, but by now the din was intense, and even Annette turned her gaze upwards, wincing, watching. The silver giant was decelerating, elongating as it dropped towards its exhaust pit; the curved flank came plainly into view. There was a diagonal crest; below, the words HETHERINGTON ORGANIZATION.

And below that, in plain black, the number 4.

Through the bedlam I heard Charlesworth's yell of triumph, and I turned to look at him. Though I can't describe his expression, I'll never forget it. I think I felt a slight shiver on that hot July afternoon. Nobody should feel like Charlesworth felt about a plain black digit. I noticed that he had dropped the leash, and I think Annette became aware of this at the same instant—because that was when she screamed.

The black beast bounded forward, covering the concrete in

giant flowing strides, head tilted back and staring fixedly at the descending ship.

"Stop him, Roger! Stop him! He'll be killed!"

And for an unthinking moment Charlesworth obeyed and ran forward while the fearsome tail pipes bellowed malevolently at him. Then he stopped and turned back, looking from Annette to me dazedly, while behind him the paracat bounded on.

Annette's voice cut through the din. "*Go on! Go on! What are you stopping for?*"

The ships seem to descend right on top of you; yet the landing areas are some distance away, far across the smooth concrete. This surprising distance is apparent when a truck or embarkation bus pulls alongside a ship.

So it was that the paracat dwindled to a frisking kitten, still looking up as it ran, hearing excitingly in its mind what we could never hear—the irresistible call from female to male, from its telepathic mate in the descending ship . . .

It never saw the edge of the exhaust pit; it was still staring eagerly upwards as if fell over the lip and disappeared from view.

The giant silver legs touched and flexed. The flames, the smoke knifed down, hit the base of the pit and bounced up again, thick and alive like yeast. The sounds diminished, the perimeter fountains puffed.

I dared to look at Annette and Charlesworth.

I could not tell what they were thinking. I could not tell what Annette was saying, because it was too fast, too bitter, too frightened, and I was too deaf.

I walked quickly to the tunnel and descended the steps. I made my way through the dark shelter and up the other side, beyond the wire where the tall dry grass waved, and it was a different world. I didn't look back, but I knew that Annette and Charlesworth were standing exactly where I had left them, etching in their memories a scene that neither of them would forget.

I had reached the main street of the town before the irony of it occurred to me. Charlesworth's moment of ultimate triumph had been turned into a defeat which might be equally ultimate.

And now there was a sprinkling of snow drifting from the greying skies, and the mountains in the distance were blurred.

I kicked idly at a clump of coarse grass which had thrust its way bravely through the decaying concrete, and thought about leaving; there was nothing for me here, now that I had done what I came to do. I had paid my last respects to the ships, and now I must get out before the desolation and the putrefaction impressed itself too deeply on me and erased the happier memories.

Number Four stood there like a cenotaph to my youth, and as I began to walk slowly towards the terminal building, I told myself I had done the right thing in coming here. I had obeyed the impulse, I had found—as I had expected to find—that things were not the same, and now I was going.

I had not expected to see anyone else here, yet.

I stopped, moved back beside the tunnel entrance as a hovercar came swaying across the concrete from the terminal buildings, heading fast in my direction. A nervousness tingled in my stomach. Maybe that was another memory, but nevertheless I was trespassing, and I had seen recently on Newspocket that the penalties for trespass had been increased lately, following a shortage of state prisoners. I couldn't understand how they had spotted me—unless someone had been scanning the landing area with binoculars.

Then I noticed four black shapes in the southern sky, and I relaxed. The car was merely the advance guard of the wrecking team, coming to size the place up. They would hardly report a sightseer to the police. All the same, I withdrew into the tunnel entrance; there was no point in taking chances. The car pulled up and sank to the ground nearby; two men climbed out, watching the approach of the ungainly airborne cranes. They were too far away for me to hear what they were saying, but one of them was pointing at the helpless ships standing around, doubtless giving instructions.

The cranes were close now, black and sinister to my prejudiced eye as they hovered above the spaceport like giant vultures. They were functional in shape; skeletal arms projecting at all angles, hooks and magnets hanging, swinging. Their highly efficient antigravity units were almost soundless; just a thin whine drifted down with the snow. They were cold and unthinking, those cranes, robotic and heartless like all antigrav vehicles, and I wanted to get away. I could not bear to witness this, their final victory over their evolutionary predecessors, this destruction of everything my childhood held beautiful.

The two men turned and walked towards me; they saw me standing there but merely nodded briefly; no doubt they were accustomed to idle bystanders at wrecking operations. The smaller man was speaking. His voice was harsh and confident, the voice of authority. He looked up, his sharp features profiled against the grey sky, a faint thin smile on his lips— and the years slipped away. . . .

The nearest crane rotated slowly above the spaceport, and the huge white letters came into view: CHARLESWORTH CONTRACTORS. I've often wondered what lies behind the single minded strength of purpose that can drive the unlikeliest man to success; Charlesworth seemed to have done very well for himself.

I almost went forward to speak to him, to renew our acquaintance, but decided not to and made for the terminal buildings instead.

Somehow, I felt we didn't have much in common, any more.

THE HERTFORD MANUSCRIPT

by Richard Cowper

Cowper combines a high quality British literary style with a background of historical understanding—and thereby comes up with a sequel to Wells' immortal Time Machine *that stands on its own.*

The death of my Great-Aunt Victoria at the advanced age of 93 topped off the longest branch of a family tree whose roots have been traced right back to the 15th Century—indeed, for those who are prepared to accept "Decressie" as a bonafide corruption of "de Crècy," well beyond that. Talking to my aunt towards the end of her life was rather like turning the pages of a Victorian family album, for as she grew older the England of her childhood seemed to glow ever more brightly in her mind's eye. In those far-off days it had been fashionable to accept the inevitability of human progress with a whole-heartedness which is almost impossible for us to imagine. In the 1990's life presented *Homo sapiens* with a series of "problems" which had to be "solved." It was as simple as that. The Edwardians merely gilded the roof of that towering pagoda of Victorian optimism which collapsed in smithereens in 1914.

James Wilkins—Great-Aunt Victoria's husband—died of trench fever in the Dardanelles in 1916. They had no children and she never married again. I learnt later from my aunt that James had been a keen member of the Fabian Society. He had also been an active partner in the antiquarian book business of Benham & Wilkins which owned premises off Old Bond Street.

Shortly after James's death, and much to her family's astonishment, Victoria announced her intention of taking over her husband's share of the business. She very soon proved herself to be an extremely capable business woman. She made a specialty of English incunabula, and throughout the 20's and 30's she built up a thriving trade with countless museums and university libraries all over the world. When the vast Hertford Collection was sold off to pay death duties in 1938, Great-Aunt Victoria had her seat reserved in the front row of the auction gallery throughout the two weeks of the sale, and in the price register published afterwards the name Wilkins was prominent among the list of buyers.

In October, 1940, a direct hit from an incendiary bomb destroyed the premises and much of the stock of Benham & Wilkins overnight. She was close to sixty at the time, living alone in Hampstead, and I remember receiving a letter from her in which she told me that she had decided to sell out. She did not sound particularly regretful about it. "No doubt it had to happen," she wrote, "and I consider myself fortunate that it did not happen to me too." I discounted the unfamiliar note of fatalism in her words as being due to shock.

She lived on in her house in Well Walk, growing perceptibly frailer as the years advanced, but with her mind still alert. I used to make a point of calling in to see her whenever I was up in town and was invariably offered China tea and caraway-seed cake for which she had a lifelong passion. On one occasion, in the late 50's, she told me she had once been "propositioned" by H.G. Wells.

"I had no idea you knew him," I said. "When was that?"

"Oh, at about the time he and Shaw and the Webbs were squabbling over the future of the Society."

"The Fabian Society?"

"Yes, of course. 1907, I think it was."

"And what was the proposition?"

She laughed. "The usual one, I gathered. He said he wished me to help him with a book he was writing on the emancipation of women." She paused and gazed out of the window. "He was a strangely attractive little man."

"But you didn't accept?"

"No. Perhaps I should have done. Of course I had met him before that—at the Huxleys'. Everyone was talking about him." She paused again and seemed for a while to lose herself in reverie, then she remarked, "Did you ever read a story of his called 'The Chronic Argonauts'?"

"I can't recall it," I said. "What was it about?"

"About a man who invents a machine which will carry him through Time."

"Oh, you mean 'The Time Machine,' Aunt."

"Indeed I don't. I'm quite sure that was the title. I'd never seen 'chronic' used in that way before. It was a serial he was writing for a magazine. He showed me a copy of the first installment. You see we both knew the man it was based on."

"I'm surprised it was based on anyone," I said.

"Oh, yes," she assured me. "A Doctor Robert Pensley. He lived in Herne Hill. Like all of us in those days he too was a great admirer of Professor Huxley."

I helped myself to another slice of seed cake. "And what did the doctor make of young Wells's portrait of him?" I asked.

"As far as I know he never read it."

"Oh? Why not?"

"He disappeared."

I blinked at her. "Just like that?"

She nodded. "It created quite a stir at the time. There were rumors that he had skipped off to America."

"And had he?"

"*I* don't think so. And neither did Wells." She chuckled—a strangely youthful sound from lips so old—and added: "I remember H.G.'s very first words to me when he learnt what had happened: 'By God, Vikki, don't you see? He's done it!'"

"And what did he mean by that?" I asked.

"Traveled in Time, of course," said Aunt Victoria in the matter-of-fact tone she might have employed in saying: "Caught the 10:15 to Portsmouth."

I am ashamed to say I laughed.

She gave me a darting, sidelong glance from her clear, gray eyes. "You think it quite impossible, of course."

"Oh, quite," I said, setting down my tea cup and wiping the cake crumbs from my fingers with my handkerchief.

"Wells didn't think so."

"Ah, yes," I said. "But then he wrote science-fiction, didn't he?"

"Well, I presume he'd just appreciated that he had the

material for an excellent story. After all, he wrote it, didn't he?"

"He wrote it *down*," she said.

"Well, there you are then. And no doubt Doctor Pensley's descendants are living happily in America to this day."

Aunt Victoria smiled faintly and let the subject drop.

I was in Melbourne, Australia, right on the other side of the globe, when I received a letter telling me that Aunt Victoria had died. The news did not come as any great surprise because I knew she had been in poor health ever since catching a severe dose of flu in the early spring, but the sense of loss I felt was real enough. Her death seemed to nudge me appreciably nearer to my own grave.

When I returned home to England, some six weeks later, it was to discover that my aunt's mortal remains were nourishing the rose bushes in Highgate cemetery and the house in Well Walk had already been sold. I also discovered a letter awaiting me. It was signed by her bank manager, who, it appeared, was the executor of her will, and it informed me that I had been left a legacy of a thousand pounds together with "a particular token of the regard in which the late Mrs. Wilkins held you."

I lost no time in traveling up to town from my house in Bristol and presenting myself at the bank manager's office. After the formal exchange of polite regrets for the sad nature of the occasion, I was handed a brown paper parcel, securely tied and sealed, with my own name written upon it in Aunt Victoria's quite remarkably firm hand. I signed the official receipt, was presented with an envelope containing a cheque for 1000 pounds, and stepped out into the street. I was not consumed by any overwhelming curiosity to discover exactly what "token of regard" the parcel contained. From the shape of it I guessed that it must be a book of some kind, and I had a shrewd suspicion that it would prove to be the photograph album which Aunt Victoria and I had often looked at together when I visited her in Well Walk.

There being nothing further to detain me in London, I took a taxi to Paddington and caught the first available train back to Bristol. Having decided to invest a modest portion of my windfall on a first-class ticket, I had the unfamiliar luxury of a whole compartment to myself, and seated there, relaxed and extremely pleased with myself and the world, I finally got round to untying the string which, I did not doubt, Aunt Victoria had fastened with her own capable hands.

I soon realized that I had been mistaken in my previous assumption. The book which emerged from beneath the layers of brown paper and newsprint in which it was wrapped had certainly been old long before the invention of photography. It measured roughly 12 inches by 9, was bound in dark brown leather, and had a heavily ridged spine of the kind which I believe is known in the antiquarian book trade as "knuckled." There was no tooling of any kind either on the covers or on the spine, in fact nothing at all on the outside of the book to indicate what its contents might be. For the life of me I could not conceive why Aunt Victoria should have left it to me.

As I turned back the front cover, I found, lying inside, a sealed envelope, inscribed with my Christian name and bearing at the bottom right-hand corner a date—June 4th, 1958.

I laid the book down on the seat beside me, slit open the envelope and extracted two sheets of the tinted notepaper which my aunt had always favoured. I put on my spectacles and read the following:

Wednesday evening

My dear Francis,

There was a point during our conversation this afternoon when I was sorely tempted to march upstairs and fetch down this book. Though I am sure you don't realize it, there was something about the way in which you dismissed the very idea of time travel as being 'Quite impossible!' that struck me as almost unbearably smug. However, second thoughts being, as usual, better than first impulses, I have decided instead that I shall leave you the book in my will. So by the time you read this letter I daresay you will already have become accustomed to thinking of me as your late Aunt rather than your Great Aunt! I confess that it makes me smile even as I write it.

From the ex-libris plate inside the front cover you will see that this book comes from the Hertford Library which was sold up in 1938. It was part of a lot consisting of some half a dozen miscellaneous 17th Century Registers which I obtained for the proverbial song simply because no one else seemed interested in them. It was not until I was going through them to make out entries for our Overseas catalogue that I noticed that one of them had stitched into the back of it about twenty flimsy sheets of paper which were quite different in texture from those which make up the rest of the volumn. Since the binding itself was indisputably 17th Century workmanship and all the other entries concerned the years 1662–1665. I started to examine these odd pages with some interest. I discovered, to my astonishment, that they constituted a sort of rough journal or diary, written in pencil, and covering a period of some three weeks in August and September, 1665.

I will not spoil my own pleasure in imagining your expression as you read them by telling you what I believe them to be. All I will say is that the Register was entered in the Hertford Catalogue in 1808 as having been purchased along with two other 'from the Estate of Jonas Smiley Esq.' To the very best of my knowledge they lay there in the library of Hertford Castle gathering dust for the next 130 years.

I trust you will find it as interesting and as instructive as I did.

Yours most affectionately,
Victoria.

I re-read the letter from beginning to end in total bewilderment. At first, I confess, I could only assume that I was the victim of some extraordinary practical joke she had chosen to play upon me, but it was so *unlike* Aunt Victoria to do anything of the kind that, in the end, I simply shrugged and picked up the book. Sure enough, pasted inside the front cover was an engraved bookplate depicting two remarkably well-developed mermaids holding aloft a shell in which reclined a grinning skull, a quill pen and an hourglass. Circumscribing this somewhat ill-assorted gathering was a fluttering banner emblazoned with the legend *EX LIBRIS HERTFORDENSIS*. So at least there seemed to be no doubt about that part of Aunt Victoria's story. I turned over the stained flyleaf and found myself contemplating an ornate sepia scrip which informed me that this was ye Register opened on November 20th 1662 for ye Hostel of Saint Barnabas in ye Parish of Wapping of whieh ye Recording Clerk was one Tobias Gurney. The first entry on the next page read: *Decd. at the 4th hr. Agnes Miller, fem. age indet. of ye fev. quot. tert.*

I ran my eye down the column which appeared to consist

almost entirely of records of deaths and then flicked on through the yellowed pages till I reached those leaves which Aunt Victoria had spoken about. I saw at once why they had caught her attention. For one thing they measured little more than 6 inches by 4, and the paper, besides being badly faded at the edges of the sheets, was ruled with faint lines. But even more striking was the difference in the handwriting. These pages were covered in a minute, cramped, cursive script quite unlike the hand of the recording clerk. If I had to select one adjective to describe it, the word would be "scholarly." In fact the tiny writing put me immediately in mind of that of J.E. Lawless, my erstwhile tutor at St. Catherine's; there were even some of the identical abbreviations—"tho." for "though"; "wd." for "would"; "shd." for "should"—which I remembered he had favored. Settling myself firmly into the corner closest to the window, I raised the book to catch the maximum amount of daylight and began to read.

Some twenty minutes before the train was due at Bristol I had reached the last entry. I find it quite impossible to describe accurately my precise state of mind at that moment. I remember becoming conscious of an acute headache, the onset of which I had, presumably, ignored while I was engrossed in my reading. I remember too that as I unhooked my spectacles and gazed out of the window I experienced a most extraordinary sense of disorientation—perhaps "displacement" would be the better word—as though the green fields and cosy Wiltshire farms beyond the tract had become mysterious, insubstantial, illusory things; mere tokens of stasis in some fantastic temporal flux. The moment passed quickly enough—the discipline of a lifetime's ingrained habit of thought soon reasserted itself—but I was left with the same excessively unpleasant sense of inner quivering that I had once endured after experiencing a minor earthquake in Thessaloniki. To say that I doubted what I most firmly believed would be putting it too strongly; to say that my philosophical foundations had been temporarily shaken would not be putting it quite strongly enough.

It will, I am sure, be maintained that I am either the instigator of—or the victim of!—some elaborate hoax. The first contention I shall perforce ignore, since, knowing it to be untrue, it does not particularly concern me. To the second I am forced to return a reluctant verdict of "Not Proven." I have had the Register examined by two separate experts in such matters and both have assured me, to my own total satisfaction, that the notebook pages which have been incorporated within it were stitched into the binding at the time when the book itself was bound up, i.e., not later than the middle of the 18th Century and, in all likelihood, a good half-century earlier. *Yet the paper of the notebook itself is, indisputably, of a type not manufactured before 1860! Ergo,* either somebody is lying or the notebook is genuine.

If we assume that some person (unknown) had wished to perpetuate such a hoax, when could it have been done? From the internal evidence certainly not before 1804. Therefore this anonymous hoaxer must have had access to the Hertford Library, have inserted his spurious material into the Register, have replaced it on the library shelf and then *done nothing at all to draw attention to it.* Since, presumably, the whole point of a hoax is to deceive as many people as possible, this strikes me as just about the most pointless hoax ever devised.

That leaves, as far as I am concerned, only my Great-Aunt Victoria. She had custody of the Register from the time of the sale in 1938 until the day of her death—ample opportunity certainly in which to have "doctored it" to her heart's content. Furthermore she, with her professional connections, would have been ideally situated to carry out such a plan had she wished to do so. This would have entailed forging the whole "diary" itself on suitable paper, having the Register broken down and the forged diary incorporated, reassembling the whole and restoring it to its original condition in such a way as to totally deceive two vastly experienced and disinterested professional experts. She would also have had to insert (or have caused to be inserted) two completely spurious entries into the Register proper, doing it in such a way that there was no observable discrepancy between those false entries and the ones which preceded and followed them. The only way in which this could have been done would have been by removing two of the original sheets, obtaining two blank sheets of the identical 17th Century rag paper, forging the entries to correspond *exactly* with those in the rest of the book, and then reassembling the whole. I am prepared to admit that all this *could* have been done, but nothing will ever succeed in convincing me that it was. Nevertheless, since such a thing is conceivably possible, I must to that extent acceed to the verdict of "Not Proven" on the second of my two counts.

Having said that, all that remains is for me to transcribe *in toto* the contents of this extraordinary document and to add, by way of an appendix, the relevant entries from the Register itself together with a few concluding observations of my own.

Although the transcript is a faithful word-for-word copy of the orginal text, I have taken the liberty of expanding the author's abbreviations, inserting the paragraphs, and tidying up the punctuation where I think it is called for. The diary commences at the top of the first page, and it is possible that a preceding page or pages were incorporated in the Register.

* * *

It is, of course, utterly pointless to go on cursing myself for my idiotic complacency, yet has there been a single waking hour in the last 48 when I have not done so? To assume, as I did, that the Morlocks* had done no more than carry out an investigation of the superficial structure of my Machine was an inexcusable indulgence in wishful thinking, bolstered, unfortunately, by my successful onward voyage and return. Yet even now I am by no means certain that the Morlocks were responsible for that microscopic fracture of the dexter polyhedron. Could it not equally well have occurred during that final frenzied battle within the pedestal of the White Sphinx? Indeed it seems more than likely. What is utterly unforgivable is that I should have failed to detect the flaw when I carried out my detailed check on Friday. Well, few men can ever have paid more dearly for wanton carelessness.

I knew that something was amiss the moment I had recovered sufficiently from my initial vertigo to scan the dials. Instead of circling smoothly around the horologe the indicator arm had developed a perceptible and disquieting lurch, first slowing and then accelerating. I realized at once that two of the quartz pillars in the quincunx were out of phase and I suspected some minor fault of alignment which it would be but the work of a moment in the laboratory to correct. Although the dials on the fascia showed that I was already well back into the 17th Century, a glance at my pocket watch informed me that my journey was less than two minutes old.

---

* *For this and similar references see* The Time Machine *by H.G. Wells.*
—*Ed.*

Very gingerly I coaxed the right-hand lever towards me and was much alarmed to observe that the pulsation of the needle at once became far more pronounced. This, together with that indescribable nausea which is seemingly an unavoidable concomitant of Time travel, produced in me a sensation that was uncomfortably close to panic. Nevertheless, I kept my head sufficiently to observe that I was not about to enter into conjunction with some massive external object and, very gently, I brought the lever back into the neutral position.

The machine was resting on the bare hillside, its brass runners buried in grass and buttercups. Above me the sun was blazing down out of a cloudless sky, and from its position relative to the meridian I judged the hour to be early afternoon. Some way down the slope of the hill below me two brown and white cows were grazing placidly, flicking their tails at the flies. As I glanced away I saw one of them raise its head and regard me with mild curiosity. So much for the 17th Century, I thought, and with a silent prayer on my lips I thrust forward the left-hand lever which would send me winging forward through the centuries to 1894. *And nothing happened!* I tried again and even risked further pressure on the right-hand lever. The result was exactly the same.

My emotions at that moment were all but identical with those I had experienced when I first looked down from the gazebo on the hillcrest above the Hall of Eloi and found my Machine was no longer standing where I had left it on the lawn before the White Sphinx. It is the fear that grips the marooned mariner when he sees the topsail finally dip below the horizon. For a minute or two I surrendered to it cravenly and then, thank Heaven! reason reasserted itself once more. I had successfully surmounted the earlier crisis: I should survive this too.

I climbed out of the saddle, stepped down into the grass, unclipped the aluminum cover and peered into the womb of the quincunx. One glance was sufficient to tell me what had happened. Of the four polyhedral quartz prisms, the second dexter one had *fractured clean in two along its plane of cleavage!*

For a long moment I simply stared at it in disbelief while the full implication of the disaster gradually dawned upon me. With it came an overwhelming awareness of the grotesque and inescapable irony of my predicament. There, a mere ten paces from where I was standing, lay my workbench, and lying upon that workbench were no fewer than *four identical quartz polyhedra*, any one of which could have been fastened into place within a matter of moments! Ten paces or two hundred and thirty years! Compared with my previous voyage it was hardly a hair-breadth of Time, and yet, for all that, those vital components might just as well have been engulfed in the swamps of the Jurassic.

I reached into the quincunx, unscrewed the two halves of the broken rod, withdrew them and examined them. I thought I could detect a minute scratch ending just where the fracture began. 'Ah, fool,' I castigated myself bitterly. 'Crass, unmitigated fool!'

I sat down in the grass with my back resting against the framework of the Machine, and tried to marshal my fragmented thoughts. It was plain enough that my only hope of escape was to obtain a replacement for that broken prism. I even derived a mite of consolation from the wry reflection that had it been the neodymium dodecahedron which had shattered I should have been lost indeed since that—chronically speaking—essential element had been discovered only in 1885! But how to set about obtaining a replacement?

I rose to my feet and consulted the fascia dials once more. A brief calculation told me that I was now in the year 1665 A.D. The date did indeed touch some faintly disturbing chord in my memory, but I was too concerned with finding a solution to my immediate problem to spare any time on tracking it to its source. Reaching into the pannier below the saddle, I next drew out the canvas knapsack and my kodak. Then, mindful of my experiences with the Morlocks, I unscrewed the two control levers, thus still further immobilizing my already impotent Machine. That done, I carefully removed the second of the dexter prisms, reasoning that, if a replacement were ever to be obtained, a complete artifact would provide a more satisfactory pattern than a broken one. These practical actions, small enough in themselves, did much to help me take that first imaginative step on the far side of the gulf, which is imperative if a traveler in Time is to preserve the full effectiveness of his intellectual faculties.

My next move was to take stock of my useful possessions. I was, it is true, somewhat better equipped than when I had first launched myself so impulsively into the Future. but since I had planned for a brief expedition into the early Holocene, it was open to question whether a patent pocket compass, a kodak, a specimen case, or a notebook and pencils would be of very much service to me in my present predicament. Far more to the point was the handful of loose change, which, by a fortunate oversight, I was still carrying in one of the thigh pockets of my knickerbockers. It amounted in all to two sovereigns, three florins, a sixpence and some assorted coppers. Apart from my fob watch, the other pockets surrendered little more than a small tin of licorice cashews, my tobacco pouch and pipe, a box of lucifers, a twin-bladed penknife and a brass-sheathed pocket lens. This latter I put to immediate use by verifying what I had already suspected concerning the microscopic cause of the fracture in the prism.

The warmth of the summer sun was striking full upon me. So I loosened the belt of my Norfolk jacket, hoisted the knapsack over my shoulder and, after bidding my Machine a truly heartfelt *au revoir*, settled my cap square on my head and set off, striding out through the buttercups across the flank of the hill in the direction of the Camberwell.

The plan of action I had settled upon was simple enough—to get to London as soon as I possibly could. It was there, if anywhere, that I might hope to find a skilled lapidary artificer whom I could prevail upon to fashion me a 4-inch polyhedral rod of rock crystal sufficiently accurate for my needs. An exact replica was obviously too much to hope for, but I reasoned that I had already sufficiently demonstrated how even a flawed rod would serve its purpose long enough to enable me to effect my return to the 19th Century.

Ten minutes brisk walking brought me within sight of the Thames basin, though the river itself I could perceive only as a tremulous silver flickering in the distance towards Rotherhithe some four miles to the northeast. I was astonished by the amount of woodland which clothed the south bank of the river from Battersea to Greenwich. Although it was largely dispersed in the form of small coppices and outgrown hedgerows, the spaces between those closest to me were filled by others yet more distant so that the general effect was to screen the city from my sight. Had I chosen to ascend to the crest of Herne Hill, I would doubtless have obtained a view of the whole panorama, but time was too precious. Leaving the hilltop windmill on my left, I descended by means of a dry and rutted cart track towards the untidy huddle of houses which I guessed must be ancient Camberwell.

The track led me down into the road, which I recognized

as connecting Camberwell with Dulwich, and so I turned to my left and headed in the general direction of Walworth. As I rounded the corner which brought me in full view of the hamlet, I was surprised to observe that a rough stockade had been erected across the road. The centerpiece of this makeshift barrier was formed by a large hay wain, on the top of which were seated three men, one of whom appeared to be shouldering a musket. I paused for a moment to take stock of the situation; then, able to make nothing of it, I approached and called out to ask whether I was on the London road. "Aye!" shouted one of the men, rising to his feet. "And keep a-going, stranger! We're all sound bodies here and by the Lord's grace will stay so."

Perplexed in the extreme, I continued moving steadily towards them, whereupon the same man shouted again, "Not one step further upon thy life!"

I halted in my tracks and stared at him—or rather at the musket which he was now pointing directly at my head!—and raised my hands to show that I carried no weapon. "I wish you no harm, good people," I cried.

"Nor we you, mister," responded the spokesman. "So get ye gone."

"But this is most uncivil," I protested. "I have urgent business to transact in London."

"Aye, and the Angel of Death likewise!" cried one of the others. "Four thousand souls been culled at last week's billing."

This extraordinary remark did what nothing else in the exchange had so far achieved. The significance of the final figure registered upon the dials of my Machine reverberated through my stunned mind like an electric alarm bell. *1665. The year of the Great Plague!*

My hands dropped to my sides as though paralyzed and I stood transfixed, wonderstruck, staring at the three men. One of them raised his fingers to his lips and whistled shrilly. A moment later I caught the excited yelping of dogs. There was an urgent cry of "Sic him! Sic him!" whereat I spun about and fled precipitately with a pack of eager curs snapping at my flying heels.

No sooner had I regained the sanctuary of the cart track than the dogs, with a few backward looks and admonitory snarls trotted off towards the village, leaving me with a painfully racing heart and the realization that my predicament was far worse than even I could have imagined. My historical knowledge of the effects of the Plague was woefully sketchy, though I did recollect from a childhood reading of Pepy's Diary that commercial life of some sort had continued in the city throughout the visitation. My longing to be quit forever of this benighted age increased a hundredfold. I resolved to strike out at once across the fields in the general direction of Southwark, avoiding, as far as humanly possible, the vicinity of any of the scattered farms or hamlets I might encounter on the way.

An hour (and several wearisome detours) brought me within sight of the Old Kent Road, along which I perceived a number of covered carts and several head of cattle being driven in the direction of London Bridge. I skirted round the edge of a cornfield, thrust my way through the hedge and, having gained the highway, set off at my best pace in the wake of this motley caravan. I soon came up with a young cattle drover, who eyed me somewhat oddly, no doubt on account of my dress, though in truth my tweed knickerbockers were perfectly recognizable descendants of his own leather breeches and woolen hose. The most obvious anachronism was my checkered cloth cap (all the men I had seen so far had been wearing either the broad-rimmed "wideawake" or the high-crowned "steeple" style of headgear favored by the Puritans). So on the pretense of wiping the sweat from my brow I removed the questionable article, stowed it away in my pocket, and gave the youth a good day. He returned my greeting civilly enough and enquired what I was traveling in. My look of perplexity led him to say, "Are ye not a pedlar?"

It seemed prudent to agree that I was, and I asked him, whether he knew of any jewelers or instrument makers still trading in the city.

He shook his head and said he supposed they must all have fled if they had the means to do so. Realizing I should get no useful information from him and anxious to push on with all possible speed, I wished him a good journey and strode off in the wake of the carts.

I was by now within plain sight of Southwark Cathedral and the Old Bridge, and for the first time since setting foot in this grim century I found myself gazing about me with real curiosity. The great river—sparkling, green, and clear in a manner all but unimaginable in 1894—was crowded with vessels of every conceivable shape and size from tiny skiffs to quite substantial merchantmen. Indeed, further down stream below the Tower I counted no fewer than 23 large craft moored out in midchannel, while a host of small rowing boats fussed around them like water beetles. As to the city itself I think what struck me most forcibly was, firstly, the grisly row of several heads adorning the battlements of the Bridge Gatehouse and, secondly, the gaiety and brightness of the waterfront houses, each decorated individually to its owner's whim. The sight of those bright reflections shimmering on the sunny water affected me so strongly that it was with a real sense of impotence and loss that I suddenly realized how, within a mere twelvemonth, the ravages of the Great Fire would have destroyed forever most of what I was now seeing. That it must be so I acknowledged, but it caused me none the less of a pang for that.

As I approached the Gatehouse, I observed a group of watchmen armed with pikes and muskets examining the contents of the incoming carts and questioning the drivers. Since pedestrians did not appear to be attracting the same attention, I strode on purposefully, only to be halted by one of the guards demanding to know my business. I told him I was a pedlar-mechanician seeking out instrument makers in the city and added that I would be obliged if he could assist me with directions.

He looked me up and down, scrutinizing my woolen necktie and my stout Highland brogues with obvious suspicion. "And whence come ye, master pedlar?" he asked.

"Canterbury," I replied glibly, offering the first likely name that came to mind.

"Be ye of sound health?"

"Indeed I am," I said, "and hopeful to remain so."

"Aye," he muttered, "with God's blessing, so are we all. Be advised by me, master, and look to peddle your wares elsewhere."

"I have no choice in the matter," I replied. "My trade is too rare." So saying, I slid my hand into my trousers pocket and jingled my coins meaningfully. "Would you happen to know of any jewelers still trading in the city?"

He squeezed his nose thoughtfully between his finger and thumb. "Ludgate's their common quarter. But the sickness lies heavy thereabouts they say. More I know not."

I thanked him for his help, drew out a penny from my pocket and handed it to him. As I hurried on to the bridge, I glanced and saw him turn the coin doubtfully between his fingers before tapping it against the steel blade of his pike.

I crossed the river without further incident, picked out the gothic spire of Old St. Paul's soaring high above the roofs to my left and knew that Ludgate lay immediately beyond it, hidden from my view. I passed through the gate at the north end of the bridge and stepped down into the city.

No sooner had I done so than the waterside breeze died away and I was assailed by a most terrible stench from the heaps of garbage and human ordure which lay scattered all down the center of the street, baking in the sun and so thick with flies that the concerted buzzing sounded like a swarm of angry bees. I felt my stomach heave involuntarily and clutched my handkerchief to my nose and mouth, marveling how the other pedestrians seemed able to proceed about their business seemingly oblivious to the poisonous stench.

I had covered barely 200 yards before I came upon a house, securely shuttered and barred, with a clumsy cross daubed upon its door in red paint and the ominous words *Lord, have mercy upon us* scrawled above it. Dozing on a stool beside it was an old man with a scarlet wooden staff resting across his knees. I observed that my fellow pedestrians were careful to give the area a wide berth, and at the risk of fouling my shoes I too edged out towards the center of the street glancing up as I did so in time to see a small white face peeping fearfully down at me from behind one of the high leaded windows. In spite of the heat I shivered and quickened my pace, taking the first available turn to the left and hurrying down what is still, I believe, called Thames Street. As soon as I saw the cathedral spire rising to my right, I turned again and headed towards it.

As I made my way along the narrow alley, I scanned the signboards on either side and eventually saw one which bore a representation of a pair of compasses. I hurried towards it only to discover that the shop was locked and barred. I squinted in through the leaded window at the selection of terrestrial globes, astrolabes, hour-glasses and astronomical rings and felt my heart sink. What earthly hope had I of finding anyone capable of supplying my needs in an age which was only just beginning to emerge from the shadows of the mediaeval? As I turned dispiritedly away, I saw an elderly gentleman emerging from a door further up the street. I waited until he came abreast of me and then accosted him politely and asked whether he knew of any instrument maker or optician still working in the neighborhood.

Perhaps something in my manner of speech or my dress intrigued him because he peered at me shrewdly from beneath the broad brim of his hat and asked me if I would care to specify exactly what it was I was looking for.

Having nothing to gain by not doing so, I told him I had urgent need of some skilled artificer capable of fashioning for me a small rod or cylinder of rock crystal.

"Why, sir," he said, "if you seek a lens grinder, then Master William Tavener is your man. His shop lies hard by St. Anne's in Carter Lane." He indicated with his cane the direction I should take, adding that he could not vouch for it that the man had not fled the City, though he believed not.

I thanked him warmly for his assistance and made haste to follow his directions. Ten minutes later I had found the shop, exactly where he had described it, with a large gilded spectacles frame hanging above it for its sign. I glanced briefly at the small display of reading lenses in the window, realized that this or nothing was what I had been seeking, and with a painfully racing heart reached for the door latch. To my inexpressible relief the door opened and I stepped over the threshold into the shop.

A small brass bell was standing on the wooden counter, and, after waiting for a minute or so, I picked it up and rang it briskly. I heard a door bang somewhere in the back regions of the shop and the sound of approaching footsteps. Finally a young woman appeared holding a baby in her arms. She stood gazing at me somberly for a moment than asked, "What is it ye seek, master?"

"Is Mr. Tavener in?" I asked. "I have some urgent business for him."

A distant voice called out: "Who is it, Bessie?"

"Robert Pensley," I supplied. "*Doctor* Robert Pensley."

I thought I detected a faint quickening of interest in her face as she passed on this information. "He'll be down to you in a minute, sir," she said.

"Does he work alone, then?"

"Th' prentices have flown this month past," she said. "I warrant I'd have followed them had it not been for father. Plague or no plague, he'll not budge."

"Have you any rats in your house?" I enquired.

"Aye, some I daresay. What house hereabouts hasn't? They swarm up from the fleet like black heathens."

"Their fleas are the plague carriers," I said. "Rid yourself of the rats and you'll be safe."

She laughed. "Lord, sir, the beasts are dying without any help from us! I found two lying stiff in the jakes this very morning."

"You didn't touch them?"

"Not I," she said. "Father hoisted them with the furnace tongs and flung 'em over the wall into the ditch."

"On no account handle them whatever you do," I said. "One bite from an infected flea and that could well be the death of you. Believe me, I know."

"They do say as it's the foul air," she said. "There's orders posted abroad for the watch to burn night fires at every street crossing—and all day long in the open yards. But father says the London air's always been as foul even when there was no plague."

"He's right," I insisted. "So do as I say, Bessie, and promise me you'll touch no dead rats; then you and your babe will both live through it safely."

She smiled. "Me, I hate the ugly brutes. Hark ye, here comes father now."

A middle-aged man with a bald crown to his head and sparse brown hair touched with grey came shuffling out of the passage at the back of the counter and nodded to me. "We've not met before, I think, sir," he said. "What is it ye seek?"

I lifted my knapsack on to the counter, unbuckled it and drew out the complete prism and the two broken pieces. "I want you to cut me an eight-faced crystal prism to these identical dimensions, Mr. Tavener," I said. "Can you do it?"

He took the whole crystal from me and held it up, twisting it this way and that as he squinted at it. "May I aske who fashioned this for ye, sir?"

"I had it cut in Italy."

" 'Tis fine workmanship. I've seen none better." And with that he handed it back to me with a smile.

"But you must keep it, Mr. Tavener," I insisted. "It is to be your pattern. The dimensions are vital, I do assure you."

"I'm sorry to disappoint ye, Doctor," he said, "but seemingly that's what I must do. Single-handed I'm so tardy in my work that it would be the best part of a three-month before I could even consider it. Why, I have grinding in hand upstairs for Master Hooke, due last month, that bids fair to keep me till the middle of next."

"Mr. Tavener," I cried desperately. "I have not traveled all this way to find you, only to be denied! Will you tell me how long it would take to cut such a prism?"

He lifted the rod again and turned it over speculatively between his fingers. "Cut *and* polish?" he enquired.

"Of course."

"Two or three days. Depending on how fine ye wanted it."

"And what would you charge?

"A guinea a day for the skilled labour."

"I'll pay you ten," I said, and the words were no sooner out of my mouth than I realized what I had said.

He peered up at me quizzically over the crystal. "Ten guineas?" he repeated slowly. "Ye'd pay me *ten gold guinea pieces?*"

I nodded. "I will. Providing you'll put the work in hand for me at once."

He looked down again at the prism and traced its beveled contours with his fingertips. I could see he was wondering what kind of man I was to have brought him such a proposition. "D'ye mind telling me why the matter is so urgent, sir?"

"You'd not believe me if I did, Mr. Tavener," I said, "but I assure you it could well be a matter of life or death. Time is of the essence."

"Well, there again, sir," he said, "I know not whether I even have such a blank to suit. Like all else, good crystal's hard to come by in these black days. But perhaps you'd care to step up into the workshop and see what there is."

"Then you *will* undertake it?"

"If I have no satisfactory blank, sir, then no amount of willing on my part will make ye one," he said. "So you'd best come up and see for yourself."

I followed him through the shop, up some dark stairs and into a long, low-beamed workroom which must surely have been cantilevered on to the back of the house. Windows ran round three sides, and two of them looked out over the graveyard of the church next door. The early evening sunlight was slanting in through a dusty drapery of cobwebs. An antique wooden treadle lathe stood against one wall. Suspended above it was a rack of tools. Instead of a fireplace there was a charcoal oven-furnace and a glass-making crucible.

The whole place was depressingly reminiscent of a Dürer engraving of an alchemist's glory hole, but while Mr. Tavener was routing in the depths of a cupboard, I examined two lenses I found lying on a bench and discovered them to be of astonishingly high quality.

Tavener emerged clasping a chunk of quartz which he brought across to the bench and laid before me. "That's Tintagel pebble," he said. "Would it do?"

I picked up the crystal and held it to the light. As far as I could tell, it was flawless. I handed it back to him and expelled my breath in a long sigh. "It will do perfectly, Mr. Tavener," I said.

At that very moment the clock in the church began to sound a chime, and without thinking I pulled my watch from my fob pocket, intending to set it by the prevailing time. I had just clicked open the gold face-guard when I noticed that Tavener's gaze was riveted on the instrument. I smiled. "You will not have seen a watch like this, I daresay, Mr. Tavener?" I detached the chain clip and held the instrument out to him.

He took it from me and turned it round wonderingly in his fingers, rather as the guard at the bridge gatehouse had turned over the penny I had given him. Then he lifted it to his ear and a look of the most profound astonishment suffused his face. It is, in truth, a fine timepiece, made by Jacques Simenon of Paris and given to me to mark my 21st anniversary by my dear mother and father. I took it back from him, opened the case with my thumbnail and showed him the jewel precision movement within. "Why, sir," he breathed, "that is a true miracle! God's truth, never in my life did I dream to see such a thing."

"I warrant it is the only one of its kind in the world to-day," I said.

"That I can well believe, sir. I doubt the King himself hath such a treasure."

"Mr. Tavener," I said slowly, "would *you* like to own that watch?"

He looked at me as if I had gone clean out of my mind and said nothing at all.

"I mean it," I said. "So anxious am I to have the prism cut that I am prepared to give you my watch in exchange for it. It is worth far more than ten guineas. Make for me a perfect copy of that prism, put it into my hand, and I will put the watch into yours. See, here is my hand in pledge of it."

Tavener looked down at the watch ticking away merrily on the bench with the yellow sunlight winking from the jeweled balance. It almost seemed to have hypnotized him. "Well?" I said. "Isn't it a fair bargain?"

"Aye, sir," he agreed at last. "I must suppose ye best know what ye are about," and with that he joined his palm to mine and we shook upon the contract.

"And when can you start?" I asked him.

"Tomorrow, God willing. But I shall have to ride to Edmonton first for pumice powder and rottenstone. I'm clean out of both of them."

"How long will that take?"

"All day, most like. 'Tis ten mile there and no less back."

"And those things you must have?"

"Aye. For cutting pebble. 'Tis not like your whoreson glass. The other grits I have enough of."

"It's not for me to teach you your business, Mr. Tavener," I said. "All I can do now is to wish you God speed."

"Believe me, I'll not tarry, sir. As it is, the lass won't care to be left."

I picked up the watch and clipped it back onto its chain. "I am just newly arrived in London, Mr. Tavener," I said, "and as yet have no lodgings. Could you perhaps recommend me to some inn close by?"

He scratched his chin. "*The Three Keys* in Lower Wharf Street is a clean house," he said. "It's just down alongside Paul's Steps. I daresay that would suit ye. The air is more wholesome by the water."

So I took my leave of him with my heart feeling a good deal lighter than it had for many hours. I soon found The Three Keys and prevailed upon the landlord to rent me an attic room overlooking the river, paying for one week's rent and board in advance with the first of my two sovereigns. I told him that the coin was a Polish *thaler*—Henderson the numismatist once told me that this coin bore a superficial resemblance to our modern sovereign—and he accepted it cheerfully enough, no doubt on account of his having frequent dealings with sailors from foreign ports. I drank a mug of ale with him and ate an excellent mutton pasty while he regaled me with horrific stories of the ravages the "visitation" was wreaking upon the city. He also told me that the ships I had seen drawn up in midstream were filled with wealthy citizens who had embarged their wives and families and would permit no one else to set foot aboard, all their daily needs being supplied by boatmen who purchased food on shore, rowed out with it, and loaded it into baskets which were then hauled up on deck.

Soon after this I retired to my room intending to take a short nap, but whether from the unaccustomed effect of the strong ale or by simple reaction to the day's exertions, I fell deeply asleep and did not wake until the next morning, though I seem dimly to recall having my dreams invaded by the sound of a handbell being rung in the street below and the jarring clatter of iron-shod cart wheels upon cobble stones.

Apart from a brief excursion this morning along the waterfront, during which I purchased for myself a less anachronistic hat with one of my three florins and a plain-fronted, linen bib shirt with another, I have spent the whole day closeted in my attic writing up this record of what must surely be one of the most extraordinary days ever spent by a 19th Century gentleman.

August 28th.

To Tavener's early, only to find the shop locked up. I waited for over half an hour hoping that at least his daughter would put in an appearance but saw nobody. I made my way round to the back of the premises and peered up at the workshop windows. The whole place seemed utterly deserted. The rest of the morning I spent wandering about the city in an agony of apprehension. Finally I returned to Carter Street, knocked on the door of the house adjoining the shop and inquired whether they knew anything of the man's whereabouts. The woman told me that Tavener, accompanied by his daughter and her child had set out early the previous morning in a small pony cart and had not been seen since. Telling myself they had been delayed at Edmonton and would surely return that afternoon, I wandered into the cathedral and, despite my own anxiety, was deeply moved by the sight of hundreds of people all kneeling in silent prayer. I read a printed proclamation which I found nailed up in the cathedral porch. It was signed by the Lord Mayor and the Sheriffs and gave a series of orders to the citizens, some of which explained the odd noises I had heard—handbells, horns blowing and the rest. Nothing more desperately ironical than the directions *to kill all dogs and cats!*—the one slender hope of keeping some of the rats out of the houses! Returned to Tavener's three times more, then finally back here feeling thoroughly depressed.

August 29th.

Spent a wretched night lying awake listening to the melancholy cries of the bellmen—*Bring out your de-a-a-d! Bring our your de-a-a-d!* Resolved to try to speak to the Mayor or the Sheriffs and attempt to persuade them to at least rescind the order for the destruction of dogs and cats. Heard the squeaking of mice—or rats!—behind the wainscot and broke out into a cold sweat of pure terror. Would I not be better advised to seek lodgings south of the river?

(later)

Still no sign or word of Tavener. Wrote him a note which I thrust under his door, urging him to contact me immediately he returns. Found another lens grinder in Cheapside, but lacking the prisms which I had left with Tavener, I could only give him a rough description of what I wanted. Since he had no suitable crystal anyway, it was so much wasted effort. However he told me that William Tavener was "a true man of his word" and that my business could not be in better hands. Consolation of a sort, I suppose, if only I could be sure that my business *was* in his hands!

A thoroughly unnerving encounter in a street (Bread St.?) linking Cheapside with Watling Street. Saw a man I took for a drunkard staggering towards me. Just before he reached me, he pitched over and fell full length on the cobbles. I hurried up to him—he was lying on his face—turned him over and saw to my horror that he had all the signs of the plague, gross swellings at the sides of his neck and dark blotches under his skin from internal bleeding. There was a trickle of blood running from the corner of his mouth, though this may well have been a result of his fall. He was still breathing—a throaty, rasping sound—and as I bent over him, he vomited up a black, evil-smelling bile—shuddered once, violently, and lay still. I looked up and saw that the narrow street, which had been busy enough when I entered it, was now completely deserted. All round me I heard the staccato sounds of doors and window shutters being clapped to. I felt for the poor devil's pulse and found nothing. I left him lying there in the street and hurried away.

When I had recovered something of my composure, I

made my way straight to the Mansion House and asked if I could speak to one of the Sheriffs or some other person of authority upon a matter of great urgency. Finally I was granted an audience with a Mr. Robinson, the Private Secretary to Sir Charles Doe. He listened patiently while I poured out my reasons for at least rescinding the order for the destruction of cats and dogs. Having heard me out, he thanked me politely and then told me that I was mistaken since it had been proved quite conclusively that the plague was transmitted by the "evil miasma" which was inhaled by these very animals and then breathed out upon their unsuspecting victims! Besides, he added with a charming smile, did I really suppose that such a tiny creature as a *flea* could carry all the monstrous weight of such appalling infection? Furthermore, if extra proof were needed, could any man deny that fleas had been skipping around London for years before the outbreak of the present calamity? "Bubonic plague," I said, "is carried by the black rat in the form of an invisible bacterium, *bacillus pestis*. When the rats die of the infection, their fleas seek out other hosts and by sucking their blood transmit the infection to them. Would you be so good as to record that fact and see that it is conveyed to Sir John Lawrence? If the authorities act promptly, thousands of innocent lives may yet be saved." Mr. Robinson smiled and nodded and scribbled something on a piece of paper. "I will see that your message is conveyed to His Lordship, Doctor Pensley," he said. "And now I really must beg ye to excuse me, for I have a great deal of most pressing business to attend to." And that was that.

August 30th.

It is now three whole days since I spoke to Tavener and still nothing. Last night, for the first time, I found myself the victim of a most dreadful depression, which I could not shake off. All day long a heavy pall of cloud has hung over the city, and my eyes are still red and inflamed from the sulfurous smoke of those infernal bonfires they light *to sweeten the air!* This afternoon I was assailed by an ungovernable panic fear that my Machine had been discovered and removed. I ran down to the waterside, paid a boatman sixpence to ferry me over to Southwark and made my way back across the fields to Herne Hill. My relief at discovering my Machine still standing exactly where I had left it—and, apparently, untouched—quite overwhelmed me. I sank down in the grass beside it and wept like a child. While I was making my return, a violent thunderstorm broke, and by the time I eventually got back to the inn I was soaked to the skin. The landlord persuaded me to drink a stiff tot of hot Hollands punch, which, though it may not be the universal specific he claims, certainly seems to have done something to lift my leaden spirits.

August 31st.

Tavener is returned!! The serving maid who attends on me in my room brought up my clothes, which had been drying overnight in the kitchen, and told me that Tavener's daughter had brought word to the innkeeper. My spirits soared like a sky lark. I was out of bed, had dressed, and was on my way to Carter Street within minutes of hearing the news. Bessie came to the shop door herself and told me that her father was already at work upstairs on my commission. Not wishing to delay him still further, I asked her to tell me what had happened. Whereupon she invited me through into their parlor and told me how they had been stopped at Stanford by a barrier across the road, similar in all respects to that which I had encountered at Camberwell. Unable to persuade the villagers to let them through, they had been forced to make a detour as far westward as Palmer's Green before they could circle back by a maze of by-lanes towards Edmonton. They had spent that night under a haystack and, on resuming their journey next morning, had reached Edmonton around noon only to find to their dismay that there a similar barricade had been erected. Her father had spent most of the afternoon parleying with the constables and had eventually prevailed upon them to allow him through. But their troubles were still not over. The dealer who normally supplied him with materials had shut up his works for the duration of "the visitation" and gone to lodge with his sister in Newmarket! Having got so far, the resourceful Tavener was not to be denied. He forced an entry into the store shed, helped himself to whatever he wanted, left some money to pay for it together with a note of explanation and, next morning, the three of them were on their way back to London.

All had gone well until, while they were descending Stanford Hill, the axle of their hired pony-cart broke. Tavener was somehow able to effect a temporary repair which enabled them to crawl back to Wood Green where they had spent the rest of that day finding a wheelwright and persuading him to replace the broken axle. This meant still further delay, and by the time the job was finished it was too late to continue to London. They spent that night in Wood Green and had set out the following day, arriving back at Carter Lane at about the same time as I was on my way back from Herne Hill.

I have recounted here briefly what Bessie Tavener spent an animated hour in describing, painting a remarkably vivid word picture of the pathetic bands of fugitives from the city whom they had encountered roaming the forest round Woodford—"living like gypsies, poor souls, with nary a scanthing of provender to keep their bones from rattling." I was moved to ask her whether she regretted having to return to London, but she said there were already many cases of plague in the outlying districts and if she was fated to die of it she would rather draw her last breath in her own house than lost among strangers. I repeated my stern warning about the rats and extracted a solemn promise from her that she would keep well clear of any place where fleas might be caught. She gave me her word readily enough, but I suspect it was more to humor me than because she believed me.

I looked in briefly upon Tavener before I left and told him how inexpressibly relieved I was to see him back. He merely nodded, gave me a shy grin, and returned to his lathe. As I stepped out into the street, which smelt mercifully sweeter for the deluge yesterday evening, I felt as though a huge and suffocating burden had been lifted from my shoulders.

Sept. 1st.

The soaking I received in the thunderstorm seems to have left me with a chill. Hardly surprising. However, I have before me one of the landlord's excellent "Hollands tonics," which is a great source of comfort. Shortly before noon I called round at Tavener's to see how the work was progressing only to find him engaged in packing up a box of lenses for a little hunch-backed fellow in a grubby wig. Tavener introduced him to me as Master Hooke. As I shook him by the hand, I thought, by way of a joke, to say: *"ut tensio sic vis,* Mr. Hooke." He gave me a most extraordinary look as if to say: "Who is this madman I have by the hand?" and the thought crossed my mind that perhaps he had not yet formulated that shortest of all Physical Laws which posterity would link to his name. Thereafter we chatted in a desultory way about the plague until he hobbled off with his box of lenses under his arm.

After he had gone, Tavener showed me how the work on the prism was progressing. The blank is already two-thirds shaped in rough, and he hopes to have that part of the work completed by this evening. Then the labor of polishing begins. In spite of my pressing him he would not give me a definite date for completion on the grounds that Tintagel pebble was notoriously slow to take a fine polish, being "hard nigh unto diamond." He is certainly a most meticulous craftsman, who obviously takes a profound—though somewhat inarticulate—pride in the quality of his work.

Sept. 2nd.

A violent bout of sweating in the night left me with a feeling of great lassitude and a severe headache. I arose late, dressed myself, went out into the street and was overcome with a fit of giddiness not unlike the vertigo I have experienced while Time traveling. I have no doubt at all that it is an unwelcome aftereffect of the chill, but I could well do without it. On my returning to the inn the landlord made my blood run cold with a story of some poor pregnant girl in Cripplegate who was nailed up in her house when one of her sisters contracted the plague. All the rest of the family were stricken down one after the other until finally, when only she was left alive, she gave birth and, with no one on hand to help her, died, not of the plague, but of a hemorrhage! With her self-delivered infant in her arms! The sheer, wanton cruelty of this policy of sealing up houses is almost beyond belief. No phrase sickens me more than the pious: " 'Tis God's will," and I must be hearing it in one form or another twenty times a day.

Sept. 3rd.

Little doubt in my mind but that I've caught a really nasty dose of influenza. I have passed all the day lying in bed, and despite the sun beating down on the tiles overhead making this attic as hot as an oven, I have spent much of the time shivering violently. When the servant girl came up to make my bed, I told her I had caught a bad chill and asked her to be good enough to fetch me up a mug of strong spiced ale. That was over three hours ago and still she has not returned.

Sept. 9th?
Hostel of St. Barnabas.

Days of nightmare. What is memory? What dream? Grey-Morlock figures bending over me, prodding at my chest, thrusting me into my clothes, carrying me downstairs with a rag soaked in brandy stuffed into my mouth. A boat. Stars swirling round in the sky above me. Squeaking of oars. Voices whispering. Waking again to find the sun hammering nails into my naked eyes. My knapsack is lying on the sand beside me. Where am I? My fumbling fingers explore my body as though it is a stranger's. My joints are all on fire, and my head feels as though a red-hot gimlet is being screwed into my brain. Beneath my armpit the outline of an unfamiliar lump. Another in my groin. *Buboes!* Pain gives way to sheer, mindless terror. I am falling backwards down the black well-shaft that has no bottom. Voices. Hands lifting me. Hands carrying me. Falling, falling without end. I open my eyes to see a stone vaulted roof arching above me. As I stare up at it, a cowled face swims into my field of vision. Its lips move. "Welcome, stranger." "Where am I?" (Is that really my own voice?) "The hostel of Saint Barnabas." "I have the plague?" The cowl nods. "Am I dying?" "We think not." Time passes. I sleep; I dream; I wake. Sleep; dream; wake. Strong, firm, gentle hands raise me and prop me back against straw-filled sacks. Soup is spooned into my mouth and a worried voice urges: "Drink, Robert." I swallow and choke. "Again." I swallow. "Again. Good i'faith. Most excellently done." "Who brought me here?" "Who knows, Robert? Friends to be sure. They could have drowned ye in the river like a puppy, for all ye could have stayed them." A pause, then: "Who is Weena?" "Weena?" "Aye. Ye called on her by the hour in your raving. Dost wish me to send word to her that ye lie here?" "She's dead." He rises from my bedside and sketches a token blessing over me. "My knapsack," I croak. "Fear not, Robert. 'Tis here." He lifts it onto my bed and then moves off down the ward. I fumble the buckle undone, extract my notebook and force myself to write a note to Tavener. Then I sleep again. When I wake next, I make this entry. It has taken me nearly three hours to complete it.

Sept. 11th.

Today Brother James trimmed my beard for me and has promised to see that my note is delivered to Tavener. He assures me too that "through God's infinite mercy" I have successfully weathered the worst of the storm. Twenty-four patients have died since I was brought in. The bell in the chapel never seems to stop its mournful tolling.

Sept. 12th.
The superstitious fear of infection is presumably what I have to thank for the fact that I still have all my possessions down to the last pencil—that and the fact that the innkeeper's livelihood was at stake. Had word got out that I had the plague, The Three Keys would now be a "sealed house."

Sept. 13th.
This afternoon I spent half an hour trying to persuade Brother Dominic, the physician, that the infection is transmitted primarily by rats and their fleas. I had hardly more success than I had with Secretary Robinson even though I thought to cite Harvey to illustrate how the bacillus was carried through the bloodstream. B.D. told me he thought it was an interesting theory but that proof was lacking. I told him that if he swabbed out his wards with a 250/1 solution of sulfuric acid, he'd soon have all the proof he needed. "And what is sulfuric acid, Robert?" On my telling him it was another name for oil of vitriol he nodded, but I suspect he was really no more convinced than Robinson had been.

Sept. 14th.
A message was brought in to me by a walking patient that a Master William Tavener was without and would speak with me but was fearful of entry. He sent word to say that the work was finished and that he had it now upon him. On hearing this I crawled off my bed, staggered the length of the ward like a drunkard and so, by painful degrees, proceeded to the hostel gate. "Tavener?" I croaked. "Is that you, man?" He stood a little way off and stared in at me. "In God's name, Doctor Pensley, ye are sadly changed!" "I'm recovered now," I said, clutching at the iron rails of the gate for support. "It's quite safe to come close." "That I durst not, Doctor," he called. "Go ye back a way and I'll push them through to ye." I did as he said, though how I contrived to remain standing is a miracle. Whereupon he ran to the gate and quickly thrust a bundle wrapped in cloth through onto the flagstones. I picked

it up, unwrapped it with shaking hands and found, lying inside, swaddled in lambswool, the two whole prisms together with the two broken pieces. *And for the life of me I could not tell the copy from the original!* My eyes filled with tears I was quite powerless to prevent. "God bless you, William Tavener!" I cried. "You are indeed a master among craftsmen!" and taking out my watch and chain, I held them up so that he could see them plainly, then laid them down upon the flagstones. He let the watch lie there while I stepped back; then he darted forward and scooped it into a leather bag he had ready for the purpose. "Farewell, Doctor," he called. "God be wi'ye!" and he was gone. Somehow I managed to stagger back to the ward and there collapsed upon my cot.

Sept. 15.

Feel too weak to write much. Obviously overdid things yesterday. The prism is a true marvel—a perfect replica. No doubt at all it will fulfill its function.

16.

Vomiting all last night. Feel v. weak.

17.

Diarrhea and vomiting.

disgust

*   *   *

There it ends. The last entry is so faintly penciled that it is very difficult to decipher. The word could possibly be read as "despair." However, the Register itself leaves us in no doubt as to the final outcome. One of the two entries for September 20th, 1665, reads: *Decd. at ye 5th hr, one Rbt. Penly* (sic) *of med. yrs. of ye black flux.* It is matched by a previous entry for September 5th: *Admi. one Penly, sick nigh unto death.*

In the weeks which followed my initial perusal of the Hertford Manuscript I took certain steps to ascertain, for my own satisfaction, whether the journal was in fact nothing more than an elaborate and pointless forgery.

My first problem was to obtain a specimen of the true Doctor Pensley's handwriting. I wrote to Somerset House and inquired whether he had left a will, only to be informed that there was no one of that name in their probate records for the years 1894–1899. I then thought to try the civil records for Herne Hill and wrote to the Camberwell Town Clerk, but again drew a blank. I could find no Pensley in the London telephone directory, and a discreet advertisement placed in the personal column of *The Times* proved just as unrewarding. However, these initial disappointments served only to spur my determination. I contacted an old friend of mine in Cambridge and asked him to consult the university records on my behalf. Within a fortnight I learnt that Robert James Pensley had been admitted to Emmanuel College as an Exhibitioner in the year 1868.

I traveled down to Cambridge and there in the college records I found at last what I had been seeking. It was not very much certainly—a mere signature—but when I laid it beside an entry in the Hertford text where the author had written out his own name, I was convinced that the writing was by the same hand. My instinctive conviction has since been confirmed by the opinion of a professional graphologist.

My next move was to consult the back files of local newspapers. The only one which still survives is *The Dulwich and District Observer*, and there in the yellowed print of the issue for the week of June 18th, 1894, tucked away among advertisements for safety bicycles and patent knife powder, I found: *Puzzling Disappearance of Well-Known Amateur Scientist.* The account, written in an excruciatingly "literary" style, described how Doctor Robert Pensley, the only surviving son of James and Martha Pensley, had vanished from his home in Herne Hill on the morning of June 7th and had not been seen or heard from since. There was a thinly veiled suggestion that the doctor had been suffering from severe mental strain brought on by overwork. His housekeeper, in an exclusive interview with "our Reporter," described how her employer was in the habit of vanishing into his laboratory "for hours on end, bless him, and all night too sometimes." There the article ended, and since I could find no further references to the mystery in any later issue, I can only suppose that the matter had been purposely hushed up.

But I could not let the matter rest there. Some strange, haunting quality in that penciled manuscript beckoned to me like a forlorn will-o'-the-wisp, and I resolved to track down as many of the historical references as it was possible to do after an interval of over three hundred years. During the past eighteen months, whenever I have had the opportunity, I have consulted ancient documents in the Guildhall, the Stationers' Hall, the British Museum, and the London Records Office in an attempt to verify what I already *felt* to be true, namely that in some wholly inexplicable manner Robert Pensley *had* succeeded in transferring himself backwards in time to the 17th Century and had there perished.

My first notable success was in establishing that one William Tavener, a member of the Guild of Spectacle Makers, had occupied premises next to the Church of St. Anne in Carter Lane. The date given was 1652. A further entry recorded that two apprentices had been bound to the aforesaid Master Tavener at premises in New Cheapside in 1668! So he, at least, seems to have escaped both the plague and the fire.

In a Victorian handbook entitled *The Inns of Elizabethan London* I came upon a reference to The Three Keys of Lower Wharf Street. Like most of the other establishments mentioned it was destroyed in the Great Fire of 1666.

The Hostel of Saint Barnabas—a Franciscan Charity Foundation—is reasonably well documented. It functioned until the early 19th Century when it was pulled down to make way for a new dockyard.

Last May, in the archives of the Mansion House, I unearthed the name of one Samuel Robinson, Esq., recorded as having been appointed to the post of *amanuensis privatus* to Sir Charles Doe, Sheriff, in the year 1663.

In 1665, Robert Hooke was certainly in London, working as "curator of Experiments" for the newly founded Royal Society, and I have no reason to doubt that he would have called upon the services of Master Tavener to supply him with his optical apparatus. Incidentally, it might not be inappropriate to point out that Robert Hooke, as well as formulating his famous Law, has also been credited with a multitude of other discoveries, among them the invention of the spring balance wheel without which the science of horology (not to mention navigation) would doubtless have languished for many years longer in the Dark Ages!

Yet, when all is said and done, such "facts" as I have been able to disinter seem to raise more questions than they answer. I feel I am forever condemned to pace the circumference of a circle which turns out to be not a circle at all but a spiral—my point of arrival is never the same as my point of departure. For to accept the Hertford Manuscript at its face value must surely mean accepting a concept in which Time is both predetermined and yet infinite, an endless snake with its tail in its own mouth, a cosmos in which the Past and the Future coexist and will continue to do so for all Eternity.

How then is it that I both *can* and *do* believe that Robert Pensley's journal, written in his own hand in the year 1665, was already lying there gathering dust on a shelf in the library of Hertford Castle for fifty years before its author had drawn his first infant breath in the year 1850? Or that he died, most horribly, on a straw pallet in a charity hospital in the district of Wapping, beside the silver Thames, clutching in his stiffening fingers a fragment of polished rock crystal which he had staked his life to obtain, only to lose the wager at the very moment when he must surely have believed that he had won?

NATURAL ADVANTAGE

Lester Del Rey

One does not see many stories from Lester Del Rey these days who is more apt to be found exercising his ability as a book critic for Analog and as an advisor on fantasy for a paperback publisher. So this one comes as a special treat—written for the fiftieth anniversary of the oldest American sf magazine—and deliberately re-creating the good old-time premise of Man the Unbeatable. It's short, it could have been a novelette, it could even have been a novel, but Del Rey says it all in an economy of space. "Up Terra!"

Star captain Anthor Sef sighed heavily and put down the trinoculars through which he had been staring. Seemingly above him, the pitted, airless satellite of the clouded planet glared coldly. He shut his eyes to rest them, then turned back to his control seat.

"No evidence of mines or colonies," he said. "If they have space flight, it must be in its infancy. That is, if there's any intelligent life at all on the primary."

"But the radio signals!" Timas Biir protested.

Theoretically, Biir should not have been in the control room; he was only cook and general handyman. But the engineer Sef had drawn for this trip was too taciturn to be company. The captain stared at the little man, surprised at the eagerness on the other's face. Biir was almost an anachronism, a left-over from the ancient family of heralds. Over his short snout and just above his third eye was a bulging forehead

114

that held his enlarged speech center, a reminder of the days when there were a hundred languages on Rum and a herald must know them all.

Sef nodded slowly. "Yes, the radio signals." He shrugged and set the controls to take them close to the primary while Biir picked up the trinoculars and stood staring through the transparent wall of the control room.

The doubly-damned radio signals! Sef sighed again. One of the exploring ships had spotted a cloud of anti-matter particles heading for a G-type star and mapped it as routine. It was only when they were heading away that they had received faint radio signals that might indicate intelligence on a planet around the star. As a result of their report, Sef had been ordered to detour on his trip to the farthest colony, adding a year to the fifteen the trip already took—almost a tenth of a lifetime.

Maybe he should have turned down the job, most star captains refused the long voyage. But it meant promotion above what his equal time in normal voyages would have brought.

"See anything?" he asked. They were approaching the planet now, making an easy half thousand miles a second.

"Lights maybe, on the darkened section. I'm not sure," Biir answered. Then he gasped faintly. "Wait—a moving glint! Outside the atmosphere!"

Sef set the controls to bring them to a halt and took the trinoculars. The precise wording Biir had used gave the velocity and curvature of the thing he had seen, and it could only be something orbiting the planet. The captain followed the other's pointing fing. The glint was showing clearly now, indicating something that was reflecting the sunlight as metal might do. His mind delineated its orbit, but he checked it, setting the delay line in the nerves from his third eye to longer and shorter time span. Then he went back to the controls and set up a course that would match orbits with whatever was there, slightly more than two hundred miles above the planet.

As they drew nearer, Sef could see that it was clearly an artificial satellite, shaped like a doughnut and spinning on a hub. Biir's exclamations drew Nuran Velos from the engine room to watch. The engineer scowled, pointing to the hub. "Control rockets. Look chemical. Primitive!"

Sef grunted. Primitive or not, it meant space travel of a sort. And his orders were to warn them, in that case. The cloud of anti-matter would begin striking their star in about ten more years, setting to blazing so fiercely that no planet could support life. Excitement over the possibility of finding the first alien intelligence had run so high in the Council that a rescue mission had been considered. But too few ships were at home and the needs of the farthest colony had prevailed. Still, the aliens had to be warned.

Across the control room, the radio broke into sudden loud noises as Biir fiddled with it. The little man began yelling into it, though no real communication was possible. Sef could see no sign of weaponry, but he approached cautiously until he had matched course five hundred feet below the hub. After that, there was nothing to do but wait.

It was nearly two hours later when the hub showed activity. Something opened and a figure came out in a space suit, carrying a hand rocket and trailing a line behind. Two arms, two legs, a bulge for a head—the simplest way for evolution to produce an intelligent land-dweller, of course. Shorter than the men of Ruum, but not greatly so.

Velos went to the emergency airlock and began opening the outer flap. The figure changed course to reach it, stopping to fix the line before entering. The airlock cycled, and the creature moved into the control room, carrying a box and studying a set of dials. It nodded, threw back the helmet and began removing its suit, its attention never wavering from the men of Ruum. It wore some kind of artificial covering, probably because it had hair only on top of its head. The naked skin was pinkish tan instead of a proper dark brown. There was almost no muzzle, and the nose stuck out above the mouth. But the shocking detail was that it had only two eyes in its small head.

"Mammalian female," Biir said in amazement. "But only two breasts."

The creature looked at him, frowning. *"My name is Ellen Richards, and I'm supposed to welcome you to our world,"* she said. The meaningless sounds were in a voice with none of the higher tones of Ruumian; the fundamentals seemed limited to a range of only a few thousand herz.

Biir began trying to establish a few words with her, but gave up. "I don't think she hears half of what I say," he commented. He tried to shift to her words, frowning as he attempted to make sense of them.

Them she stretched her mouth into an upward curve and

held out a small dial on her wrist, pointing to the hands that circled it and making motions. She pointed back to the satellite, motioned over the dial, and made a sweeping gesture. Even Sef could see she was indicating that she'd leave and be back in—hmmm—about three hours. Their time units were shorter than his, but not hard to translate roughly.

There were a lot of signals in various radio frequencies going on between the satellite and the planet after she had gone. Some decoded to the sounds she had made; others on different frequencies were meaningless to Sef. He gave up listening when Biir brought in lunch.

Establishing communication was going to be a problem, Sef realized. Well, that was why Biir had been sent on this trip; he had the brain development to handle language skills and memory. Sef forgot about it and turned his thoughts to the strange creature with only two eyes. Two! Enough for spatial depth perception, but not for time depth perception. Without the third eye and the brain development that integrated the extra, delayed vision, they could never see movement, never detect the exact curvature of the path of an object thrown at them, never determine precise velocities. How could such creatures have survived through their early development? They were a race of no real vision!

The female returned at the promised time, pulling a much heavier cord with her. Two others followed, and they began dragging boxes across space before entering the airlock. Once inside, she removed her suit, but they merely piled the boxes on the floor, stared at the Ruumians, and motioned that they were leaving. Males, Sef decided, wishing he could see their anatomy; but the coverings they wore in place of hair would have prevented that, anyhow.

The female opened one box and began lifting out volumes of bound sheets, all covered with marks in columns. She pointed to the radio that was faintly humming, then at the sheets. Sef considered it, then nodded, remembering with surprise that nodding was a gesture she had also used. It seemingly had meant the same as his, surprisingly. Anyhow, apparently she was trying to indicate that the printing on the sheets had been sent by radio from the planet and executed on the satellite. Sensible. So now they had a word list, for whatever good it might do.

Another box contained reels of tape. Velos examined it and nodded. "Magnetic film, I think. Too wide. Primitive."

The last box held a machine, about a foot square and two feet high. There were switches and other indications that something inside was probably electronic. But above it, where dials should have been, was a strange blank face of glass. With a decent keyboard and numbered dials, it could have

Sef jumped, sucking in his breath. Where the blank glass had been was a little man of her race, not ten inches high! It wasn't a doll, either; it moved like a living thing. *"One,"* the box said. *"One and one are two. One and two are three."* With each word, the top of the glass showed characters like those on the pages and the little man illustrated with his fin-been a calculator like the one Velos used to solve arithmetical problems. She placed it on the table, inserted a reel, and pressed a switch.
gers.

Then Sef saw his mistake. There was time depth, but no spacial depth. It was as if a draftsman had drawn a schematic diagram of a creature for some odd reason, then filled in every detail of tone and color on the paper, and somehow made it move!

Velos shoved the captain aside and stared at the thing. For the first time, the engineer was clearly struck by emotion.

The female drew the hair ridges over her two eyes together, then reached to shut the machine off. She took something from a large pocket in the stuff she wore over her skin and held it out. It seemed merely a scrap of the odd paper on which the words were printed. The Velos turned it over and swore in amazement.

There was no depth, no movement. But when Sef closed his upper and one side eye, it began to make sense. It showed one of her people. But it was only fractions of an inch thick! *"Picture,"* the girl said.

Biir examined it with less surprise. "I've heard of draftsmen who play around with things like this experimentally. But the results always look flat and dead when they sketch anything but the simplest things. So does this, of course. But such detail!"

The female's eyebrows were still together, but she motioned to the machine, resetting the reel. She took the first volume and pointed to the words as the machine started from the beginning. Biir moved beside her and followed her motions carefully as she demonstrated the machine. When he nodded, she indicated the dial on her wrist again, then pointed to the airlock.

After she left, Biir stayed by the machine, sounding the words and studying the printed sheets. Several times he reset the tape. Then at last he put it aside and began on the next.

Sef left him alone with his job, trying to figure how they got the moving "pictures" onto the screen; it was too much for his imagination. For want of anything better, he began following the language lesson as Biir went back to the first reel again.

"Impossible," Biir said finally, as he reluctantly turned off the device and sketched his tired back. "Sef, they don't have any tense in their nouns and adjectives. Even the verbs have only past indefinite, present indefinite, and future indefinite. There is no real time sense at all. And yet, it seems to work. And the words! They make one word serve for every condition of a knife. One! Not a separate one for each type of motion of the knife. They must get by with less that five thousand basic words!"

"How many do we use?" Sef asked.

Biir thought it over. "Half a million basic, perhaps. A cultured man uses seven or eight times that many, counting all the finer shades. A good herald used to know a million in twenty or so languages. Sef, I can memorize these overnight!"

Sef nodded doubtfully. Even he, who hadn't finished language school and hadn't been permitted to begin his other education until he was eight years old, could force himself to learn a few thousand a day. He got up and started for his cabin to get some needed sleep, then he swore to himself and joined the cook again. The language was even crazier than Biir had said, but there was something fascinating about it. Finally, though, he gave up and left the little man busily hunting back and forth among his reels.

When the female came back the next shift, she looked at the mess of reels beside Biir and grasped. "What in *hell* did you do? Start from the wrong end?"

"*Hell* was not among the words," Biir said. "I did the—those things—from the top to the bottom the first time."

Surprisingly, Sef could understand. The words came too fast for him to follow easily, but he managed. It was worse than trying to talk baby language—but sense could be conveyed. He fumbled through his memory. "Why had you—you men things—this ready? Expecting—expected you as men things?"

She stared, then lifted her shoulders. "It was some project a student—a student in final education—did to get his degree—his right to be a teacher. We had the program sent up from Earth. It is called 'an attempt at devising a program of language instruction for hypothetical aliens'—or some such."

Biir apparently understood enough of it to translate. Sef hesitated. Obviously, they could exchange information, and it was now his duty to issue his warning and leave. But somehow, passing on the message that would doom most of this world—and probably the female—didn't come as easily as he had thought.

Velos gave him an excuse to ponder further by demanding to know how the pictures appeared on the screen. Sef listened absently as Biir struggled to translate. Apparently the fact that the creatures could see no time depth made them fond of images of themselves that no Ruumian could accept—dead, frozen ones. That led to photography. And when they had radio, they wanted better. As a result, they invented television and videotape. He filed the words in his memory.

"All that in such a little box?" Velos asked doubtfully.

"Heavens, most of the box is empty." She pulled her eyebrows together, then began trying to explain how thousands of transistors and other parts could be put on a tiny chip by things called photo-reduction and photoetching. More pictures!

She gave up when Velos wanted more details. "You should talk to the scientists, though maybe I could get you some books from the library. I only work in administration."

Sef sighed. He could put it off no longer. "Scientists? Men that look at stars, think how to go through space?" She nodded, and he stood up. "Then take me to them. I know bad things about your star. I must talk with scientists!"

She seemed doubtful at first, but as Biir passed on a little more information, she nodded. It would take time to get the scientists together. She would give a signal from the hub of the station when everything was ready.

Velos watched her leave and turned to Sef. "I want to go with you." He listened to Sef's refusal unhappily, but nodded. Someone had to stay on the ship, and Biir was needed to translate. "Then get me those books she mentioned—all you can. Somehow I'll learn to read them!"

Sef and Biir were already suited up when Ellen's signal came. They pulled themselves across on the line and followed her through the airlock. Inside, there was a strange odor. Well, if she could breathe his air safely, hers should not harm him. He followed her, studying the alien technology as they passed upward through the station. Maybe Velos should have come. But that could be remedied later.

About twenty of the creatures were waiting, a mixture of male and female. Ellen silenced them and led Sef toward a position at the front of the crowded room.

He gave them the message and the facts, undiluted. The great cloud of anti-matter would strike their star in ten of their years, triggering it into dangerous activity; and some of the cloud would strike their atmosphere, causing lethal amounts of gamma radiation. He gave them the readings of the first ship to discover the cloud, and tried to explain why his people could do little but warn them. There was no way to send a signal across more than a hundred light years of space, nor did they have ships enough to rescue this world.

"Your ship is here!" someone yelled, and Sef had expected it:

But another man rose quickly. "We know the size of that ship. We couldn't put more than a hundred people aboard with supplies to last a year. That's not nearly enough to insure a gene pool that has a chance of survival for the race. And damn it, I resent having the suggestion made to a—a man who has come here to warn us!"

There were cries of what must be approval. There was no panic, so far as Sef could see. Maybe there would be when the general population learned the truth, but these were highly trained and self-controlled individuals.

Eventually, he had answered all their questions as best he could. Some of them were already leaving the room as Ellen led Sef and Biir away.

Back on his ship, Sef sat trying to sort out what he had learned and raging at his futility. He had found himself liking and respecting those beings. The idea of having the first intelligent race his people had discovered die before they could meet properly was unthinkable. Yet it was hopeless.

The aliens had only rockets, powered by chemical means

now. And while Sef had learned they had crude fusion power, they had no good way to apply it as thrust.

Damn it, as the man had said, it was unfair! His people were no better than these, probably—certainly no more intelligent.

Yet his race had been given a natural advantage these beings could never have. His kind saw time and evolved complex brain structures to utilize that sense of time because some three-eyed ancestral form had survived eons ago. It was because of that gift that they had been able to develop the exchange forces that held time inside their ships to the normal rate, while distorting it externally until their ships could cross space twenty times faster than light. And it was that natural advantage that had let them learn the nature of time in the atomic nucleus, to turn all of any mass into pure energy.

By the Ancient Dust, if it could have helped them, he would have dumped his cargo and taken all he could to the nearest habitable planet—the colony world toward which he was headed. Then they could have killed him on the colony, if they liked; a race was more important than one man!

Velos came in on his dark mood, asking if he had secured any of the books. Sef started to brush him aside.

Then he swore, and made up his mind. "No, but you'll get them—everything they have," he promised.

It couldn't help the race of beings who called themselves human. There wasn't time enough. But it might give them hope during the ugly years when they needed it. He could do that much, at least. And if the Council disagreed with his decision, let the Council do what they liked to him.

Sef had slept and eaten when a delegation came to his ship. There were only three of them, and one was the man who had rebuked the other.

"We've checked discretely," that man—Brewster, he called himself—announced. "And we've found more evidence than we like. There have been reports of strong X-ray emissions in the area where you place the cloud for several years. Probably caused when it hits the dust in space. And it's moving as you said. Now, how much can you tell us—or show us—of your ship? And can we build ones much bigger?"

"You don't have time enough!" Sef protested when it had been translated. "Even experts take years to build one ship."

"When there's no other solution, we'll make time!"

Sef nodded. Now he should explain enough of the time fields to show them how impossible it all was. Or he should promise them, and then flee into space. The Council would never approve of any other decision.

"You can't build bigger ships," he said at last. "We've tried, and the fields we use simply collapse beyond a certain size. But while I don't know enough to help you, I carry a good technical library on board. I'll trade you my books for yours. But I warn you that our language may prove impossible for you to learn."

Another man grinned suddenly. "Translate your thousand most important words and we'll dig the rest out with our computers. Give us your basic mathematics, and we'll solve the rest."

Biir looked at the captain sadly when the men were gone. "You will regret that," he warned.

"Would you have done otherwise?" Sef asked, and there was no answer.

Later, boxes of things called microfiche copies and readers for the three of them began coming from the station. Men came aboard with equipment and began making microfiche copies of the ship's three hundred odd volumes, while Biir and Velos slaved over the word list and mathematics introduction. There were far more books from the station than Sef had thought possible. Some were stored in an empty fuel hold, but the control room was still littered with boxes.

Brewster came last, and Sef let the man take and squeeze his hand in a gesture that was obviously meant as friendship. Then he went to the control board and began setting up their course for the colony, more than two years away. There was still ten years of traveling before they would see Ruum again.

At least, they would be less bored than usual. Velos was already moving toward the thing with the screen, to attempt learning enough English to read the technical books. And he and Biir could learn to read the others. It would keep them busy. And if the race on the planet behind them had to perish, at least someone would remember them and carry back their records to be preserved on Ruum.

By the time they reached the colony, they had decided to use nothing but English among themselves; it was not as bad as it had seemed. Only rarely was it necessary to resort to Ruumian words to express some exact meaning. And such use increased their fluency. It came as almost a surprise when they landed to hear again the speech of Ruum.

There were more shocking things, however. The colony was going sour. The land under cultivation was hardly more than that shown on the maps of a century ago. There was barely enough of the needed silver mined and smelted to fill the hold of the ship. And the men were sullen, grumbling about everything; some even tried to bribe Sef to take them back with him.

The colony was too far from Ruum, and the ships that offered the only communication were too rare. Anyhow, Sef suspected that the men who had volunteered to come so far away from their native world on the first three fleets had not been the most suitable ones. There was no pride in them now. They were uncurried and most of them stank of accumulated dirtiness.

It was good to watch the world fade behind them and head directly toward Ruum. The three men settled back into their routine. Sef still had a long ways to go before he could begin to appreciate the material that was supposed to be fiction. The history books had been hard enough.

Biir called their attention to the date at dinner. The ten years had passed, and the cloud must be striking the star the men called the Sun. They ate little that time, and Sef spent long hours afterward staring at the star of Ruum only months ahead of them. Finally he found a novel on the last days of Pompeii. Somehow, it was much easier to understand than on his first reading of it.

By the time they were within radio hailing distance, they began packing the microfiche boxes and trying to tidy up the control room for the routine inspection that would follow the normal perfunctory acknowledgment and congratulations. Ruum had known space flight too long to be excited. They were assigned their orbit around the planet and told to wait. And the waiting dragged on, which was not normal.

When the little ship drew near them and began to match orbits, it was not the regular type of inspector's gig, either. Instead, it was a two-man ship, and it carried the bands of distinctive color that could only be used on the specials assigned to members of the Council.

"Damn!" Sef said, the word coming automatically to his lips now.

Biir stared out at the ship as it matched course and began

sending out a passenger tube toward their airlock. "They couldn't have learned about your decision, Sef. That's impossible. It must be some special inspection."

Sef nodded, unconvinced. He'd thought on numerous occasions of what he must tell the Council about his turning all their scientific knowledge over to an alien race. But his plans were still unformed. Perhaps there was no way he could justify it.

The airlock cycled, and a short figure in an alien spacesuit entered, beginning at once to remove the helmet.

"Ellen Richards!"

"It's Ellen Farnum now," she told him. "I got married. Sef, it's good to see you again."

He let her take his hand and squeeze it, staring at her, puzzled vaguely by her accent. Then he realized that the accent must be his, not hers.

"You built a ship," he guessed at last. "But so quickly . . ."

She nodded, making a sound that his reading told him must be laughter. "Well, let's say we converted a ship. It's over there, in a Trojan orbit with your little moon. You know about such orbits?"

"Equilateral triangle of two satellites to the primary," Velos said.

She nodded. "Over there. You can just see it shining, if you know where to look. We hollowed out an asteroid named Juno to give us living quarters and came in that. And that gives us all the fuel we can ever use to drive it. After all, it's more than a hundred miles in diameter. Of course, your Council was a little shocked when we first took up orbit. But once we got into communication with them and they picked up enough English to begin exchanging knowledge, they were delighted. One of them sent his private ship and chauffeur to bring me out. I was determined to be the first to greet you."

Sef held up a hand to stop the flow of words that came faster than he could assimilate, but it was Velos again who interrupted. "Impossible. No field can cover such a diameter. It—"

"Not the field you used, of course." She frowned a moment. "All right, I'll try to explain. After we had a chance to learn your time theories, we found we had a big advantage over you. The way you see conditioned you to think of time in only one way—sort of in pictures. It was like the men who tried to understand the atom by picturing it, which won't work. So we, working without any preconceptions, found other ways of treating your theories. The one we found gets better as it gets bigger. And faster, too. We made the trip in four months, taking it easy."

"With how many people?" Sef asked. He was remembering Brewster's statement about the size of population needed to keep the gene pool of the race at a survival level. But with a whole planetoid to carry them here, there could be far more than enough people saved from the disaster of their world.

Her answer surprised him. "About eighty."

He sighed, and heard Birr's echoing sigh beside him.

"Only eighty—out of all your billions," the little man said softly.

She stared at them as if unaware of their meaning. Then she laughed again, easily, without a tinge of sorrow.

"Oh, I see. No, this was only a little trip to establish relations with your world—and to thank you, Sef. We moved Earth, the Sun and the planets out to a safe place almost two years ago."

THE BICENTENNIAL MAN

by Isaac Asimov

Asimov begins this special novelette of the year past with his famous laws of robotics—and then, as is his custom, proceeds to see how far he can twist those laws. At what point does a thinking machine develop an ego? And what would such a self-conscious device desire above anything else?

The Three Laws of Robotics

1. A robot may not injure a human being, or, through inaction, allow a human being to come to harm.

2. A robot must obey the orders given it by human beings except where such orders would conflict with the First Law.

3. A robot must protect its own existence as long as such protection does not conflict with the First or Second Law.

1

Andrew Martin said, "Thank you," and took the seat offered him. He didn't look driven to the last resort, but he had been.

He didn't, actually, look anything, for there was a smooth blankness to his face, except for the sadness one imagined one saw in his eyes. His hair was smooth, light brown, rather fine; and he had no facial hair. He looked freshly and cleanly shaved. His clothes were distinctly old-fashioned, but neat, and predominantly a velvety red-purple in color.

Facing him from behind the desk was the surgeon. The

nameplate on the desk included a fully identifying series of letters and numbers which Andrew didn't bother with. To call him Doctor would be quite enough.

"When can the operation be carried through, Doctor?" he asked.

Softly, with that certain inalienable note of respect that a robot always used to a human being, the surgeon said, "I am not certain, sir, that I understand how or upon whom such an operation could be performed."

There might have been a look of respectful intransigence on the surgeon's face, if a robot of his sort, in lightly bronzed stainless steel, could have such an expression—or any expression.

Andrew Martin studied the robot's right hand, his cutting hand, as it lay motionless on the desk. The fingers were long and were shaped into artistically metallic, looping curves so graceful and appropriate that one could imagine a scalpel fitting them and becoming, temporarily, one piece with them. There would be no hesitation in his work, no stumbling, no quivering, no mistakes. That confidence came with specialization, of course, a specialization so fiercely desired by humanity that few robots were, any longer, independently brained. A surgeon, of course, would have to be. But this one, though brained, was so limited in his capacity that he did not recognize Andrew, had probably never heard of him.

"Have you ever thought you would like to be a man?" Andrew asked.

The surgeon hesitated a moment, as though the question fitted nowhere in his allotted positronic pathways. "But I am a robot, sir."

"Would it be better to be a man?"

"It would be better, sir, to be a better surgeon. I could not be so if I were a man, but only if I were a more advanced robot. I would be pleased to be a more advanced robot."

"It does not offend you that I can order you about? That I can make you stand up, sit down, move right or left, by merely telling you to do so?"

"It is my pleasure to please you, sir. If your orders were to interfere with my functioning with respect to you or to any other human being, I would not obey you. The First Law, concerning my duty to human safety, would take precedence over the Second Law relating to obedience. Otherwise, obedience is my pleasure. Now, upon whom am I to perform this operation?"

"Upon me," Andrew said.

"But that is impossible. It is patently a damaging operation."

"That does not matter," said Andrew, calmly.

"I must not inflict damage," said the surgeon.

"On a human being, you must not," said Andrew, "but I, too, am a robot."

2

Andrew had appeared much more a robot when he had first been manufactured. He had then been as much a robot in appearance as any that had ever existed—smoothly designed and functional.

He had done well in the home to which he had been brought in those days when robots in households, or on the planet altogether, had been a rarity. There had been four in the home: Sir and Ma'am and Miss and Little Miss. He knew their names, of course, but he never used them. Sir was Gerald Martin.

His own serial number was NDR- . . . He eventually forgot the numbers. It had been a long time, of course; but if he had wanted to remember, he could not have forgotten. He had not wanted to remember.

Little Miss had been the first to call him Andrew, because she could not use the letters, and all the rest followed her in doing so.

Little Miss . . . She had lived for ninety years and was long since dead. He had tried to call her Ma'am once, but she would not allow it. Little Miss she had been to her last day.

Andrew had been intended to perform the duties of a valet, a butler, even a lady's maid. Those were the experimental days for him and, indeed, for all robots anywhere save in the industrial and exploratory factories and stations off Earth.

The Martins enjoyed him, and half the time he was prevented from doing his work because Miss and Little Miss wanted to play with him. It was Miss who first understood how this might be arranged. "We order you to play with us and you must follow orders."

"I am sorry, Miss, but a prior order from Sir must surely take precedence."

But she said, "Daddy just said he *hoped* you would take care of the cleaning. That's not much of an order. I *order* you."

Sir did not mind. Sir was fond of Miss and of Little Miss, even more than Ma'am was; and Andrew was fond of them, too. At least, the effect they had upon his actions were those which in a human being would have been called the result of fondness. Andrew thought of it as fondness for he did not know any other word for it.

It was for Little Miss that Andrew had carved a pendant out of wood. She had ordered him to. Miss, it seemed, had received an ivorite pendant with scrollwork for her birthday and Little Miss was unhappy over it. She had only a piece of wood, which she gave Andrew together with a small kitchen knife.

He had done it quickly and Little Miss had said, "That's *nice*, Andrew. I'll show it to Daddy."

Sir would not believe it. "Where did you really get this, Mandy?" Mandy was what he called Little Miss. When Little Miss assured him she was really telling the truth, he turned to Andrew. "Did you do this, Andrew?"

"Yes, Sir."

"The design, too?"

"Yes, Sir."

"From what did you copy the design?"

"It is a geometric representation, Sir, that fits the grain of the wood."

The next day, Sir brought him another piece of wood—a larger one—and an electric vibro-knife. "Make something out of this, Andrew. Anything you want to," he said.

Andrew did so as Sir watched, then looked at the product a long time. After that, Andrew no longer waited on tables. He was ordered to read books on furniture design instead, and he learned to make cabinets and desks.

"These are amazing productions, Andrew," Sir soon told him.

"I enjoy doing them, Sir," Andrew admitted.

"Enjoy?"

"It makes the circuits of my brain somehow flow more easily. I have heard you use the word 'enjoy' and the way you use it fits the way I feel. I enjoy doing them, Sir."

3

Gerald Martin took Andrew to the regional offices of the United States Robots and Mechanical Men Corporation. As a member of the Regional Legislature he had no trouble at all in gaining an interview with the chief robopsychologist. In fact, it was only as a member of the Regional Legislature that he qualified as a robot owner in the first place—in those early days when robots were rare.

Andrew did not understand any of this at the time. But in later years, with greater learning, he could review that early scene and understand it in its proper light.

The robopsychologist, Merton Mansky, listened with a growing frown and more than once managed to stop his fingers at the point beyond which they would have irrevocably drummed on the table. He had drawn features and a lined forehead, but he might actually have been younger than he looked.

"Robotics is not an exact art, Mr. Martin," Mansky explained. "I cannot explain it to you in detail, but the mathematics governing the plotting of the positronic pathways is far too complicated to permit of any but approximate solutions. Naturally, since we build everything around the Three Laws, those are incontrovertible. We will, of course, replace your robot—"

"Not at all," said Sir. "There is no question of failure on his part. He performs his assigned duties perfectly. The point is he also carves wood in exquisite fashion and never the same twice. He produces works of art."

Mansky looked confused. "Strange. Of course, we're at you think?"

"See for yourself." Sir handed over a little sphere of wood tempting generalized pathways these days. Really creative, on which there was a playground scene in which the boys and girls were almost too small to make out, yet they were in perfect proportion and they blended so naturally with the grain that it, too, seemed to have been carved.

Mansky was incredulous. "*He* did that?" He handed it back with a shake of his head. "The luck of the draw. Something in the pathways."

"Can you do it again?"

"Probably not. Nothing like this has ever been reported."

"Good! I don't in the least mind Andrew's being the only one."

"I suspect that the company would like to have your robot back for study," Mansky said.

"Not a chance!" Sir said with sudden grimness. "Forget it." He turned to Andrew, "Let's go home, now."

"As you wish, Sir," said Andrew.

4

Miss was dating boys and wasn't about the house much. It was Little Miss, not as little as she once was, who filled Andrew's horizon now. She never forgot that the very first piece of wood carving he had done had been for her. She kept it on a silver chain about her neck.

It was she who first objected to Sir's habit of giving away Andrew's work. "Come on, Dad, if anyone wants one of them, let him pay for it. It's worth it."

"It isn't like you to be greedy, Mandy."

"Not for us, Dad. For the artist."

Andrew had never heard the word before, and when he had a moment to himself he looked it up in the dictionary.

Then there was another trip, this time to Sir's lawyer.

"What do you think of this, John?" Sir asked.

The lawyer was John Feingold. He had white hair and a pudgy belly, and the rims of his contact lenses were tinted a bright green. He looked at the small plaque Sir had given him. "This is beautiful. But I've already heard the news. Isn't this a carving made by your robot? The one you've brought with you."

"Yes, Andrew does them. Don't you, Andrew?"

"Yes, Sir," said Andrew.

"How much would you pay for that, John?" Sir asked.

"I can't say. I'm not a collector of such things."

"Would you believe I have been offered two hundred and fifty dollars for that small thing. Andrew has made chairs that have sold for five hundred dollars. There's two hundred thousand dollars in the bank from Andrew's products."

"Good heavens, he's making you rich, Gerald."

"Half rich," said Sir. "Half of it is in an account in the name of Andrew Martin."

"The robot?"

"That's right, and I want to know if it's legal."

"Legal . . . ?" Feingold's chair creaked as he leaned back in it. "There are no precedents, Gerald. How did your robot sign the necessary papers?"

"He can sign his name, so I brought in the signature. I didn't bring him along, however. Now, is there anything further that ought to be done?"

"Um." Feingold's eyes seemed to turn inward for a moment. Then he said, "Well, we can set up a trust to handle all finances in his name and that will place a layer of insullation between him and the hostile world. Beyond that, my advice is you do nothing. No one has stopped you so far. If anyone objects, let *him* bring suit."

"And will you take the case if the suit is brought?"

"For a retainer, certainly."

"How much?"

"Something like that," Feingold said, and pointed to the wooden plaque.

"Fair enough," said Sir.

Feingold chuckled as he turned to the robot. "Andrew, are you pleased that you have money?"

"Yes, sir."

"What do you plan to do with it?"

"Pay for things, sir, which otherwise Sir would have to pay for. It would save him expense, sir."

5

Such occasions arose. Repairs were expensive, and revisions were even more so. With the years, new models of robots were produced and Sir saw to it that Andrew had the advantage of every new device, until he was a model of metallic excellence. It was all done at Andrew's expense. Andrew insisted on that.

Only his positronic pathways were untouched. Sir insisted on that.

"The new models aren't as good as you are, Andrew," he said. "The new robots are worthless. The company has learned to make the pathways more precise, more closely on the nose, more deeply on the track. The new robots don't shift. They do what they're designed for and never stray. I like you better."

"Thank you, Sir."

"And it's your doing, Andrew, don't you forget that. I am certain Mansky put an end to generalized pathways as soon as he had a good look at you. He didn't like the unpredictability. Do you know how many times he asked for you back so he could place you under study? Nine times! I never let him have you, though; and now that he's retired, we may have some peace."

So Sir's hair thinned and grayed and his face grew pouchy, while Andrew looked even better than he had when he first joined the family. Ma'am had joined an art colony somewhere in Europe, and Miss was a poet in New York. They wrote sometimes, but not often. Little Miss was married and lived not far away. She said she did not want to leave Andrew. When her child, Little Sir, was born, she let Andrew hold the bottle and feed him.

With the birth of a grandson, Andrew felt that Sir finally had someone to replace those who had gone. Therefore, it would not be so unfair now to come to him with the request.

"Sir, it is kind of you to have allowed me to spend my money as I wished."

"It was your money, Andrew."

"Only by your voluntary act, Sir. I do not believe the law would have stopped you from keeping it all."

"The law won't persuade me to do wrong, Andrew."

"Despite all expenses, and despite taxes, too, Sir, I have nearly six hundred thousand dollars."

"I know that, Andrew."

"I want to give it to you, Sir."

"I won't take it, Andrew."

"In exchange for something you can give me, Sir."

"Oh? What is that, Andrew?"

"My freedom, Sir."

"Your—"

"I wish to buy my freedom, Sir."

6

It wasn't that easy. Sir had flushed, had said, "For God's sake!" Then he had turned on his heel and stalked away.

It was Little Miss who finally brought him round, defiantly and harshly—and in front of Andrew. For thirty years no one had ever hesitated to talk in front of Andrew, whether or not the matter involved Andrew. He was only a robot.

"Dad, why are you taking this as a personal affront? He'll still be here. He'll still be loyal. He can't help that; it's built in. All he wants is a form of words. He wants to be called free. Is that so terrible? Hasn't he earned this chance? Heavens, he and I have been talking about it for years!"

"Talking about it for years, have you?"

"Yes, and over and over again he postponed it for fear he would hurt you. I *made* him put the matter up to you."

"He doesn't know what freedom is. He's a robot."

"Dad, you don't know him. He's read everything in the library. I don't know what he feels inside, but I don't know what *you* feel inside either. When you talk to him you'll find he reacts to the various abstractions as you and I do, and what else counts? If someone else's reactions are like your own, what more can you ask for?"

"The law won't take that attitude," Sir said, angrily. "See here, you!" He turned to Andrew with a deliberate grate in his voice. "I can't free you except by doing it legally. If this gets into the courts, you not only won't get your freedom but the law will take official cognizance of your money. They'll tell you that a robot has no right to earn money. Is this rigmarole worth losing your money?"

"Freedom is without price, Sir," said Andrew. "Even the chance of freedom is worth the money."

7

It seemed the court might also take the attitude that freedom was without price, and might decide that for no price, however great, could a robot buy its freedom.

The simple statement of the regional attorney who represented those who had brought a class action to oppose the freedom was this: "The word 'freedom' has no meaning when applied to a robot. Only a human being can be free." He said it several times, when it seemed appropriate; slowly, with his hand coming down rhythmically on the desk before him to mark the words.

Little Miss asked permission to speak on behalf of Andrew.

She was recognized by her full name, something Andrew had never heard pronounced before: "Amanda Laura Martin Charney may approach the bench."

"Thank you, Your Honor. I am not a lawyer and I don't know the proper way of phrasing things, but I hope you will listen to my meaning and ignore the words.

"Let's understand what it means to be free in Andrew's case. In some ways, he *is* free. I think it's at least twenty years since anyone in the Martin family gave him an order to do something that we felt he might not do of his own accord. But we can, if we wish, give him an order to do anything, couching it as harshly as we wish, because he is a machine that belongs to us. Why should we be in a position to do so, when he has served us so long, so faithfully, and has earned so much money for us? He owes us nothing more. The debit is entirely on the other side.

"Even if we were legally forbidden to place Andrew in involuntary servitude, he would still serve us voluntarily. Making him free would be a trick of words only, but it would mean much to him. It would give him everything and cost us nothing."

For a moment the judge seemed to be suppressing a smile. "I see your point, Mrs. Charney. The fact is that there is no binding law in this respect and no precedent. There is, however, the unspoken assumption that only a man may enjoy freedom. I can make new law here, subject to reversal in a higher court; but I cannot lightly run counter to that assumption. Let me address the robot. Andrew!"

"Yes, Your Honor."

It was the first time Andrew had spoken in court, and the judge seemed astonished for a moment at the human timbre of his voice.

"Why do you want to be free, Andrew? In what way will this matter to you?"

"Would you wish to be a slave, Your Honor," Andrew asked.

"But you are not a slave. You are a perfectly good robot—a genius of a robot, I am given to understand, capable of an artistic expression that can be matched nowhere. What more could you do if you were free?"

"Perhaps no more than I do now, Your Honor, but with greater joy. It has been said in this courtroom that only a human being can be free. It seems to me that only someone who *wishes* for freedom can be free. I wish for freedom."

And it was that statement that cued the judge. The crucial sentence in his decision was "There is no right to deny freedom to any object with a mind advanced enough to grasp the concept and desire the state."

It was eventually upheld by the World Court.

8

Sir remained displeased, and his harsh voice made Andrew feel as if he were being short-circuited. "I don't want your damned money, Andrew. I'll take it only because you won't feel free otherwise. From now on, you can select your own jobs and do them as you please. I will give you no orders, except this one: Do as you please. But I am still responsible for you. That's part of the court order. I hope you understand that."

Little Miss interrupted. "Don't be irascible, Dad. The responsibility is no great chore. You know you won't have to do a thing. The Three Laws still hold."

"Then how is he free?"

"Are not human beings bound by their laws, Sir?" Andrew replied.

"I'm not going to argue." Sir left the room, and Andrew saw him only infrequently after that.

Little Miss came to see him frequently in the small house that had been built and made over for him. It had no kitchen, of course, nor bathroom facilities. It had just two rooms; one was a library and one was a combination storeroom and workroom. Andrew accepted many commissions and worked harder as a free robot than he ever had before, till the cost of the house was paid for and the structure was signed over to him.

One day Little Sir—no, 'George!'—came. Little Sir had insisted on that after the court decision. "A free robot doesn't call anyone Little Sir," George had said. "I call you Andrew. You must call me George."

His preference was phrased as an order, so Andrew called him George—but Little Miss remained Little Miss.

One day when George came alone, it was to say that Sir was dying. Little Miss was at the bedside, but Sir wanted Andrew as well.

Sir's voice was still quite strong, though he seemed unable to move much. He struggled to raise his hand.

"Andrew," he said, "Andrew— Don't help me, George. I'm only dying; I'm not crippled. Andrew, I'm glad you're free. I just wanted to tell you that."

Andrew did not know what to say. He had never been at the side of someone dying before, but he knew it was the human way of ceasing to function. It was an involuntary and irreversible dismantling, and Andrew did not know what to say that might be appropriate. He could only remain standing, absolutely silent, absolutely motionless.

When it was over, Little Miss said to him, "He may not have seemed friendly to you toward the end, Andrew, but he was old, you know; and it hurt him that you should want to be free."

Then Andrew found the words. "I would never have been free without him, Little Miss."

9

Only after Sir's death did Andrew begin to wear clothes. He began with an old pair of trousers at first, a pair that George had given him.

George was married now, and a lawyer. He had joined Feingold's firm. Old Feingold was long since dead, but his daughter had carried on. Eventually the firm's name became Feingold and Martin. It remained so even when the daughter retired and no Feingold took her place. At the time Andrew first put on clothes, the Martin name had just been added to the firm.

George had tried not to smile the first time he saw Andrew attempting to put on trousers, but to Andrew's eyes the smile was clearly there. George showed Andrew how to manipulate the static charge to allow the trousers to open, wrap about his lower body, and move shut. George demonstrated on his own trousers, but Andrew was quite aware it would take him a while to duplicate that one flowing motion.

"But why do you want trousers, Andrew? Your body is so beautifully functional it's a shame to cover it—especially when you needn't worry about either temperature control or modesty. And the material doesn't cling properly—not to metal."

Andrew held his ground. "Are not human bodies beautifully functional, George? Yet you cover yourselves."

"For warmth, for cleanliness, for protection, for decorativeness. None of that applies to you."

"I feel bare without clothes. I feel different, George," Andrew responded.

"Different! Andrew, there are millions of robots on Earth now. In this region, according to the last census, there are almost as many robots as there are men."

"I know, George. There are robots doing every conceivable type of work."

"And none of them wear clothes."

"And none of them are free, George."

Little by little, Andrew added to his wardrobe. He was inhibited by George's smile and by the stares of the people who commissioned work.

He might be free, but there was built into Andrew a carefully detailed program concerning his behavior to people, and it was only by the tiniest steps that he dared advance; open disapproval would set him back months. Not everyone accepted Andrew as free. He was incapable of resenting that, and yet there was a difficulty about his thinking process when he thought of it. Most of all, he tended to avoid putting on clothes—or too many of them—when he thought Little Miss might come to visit him. She was older now and was often away in some warmer climate, but when she returned the first thing she did was visit him.

On one of her visits, George said, ruefully, "She's got me, Andrew. I'll be running for the legislature next year. 'Like grandfather,' she says, 'like grandson.' "

"Like grandfather . . ." Andrew stopped, uncertain.

"I mean that I, George, the grandson, will be like Sir, the grandfather, who was in the legislature once."

"It would be pleasant, George, if Sir were still—" He paused, for he did not want to say, "in working order." That seemed inappropriate.

"Alive," George said. "Yes, I think of the old monster now and then, too."

Andrew often thought about this conversation. He had noticed his own incapacity in speech when talking with George. Somehow the language had changed since Andrew had come into being with a built-in vocabulary. Then, too, George used a colloquial speech, as Sir and Little Miss had not. Why should he have called Sir a monster when surely that word was not appropriate. Andrew could not even turn to his own books for guidance. They were old, and most dealt with woodworking, with art, with furniture design. There was none on language, none on the ways of human beings.

Finally, it seemed to him that he must seek the proper books; and as a free robot, he felt he must not ask George. He would go to town and use the library. It was a triumphant decision and he felt his electropotential grow distinctly higher until he had to throw in an impedance coil.

He put on a full costume, including even a shoulder chain of wood. He would have preferred the glitter plastic, but George had said that wood was much more appropriate and that polished cedar was considerably more valuable as well.

He had placed a hundred feet between himself and the house before gathering resistance brought him to a halt. He shifted the impedance coil out of circuit, and when that did not seem to help enough he returned to his home and on a piece of notepaper wrote neatly, "I have gone to the library," and placed it in clear view on his worktable.

10

Andrew never quite got to the library.

He had studied the map. He knew the route, but not the appearance of it. The actual landmarks did not resemble the symbols on the map and he would hesitate. Eventually, he thought he must have somehow gone wrong, for everything looked strange.

He passed an occasional field-robot, but by the time he decided he should ask his way none were in sight. A vehicle passed and did not stop.

Andrew stood irresolute, which meant calmly motionless, for coming across the field toward him were two human beings.

He turned to face them, and they altered their course to meet him. A moment before, they had been talking loudly. He had heard their voices. But now they were silent. They had the look that Andrew associated with human uncertainty; and they were young, but not very young. Twenty, perhaps? Andrew could never judge human age.

"Would you describe to me the route to the town library, sirs?"

One of them, the taller of the two, whose tall hat lengthened him still farther, almost grotesquely, said, not to Andrew, but to the other, "It's a robot."

The other had a bulbous nose and heavy eyelids. He said, not to Andrew but to the first, "It's wearing clothes."

The tall one snapped his fingers. "It's the free robot. They have a robot at the old Martin place who isn't owned by anybody. Why else would it be wearing clothes?"

"Ask it," said the one with the nose.

"Are you the Martin robot?" asked the tall one.

"I am Andrew Martin, sir," Andrew said.

"Good. Take off your clothes. Robots don't wear clothes." He said to the other, "That's disgusting. Look at him!"

Andrew hesitated. He hadn't heard an order in that tone of voice in so long that his Second Law circuits had momentarily jammed.

The tall one repeated, "Take off your clothes. I order you."

Slowly, Andrew began to remove them.

"Just drop them," said the tall one.

The nose said, "If it doesn't belong to anyone, it could be ours as much as someone else's."

"Anyway," said the tall one, "who's to object to anything we do. We're not damaging property." He turned to Andrew. "Stand on your head."

"The head is not meant—" Andrew began.

"That's an order. If you don't know how, try anyway."

Andrew hesitated again, then bent to put his head on the ground. He tried to lift his legs but fell, heavily.

The tall one said, "Just lie there." He said to the other, "We can take him apart. Ever take a robot apart?"

"Will he let us?"

"How can he stop us?"

There was no way Andrew could stop them, if they ordered him in a forceful enough manner not to resist. The Second Law of obedience took precedence over the Third Law of self-preservation. In any case, he could not defend himself without possibly hurting them, and that would mean breaking the First Law. At that thought, he felt every motile unit contract slightly and he quivered as he lay there.

The tall one walked over and pushed at him with his foot. "He's heavy. I think we'll need tools to do the job."

The nose said, "We could order him to take himself apart. It would be fun to watch him try."

"Yes," said the tall one, thoughtfully, "but let's get him off the road. If someone comes along—"

It was too late. Someone had, indeed, come along and it was George. From where he lay, Andrew had seen him topping a small rise in the middle distance. He would have liked to signal him in some way, but the last order had been "Just lie there!"

George was running now, and he arrived on the scene

somewhat winded. The two young men stepped back a little and then waited thoughtfully.

"Andrew, has something gone wrong?" George asked, anxiously.

Andrew replied, "I am well, George."

"Then stand up. What happened to your clothes?"

"That your robot, Mac?" the tall young man asked.

George turned sharply. "He's no one's robot. What's been going on here."

"We politely asked him to take his clothes off. What's that to you, if you don't own him."

George turned to Andrew. "What were they doing, Andrew?"

"It was their intention in some way to dismember me. They were about to move me to a quiet spot and order me to dismember myself."

George looked at the two young men, and his chin trembled.

The young men retreated no farther. They were smiling.

The tall one said, lightly, "What are you going to do, pudgy? Attack us?"

George said, "No. I don't have to. This robot has been in my family for over seventy-five years. He knows us and he values us more than he values anyone else. I am going to tell him that you two are threatening my life and that you plan to kill me. I will ask him to defend me. In choosing between me and you two, he will choose me. Do you know what will happen to you when he attacks you?"

The two were backing away slightly, looking uneasy.

George said, sharply, "Andrew, I am in danger and about to come to harm from these young men. Move toward them!"

Andrew did so, and the young men did not wait. They ran.

"All right, Andrew, relax," George said. He looked unstrung. He was far past the age where he could face the possibility of a dustup with one young man, let alone two.

"I couldn't have hurt them, George. I could see they were not attacking you."

"I didn't order you to attack them. I only told you to move toward them. Their own fears did the rest."

"How can they fear robots?"

"It's a disease of mankind, one which has not yet been cured. But never mind that. What the devil are you doing here, Andrew? Good thing I found your note. I was just on the point of turning back and hiring a helicopter when I found you. How did you get it into your head to go to the library? I would have brought you any books you needed."

"I am a—" Andrew began.

"Free robot. Yes, yes. All right, what did you want in the library?"

"I want to know more about human beings, about the world, about everything. And about robots, George. I want to write a history about robots."

George put his arm on the other's shoulder. "Well, let's walk home. But pick up your clothes first. Andrew, there are a million books on robotics and all of them include histories of the science. The world is growing saturated not only with robots but with information about robots."

Andrew shook his head, a human gesture he had lately begun to adopt. "Not a history of robotics, George. A history of *robots*, by a robot. I want to explain how robots feel about what has happened since the first ones were allowed to work and live on Earth."

George's eyebrows lifted, but he said nothing in direct response.

11

Little Miss was just past her eighty-third birthday, but there was nothing about her that was lacking in either energy or determination. She gestured with her cane oftener than she propped herself with it.

She listened to the story in a fury of indignation. "George, that's horrible. Who were those young ruffians?"

"I don't know. What difference does it make? In the end they did not do any damage."

"They might have. You're a lawyer, George; and if you're well off, it's entirely due to the talents of Andrew. It was the money *he* earned that is the foundation of everything we have. He provides the continuity for this family, and I will *not* have him treated as a wind-up toy."

"What would you have me do, Mother?" George asked.

"I said you're a lawyer. Don't you listen? You set up a test case somehow, and you force the regional courts to declare for robot rights and get the legislature to pass the necessary bills. Carry the whole thing to the World Court, if you have to. I'll be watching, George, and I'll tolerate no shirking."

She was serious, so what began as a way of soothing the fearsome old lady became an involved matter with enough legal entanglement to make it interesting. As senior partner of Feingold and Martin, George plotted strategy. But he left the actual work to his junior partners, with much of it a matter for his son, Paul, who was also a member of the firm and who reported dutifully nearly every day to his grandmother. She, in turn, discussed the case every day with Andrew.

Andrew was deeply involved. His work on his book on robots was delayed, and delayed again, as he pored over the legal arguments and even, at times, made very diffident suggestions. "George told me that day I was attacked that human beings have always been afraid of robots," he said one day. "As long as they are, the courts and the legislatures are not likely to work hard on behalf of robots. Should not something be done about public opinion?"

So while Paul stayed in court, George took to the public platform. It gave him the advantage of being informal, and he even went so far sometimes as to wear the new, loose style of clothing which he called drapery.

Paul chided him, "Just don't trip over it on stage, Dad."

George replied, despondently, "I'll try not to."

He addressed the annual convention of holo-news editors on one occasion and said, in part: "If, by virtue of the Second Law, we can demand of any robot unlimited obedience in all respects not involving harm to a human being, then any human being, *any* human being, has a fearsome power over any robot, *any* robot. In particular, since Second Law supersedes Third Law, *any* human being can use the law of obedience to overcome the law of self-protection. He can order any robot to damage itself or even to destroy itself for any reason, or for no reason.

"Is this just? Would we treat an animal so? Even an inanimate object which had given us good service has a claim on our consideration. And a robot is not insensitive; it is not an animal. It can think well enough so that it can talk to us, reason with us, joke with us. Can we treat them as friends, can we work together with them, and not give them some of the fruits of that friendship, some of the benefits of co-working?

"If a man has the right to give a robot any order that does not involve harm to a human being, he should have the decency never to give a robot any order that involves harm to a robot, unless human safety absolutely requires it. With great power goes great responsibility, and if the robots have Three Laws to protect men, is it too much to ask that men have a law or two to protect robots?"

Andrew was right. It was the battle over public opinion that held the key to courts and legislature. In the end, a law was passed that set up conditions under which robot-harming orders were forbidden. It was endlessly qualified and the punishments for violating the law were totally inadequate, but the principle was established. The final passage by the World Legislature came through on the day of Little Miss' death.

That was no coincidence. Little Miss held on to life desperately during the last debate and let go only when word of victory arrived. Her last smile was for Andrew. Her last words were, "You have been good to us, Andrew." She died with her hand holding his, while her son and his wife and children remained at a respectful distance from both.

12

Andrew waited patiently when the receptionist-robot disappeared into the inner office. The receptionist might have used the holographic chatterbox, but unquestionably it was perturbed by having to deal with another robot rather than with a human being.

Andrew passed the time revolving the matter in his mind: Could "unroboted" be used as an analog of "unmanned," or had unmanned become a metaphoric term sufficiently divorced from its original literal meaning to be applied to robots—or to women for that matter? Such problems frequently arose as he worked on his book on robots. The trick of thinking out sentences to express all complexities had undoubtedly increased his vocabulary.

Occasionally, someone came into the room to stare at him and he did not try to avoid the glance. He looked at each calmly, and each in turn looked away.

Paul Martin finally emerged. He looked surprised, or he would have if Andrew could have made out his expression with certainty. Paul had taken to wearing the heavy makeup that fashion was dictating for both sexes. Though it made sharper and firmer the somewhat bland lines of Paul's face, Andrew disapproved. He found that disapproving of human beings, as long as he did not express it verbally, did not make him very uneasy. He could even write the disapproval. He was sure it had not always been so.

"Come in, Andrew. I'm sorry I made you wait, but there was something I *had* to finish. Come in. You had said you wanted to talk to me, but I didn't know you meant here in town."

"If you were busy, Paul, I am prepared to continue to wait."

Paul glanced at the interplay of shifting shadows on the dial on the wall that served as timepiece and said, "I can make some time. Did you come alone?"

"I hired an automatobile."

"Any trouble?" Paul asked, with more than a trace of anxiety.

"I wasn't expecting any. My rights are protected."

Paul looked all the more anxious for that. "Andrew, I've explained that the law is unenforceable, at least under most conditions. And if you insist on wearing clothes, you'll run into trouble eventually; just like that first time."

"And *only* time, Paul. I'm sorry you are displeased."

"Well, look at it this way: you are virtually a living legend, Andrew, and you are too valuable in many different ways for you to have any right to take chances with yourself. By the way, how's the book coming?"

"I am approaching the end, Paul. The publisher is quite pleased."

"Good!"

"I don't know that he's necessarily pleased with the book as a book. I think he expects to sell many copies because it's written by a robot and that's what pleases him."

"Only human, I'm afraid."

"I am not displeased. Let it sell for whatever reason, since it will mean money and I can use some."

"Grandmother left you—"

"Little Miss was generous, and I'm sure I can count on the family to help me out further. But it is the royalties from the book on which I am counting to help me through the next step."

"What next step is that?"

"I wish to see the head of U.S. Robots and Mechanical Men Corporation. I have tried to make an appointment; but so far I have not been able to reach him. The Corporation did not cooperate with me in the writing of the book, so I am not surprised, you understand."

Paul was clearly amused. "Cooperation is the last thing

you can expect. They didn't cooperate with us in our great fight for robot rights. Quite the reverse, and you can see why. Give a robot rights and people may not want to buy them."

"Nevertheless," said Andrew, "if *you* call them, you may be able to obtain an interview for me."

"I'm no more popular with them than you are, Andrew."

"But perhaps you can hint that by seeing me they may head off a campaign by Feingold and Martin to strengthen the rights of robots further."

"Wouldn't that be a lie, Andrew?"

"Yes, Paul, and I can't tell one. That is why you must call."

"Ah, you can't lie, but you can urge me to tell a lie, is that it? You're getting more human all the time, Andrew."

13

The meeting was not easy to arrange, even with Paul's supposedly weighted name. But it finally came about. When it did, Harley Smythe-Robertson, who, on his mother's side, was descended from the original founder of the corporation and who had adopted the hyphenation to indicate it, looked remarkably unhappy. He was approaching retirement age and his entire tenure as president had been devoted to the matter of robot rights. His gray hair was plastered thinly over the top of his scalp; his face was not made up, and he eyed Andrew with brief hostility from time to time.

Andrew began the conversation. "Sir, nearly a century ago, I was told by a Merton Mansky of this corporation that the mathematics governing the plotting of the positronic pathways was far too complicated to permit of any but approximate solutions and that, therefore, my own capacities were not fully predictable."

"That was a century ago." Smythe-Robertson hesitated, then said icily, "*Sir*. It is true no longer. Our robots are made with precision now and are trained precisely to their jobs."

"Yes," said Paul, who had come along, as he said, to make sure that the corporation played fair, "with the result that my receptionist must be guided at every point once events depart from the conventional, however slightly."

"You would be much more displeased if it were to improvise," Smythe-Robertson said.

"Then you no longer manufacture robots like myself which are flexible and adaptable."

"No longer."

"The research I have done in connection with my book," said Andrew, "indicates that I am the oldest robot presently in active operation."

"The oldest presently," said Smythe-Robertson, "and the oldest ever. The oldest that will ever be. No robot is useful after the twenty-fifth year. They are called in and replaced with newer models."

"No robot as presently manufactured is useful after the *twentieth* year," said Paul, with a note of sarcasm creeping into his voice. "Andrew is quite exceptional in this respect."

Andrew, adhering to the path he had marked out for himself, continued, "As the oldest robot in the world and the most flexible, am I not unusual enough to merit special treatment from the company?"

"Not at all," Smythe-Robertson said, freezing up. "Your unusualness is an embarrassment to the company. If you were on lease, instead of having been an outright sale through some mischance, you would long since have been replaced."

"But that is exactly the point," said Andrew. "I am a free robot and I own myself. Therefore I come to you and ask you to replace me. You cannot do this without the owner's consent. Nowadays, that consent is extorted as a condition of the lease, but in my time this did not happen."

Smythe-Robertson was looking both startled and puzzled, and for a moment there was silence. Andrew found himself staring at the hologram on the wall. It was a death mask of Susan Calvin, patron saint of all roboticists. She had been dead for nearly two centuries now, but as a result of writing his book Andrew knew her so well he could half persuade himself that he had met her in life.

Finally Smythe-Robertson asked, "How can I replace you for you? If I replace you, as robot, how can I donate the new robot to you as owner since in the very act of replacement you cease to exist." He smiled grimly.

"Not at all difficult," Paul interposed. "The seat of Andrew's personality is his positronic brain and it is the one part that cannot be replaced without creating a new robot. The positronic brain, therefore, is Andrew the owner. Every other part of the robotic body can be replaced without affecting the robot's personality, and those other parts are the brain's possessions. Andrew, I should say, wants to supply his brain with a new robotic body."

"That's right," said Andrew, calmly. He turned to Smythe-Robertson. "You have manufactured androids, haven't you? Robots that have the outward appearance of humans, complete to the texture of the skin?"

"Yes, we have. They worked perfectly well, with their synthetic fibrous skins and tendons. There was virtually no metal anywhere except for the brain, yet they were nearly as tough as metal robots. They were tougher, weight for weight."

Paul looked interested. "I didn't know that. How many are on the market?"

"None," said Smythe-Robertson. "They were much more expensive than metal models and a market survey showed they would not be accepted. They looked too human."

Andrew was impressed. "But the corporation retains its expertise, I assume. Since it does, I wish to request that I be replaced by an organic robot, an android."

Paul looked surprised. "Good Lord!" he said.

Smythe-Robertson stiffened. "Quite impossible!"

"Why is it impossible?" Andrew asked. "I will pay any reasonable fee, of course."

"We do not manufacture androids."

"You do not *choose* to manufacture androids," Paul interjected quickly. "That is not the same as being unable to manufacture them."

"Nevertheless," Smythe-Robertson responded, "the manufacture of androids is against public policy."

"There is no law against it," said Paul.

"Nevertheless, we do not manufacture them—and we will not."

Paul cleared his throat. "Mr. Smythe-Robertson," he said, "Andrew is a free robot who comes under the purview of the law guaranteeing robot rights. You are aware of this, I take it?"

"Only too well."

"This robot, as a free robot, chooses to wear clothes. This results in his being frequently humiliated by thoughtless human beings despite the law against the humiliation of robots. It is difficult to prosecute vague offenses that don't meet with the general disapproval of those who must decide on guilt and innocence."

"U.S. Robots understood that from the start. Your father's firm unfortunately did not."

"My father is dead now, but what I see is that we have here a clear offense with a clear target."

"What are you talking about?" said Smythe-Robertson.

"My client, Andrew Martin—he has just become my client—is a free robot who is entitled to ask U.S. Robots and Mechanical Men Corporation for the right of replacement, which the corporation supplies to anyone who owns a robot for more than twenty-five years. In fact, the corporation insists on such replacement."

Paul was smiling and thoroughly at ease. "The positronic brain of my client," he went on, "is the owner of the body of my client—which is certainly more than twenty-five years old. The positronic brain demands the replacement of the body and offers to pay any reasonable fee for an android body as that replacement. If you refuse the request, my client undergoes humiliation and will sue.

"While public opinion would not ordinarily support the claim of a robot in such a case, may I remind you that U.S. Robots is not popular with the public generally. Even those who most use and profit from robots are suspicious of the corporation. This may be a hangover from the days when robots were widely feared. It may be resentment against the power and wealth of U.S. Robots, which has a worldwide monopoly. Whatever the cause may be, the resentment exists. I think you will find that you would prefer not to be faced with a lawsuit, particularly since my client is wealthy and will live for many more centuries and will have no reason to refrain from fighting the battle forever."

Smythe-Robertson had slowly reddened. "You are trying to force—"

"I force you to do nothing," said Paul. "If you wish to refuse to accede to my client's reasonable request, you may by all means do so and we will leave without another word. But we will sue, as is certainly our right, and you will find that you will eventually lose."

"Well . . ."

"I see that you are going to accede," said Paul. "You may hesitate but you will come to it in the end. Let me assure you, then, of one further point: If, in the process of transferring my client's positronic brain from his present body to an organic one, there is any damage, however slight, then I will never rest until I've nailed the corporation to the ground. I will, if necessary, take every possible step to mobilize public opinion against the corporation if one brainpath of my client's platinum-iridium essence is scrambled." He turned to Andrew and asked, "Do you agree to all this, Andrew?"

Andrew hesitated a full minute. It amounted to the approval of lying, of blackmail, of the badgering and humiliation of a human being. But not physical harm, he told himself, not physical harm.

He managed at last to come out with a rather faint "Yes."

14

He felt as though he were being constructed again. For days, then for weeks, finally for months, Andrew found himself not himself somehow, and the simplest actions kept giving rise to hesitation.

Paul was frantic. "They've damaged you, Andrew. We'll have to institute suit!"

Andrew spoke very slowly. "You . . . mustn't. You'll never be able to prove . . . something . . . like m-m-m-m—"

"Malice?"

"Malice. Besides, I grow . . . stronger, better. It's the tr-tr-tr—"

"Tremble?"

"Trauma. After all, there's never been such an op-op-op-. . . before."

Andrew could feel his brain from the inside. No one else could. He knew he was well, and during the months that it took him to learn full coordination and full positronic interplay he spent hours before the mirror.

Not quite human! The face was stiff—too stiff—and the motions were too deliberate. They lacked the careless, free flow of the human being, but perhaps that might come with time. At least now he could wear clothes without the ridiculous anomaly of a mental face going along with it.

Eventually, he said, "I will be going back to work."

Paul laughed. "That means you are well. What will you be doing? Another book?"

"No," said Andrew, seriously. "I live too long for any one career to seize me by the throat and never let me go. There was a time when I was primarily an artist, and I can still turn to that. And there was a time when I was a historian, and I can still turn to that. But now I wish to be a robobiologist."

"A robopsychologist, you mean."

"No. That would imply the study of positronic brains, and at the moment I lack the desire to do that. A robobiologist, it seems to me, would be concerned with the working of the body attached to that brain."

"Wouldn't that be a roboticist?"

"A roboticist works with a metal body. I would be studying an organic humanoid body, of which I have the only one, as far as I know."

"You narrow your field," said Paul, thoughtfully. "As an artist, all conception is yours; as a historian you deal chiefly with robots; as a robobiologist, you will deal with yourself."

Andrew nodded. "It would seem so."

Andrew had to start from the very beginning, for he knew nothing of ordinary biology and almost nothing of science. He became a familiar sight in the libraries, where he sat at the electronic indices for hours at a time, looking perfectly normal in clothes. Those few who knew he was a robot in no way interfered with him.

He built a laboratory in a room which he added to his house; and his library grew, too.

Years passed, and Paul came to him one day and said, "It's a pity you're no longer working on the history of robots. I understand U.S. Robots is adopting a radically new policy."

Paul had aged, and his deteriorating eyes had been replaced with photoptic cells. In that respect, he had drawn closer to Andrew.

"What have they done?" Andrew asked.

"They are manufacturing central computers, gigantic positronic brains, really, which communicate with anywhere from a dozen to a thousand robots by microwave. The robots themselves have no brains at all. They are the limbs of the gigantic brain, and the two are physically separate."

"Is that more efficient."

"U.S. Robots claims it is. Smythe-Robertson established the new direction before he died, however, and it's my notion that it's a backlash at you. U.S. Robots is determined that they will make no robots that will give them the type of trouble you have, and for that reason they separate brain and body. The brain will have no body to wish changed; the body will have no brain to wish anything.

"It's amazing, Andrew," Paul went on, "the influence you have had on the history of robots. It was your artistry that encouraged U.S. Robots to make robots more precise and specialized; it was your freedom that resulted in the establishment of the principle of robotic rights; it was your insistence on an android body that made U.S. Robots switch to brain-body separation."

Andrew grew thoughtful. "I suppose in the end the corporation will produce one vast brain controlling several billion robotic bodies. All the eggs will be in one basket. Dangerous. Not proper at all."

"I think you're right," said Paul, "but I don't suspect it will come to pass for a century at least and I won't live to see it. In fact, I may not live to see next year."

"Paul!" cried Andrew, in concern.

Paul shrugged. "Men are mortal, Andrew. We're not like you. It doesn't matter too much, but it does make it important to assure you on one point. I'm the last of the human Martins. The money I control personally will be left to the trust in your name, and as far as anyone can foresee the future, you will be economically secure."

"Unnecessary," Andrew said, with difficulty. In all this time, he could not get used to the deaths of the Martins.

"Let's not argue. That's the way it's going to be. Now, what are you working on?"

"I am designing a system for allowing androids—myself—to gain energy from the combustion of hydrocarbons, rather than from atomic cells."

Paul raised his eyebrows. "So that they will breathe and eat?"

"Yes."

"How long have you been pushing in that direction?"

"For a long time now, but I think I have finally designed an adequate combustion chamber for catalyzed controlled breakdown."

"But why, Andrew? The atomic cell is surely infinitely better."

"In some ways, perhaps. But the atomic cell is inhuman."

15

It took time, but Andrew had time. In the first place, he did not wish to do anything till Paul had died in peace. With the death of the great-grandson of Sir, Andrew felt more nearly exposed to a hostile world and for that reason was all the more determined along the path he had chosen.

Yet he was not really alone. If a man had died, the firm of Feingold and Martin lived, for a corporation does not die any more than a robot does.

The firm had its directions and it followed them soullessly. By way of the trust and through the law firm, Andrew continued to be wealthy. In return for their own large annual retainer, Feingold and Martin involved themselves in the legal aspects of the new combustion chamber. But when the time came for Andrew to visit U.S. Robots and Mechanical Men Corporation, he did it alone. Once he had gone with Sir and once with Paul. This time, the third time, he was alone and manlike.

U.S. Robots had changed. The actual production plant had been shifted to a large space station, as had grown to be the case with more and more industries. With them had gone many robots. The Earth itself was becoming parklike, with its one-billion-person population stabilized and perhaps not more than thirty percent of its at-least-equally-large robot population independently brained.

The Director of Research was Alvin Magdescu, dark of complexion and hair, with a little pointed beard and wearing nothing above the waist but the breastband that fashion dictated. Andrew himself was well covered in the older fashion of several decades back.

Magdescu offered his hand to his visitor. "I know you, of course, and I'm rather pleased to see you. You're our most notorious product and it's a pity old Smythe-Robertson was so set against you. We could have done a great deal with you."

"You still can," said Andrew.

"No, I don't think so. We've past the time. We've had robots on Earth for over a century, but that's changing. It will be back to space with them, and those that stay here won't be brained."

"But there remains myself, and I stay on Earth."

"True, but there doesn't seem to be much of the robot about you. What new request have you?"

"To be still less a robot. Since I am so far organic, I wish an organic source of energy. I have here the plans . . ."

Magdescu did not hasten through them. He might have intended to at first, but he stiffened and grew intent. At one point, he said, "This is remarkably ingenious. Who thought of all this?"

"I did," Andrew replied.

Magdescu looked up at him sharply, then said, "It would amount to a major overhaul of your body, and an experimental one, since such a thing has never been attempted before. I advise against it. Remain as you are."

Andrew's face had limited means of expression, but impatience showed plainly in his voice. "Dr. Magdescu, you miss the entire point. You have no choice but to accede to my request. If such devices can be built into my body, they can be built into human bodies as well. The tendency to lengthen human life by prosthetic devices has already been remarked on. There are no devices better than the ones I have designed or am designing.

"As it happens, I control the patents by way of the firm of Feingold and Martin. We are quite capable of going into business for ourselves and of developing the kind of prosthetic devices that may end by producing human beings with many of the properties of robots. Your own business will then suffer.

"If, however, you operate on me now and agree to do so under similar circumstances in the future, you will receive permission to make use of the patents and control the technology of both robots and of the prosthetization of human beings. The initial leasing will not be granted, of course, until after the first operation is completed successfully, and after enough time has passed to demonstrate that it is indeed successful."

Andrew felt scarcely any First Law inhibition to the stern conditions he was setting a human being. He was learning to reason that what seemed like cruelty might, in the long run, be kindness.

Magdescu was stunned. "I'm not the one to decide something like this. That's a corporate decision that would take time."

"I can wait a reasonable time," said Andrew, "but only a reasonable time." And he thought with satisfaction that Paul himself could not have done it better.

16

It took only a reasonable time, and the operation was a success.

"I was very much against the operation, Andrew," Magdescu said, "but not for the reasons you might think. I was not in the least against the experiment, if it had been on someone else. I hated risking *your* positronic brain. Now that you have the positronic pathways interacting with simulated nerve pathways, it might have been difficult to rescue the brain intact if the body had gone bad."

"I had every faith in the skill of the staff at U.S. Robots," said Andrew. "And I can eat now."

"Well, you can sip olive oil. It will mean occasional cleanings of the combustion chamber, as we have explained to you. Rather an uncomfortable touch, I should think."

"Perhaps, if I did not expect to go further. Self-cleaning is not impossible. In fact, I am working on a device that will deal with solid food that may be expected to contain incombustible fractions—indigestible matter, so to speak, that will have to be discarded."

"You would then have to develop an anus."

"Or the equivalent."

"What else, Andrew . . . ?"

"Everything else."

"Genitalia, too."

"Insofar as they will fit my plans. My body is a canvas on which I intend to draw . . ."

Magdescu waited for the sentence to be completed, and when it seemed that it would not be, he completed it himself. "A man?"

"We shall see," Andrew said.

"That's a puny ambition, Andrew. You're better than a man. You've gone downhill from the moment you opted to become organic."

"My brain has not suffered."

"No, it hasn't. I'll grant you that. But, Andrew, the whole new breakthrough in prosthetic devices made possible by your patents is being marketed under your name. You're recognized as the inventor and you're being honored for it—as you should be. Why play further games with your body?"

Andrew did not answer.

The honors came. He accepted membership in several learned societies, including one that was devoted to the new science he had established—the one he had called robobiology but which had come to be termed prosthetology. On the one hundred and fiftieth anniversary of his construction, a testimonial dinner was given in his honor at U.S. Robots. If Andrew saw an irony in this, he kept it to himself.

Alvin Magdescu came out of retirement to chair the dinner. He was himself ninety-four years old and was alive because he, too, had prosthetized devices that, among other things, fulfilled the function of liver and kidneys. The dinner reached its climax when Magdescu, after a short and emotional talk, raised his glass to toast The Sesquicentennial Robot.

Andrew had had the sinews of his face redesigned to the point where he could show a human range of emotions, but he sat through all the ceremonies solemnly passive. He did not like to be a Sesquicentennial Robot.

17

It was prosthetology that finally took Andrew off the Earth.

In the decades that followed the celebration of his sesquicentennial, the Moon had come to be a world more Earthlike than Earth in every respect but its gravitational pull; and in its underground cities there was a fairly dense population. Prosthetized devices there had to take the lesser gravity into account. Andrew spent five years on the Moon working with local prosthetologists to make the necessary adaptations. When not at his work, he wandered among the robot population, every one of which treated him with the robotic obsequiousness due a man.

He came back to an Earth that was humdrum and quiet in comparison, and visited the offices of Feingold and Martin to announce his return.

The current head of the firm, Simon DeLong, was surprised. "We had been told you were returning, Andrew"—he had almost said Mr. Martin—"but we were not expecting you till next week."

"I grew impatient," said Andrew, briskly. He was anxious to get to the point. "On the Moon, Simon, I was in charge of a research team of twenty human scientists. I gave orders that no one questioned. The Lunar robots deferred to me as they would to a human being. Why, then, am I not a human being?"

A wary look entered DeLong's eyes. "My dear Andrew, as you have just explained, you are treated as a human being by both robots *and* human beings. You are, therefore, a human being *de facto*."

"To be a human being *de facto* is not enough. I want not

only to be treated as one, but to be legally identified as one. I want to be a human being *de jure*."

"Now, that is another matter," DeLong said. "There we would run into human prejudice and into the undoubted fact that, however much you may be *like* a human being, you are *not* a human being."

"In what way not?" Andrew asked. "I have the shape of a human being and organs equivalent to those of a human being. My organs, in fact, are identical to some of those in a prosthetized human being. I have contributed artistically, literarily, and scientifically to human culture as much as any human being now alive. What more can one ask?"

"I myself would ask nothing more. The trouble is that it would take an act of the World Legislature to define you as a human being. Frankly, I wouldn't expect that to happen."

"To whom on the Legislature could I speak?"

"To the Chairman of the Science and Technology Committee, perhaps."

"Can you arrange a meeting?"

"But you scarcely need an intermediary. In your position, you can—"

"No. *You* arrange it." It didn't even occur to Andrew that he was giving a flat order to a human being. He had grown so accustomed to that on the Moon. "I want him to know that the firm of Feingold and Martin is backing me in this to the hilt."

"Well, now—"

"To the hilt, Simon. In one hundred and seventy-three years I have in one fashion or another contributed greatly to this firm. I have been under obligation to individual members of the firm in times past. I am not, now. It is rather the other way around now and I am calling in my debts."

"I will do what I can," DeLong said.

18

The Chairman of the Science and Technology Committee was from the East Asian region and was a woman. Her name was Chee Li-hsing and her transparent garments—obscuring what she wanted obscured only by their dazzle—made her look plastic-wrapped.

"I sympathize with your wish for full human rights," she said. "There have been times in history when segments of the human population fought for full human rights. What rights, however, can you possibly want that you do not have?"

"As simple a thing as my right to life," Andrew stated. "A robot can be dismantled at any time."

"A human being can be executed at any time."

"Execution can only follow due process of law. There is no trial needed for my dismantling. Only the word of a human being in authority is needed to end me. Besides . . . besides . . ." Andrew tried desperately to allow no sign of pleading, but his carefully designed tricks of human expression and tone of voice betrayed him here. "The truth is I want to be a man. I have wanted it through six generations of human beings."

Li-hsing looked up at him out of darkly sympathetic eyes. "The Legislature can pass a law declaring you one. They could pass a law declaring that a stone statue be defined as a man. Whether they will actually do so is, however, as likely in the first case as the second. Congresspeople are as human as the rest of the population and there is always that element of suspicion against robots."

"Even now?"

"Even now. We would all allow the fact that you have earned the prize of humanity, and yet there would remain the fear of setting an undesirable precedent."

"What precedent? I am the only free robot, the only one of my type, and there will never be another. You may consult U.S. Robots."

" 'Never' is a long word, Andrew—or, if you prefer, Mr. Martin—since I will gladly give you my personal accolade as man. You will find that most congresspeople will not be so willing to set the precedent, no matter how meaningless such a precedent might be. Mr. Martin, you have my sympathy, but I cannot tell you to hope. Indeed . . ."

She sat back and her forehead wrinkled. "Indeed, if the issue grows too heated, there might well arise a certain sentiment, both inside the Legislature and outside, for that dismantling you mentioned. Doing away with you could turn out to be the easiest way of resolving the dilemma. Consider that before deciding to push matters."

Andrew stood firm. "Will no one remember the technique of prosthetology, something that is almost entirely mine?"

"It may seem cruel, but they won't. Or if they do, it will be remembered against you. People will say you did it only for

yourself. It will be said it was part of a campaign to roboti-
cize human beings, or to humanify robots; and in either case
evil and vicious. You have never been part of a political hate
campaign, Mr. Martin; but I tell you that you would be the
object of vilification of a kind neither you nor I would credit,
and there would be people to believe it all. Mr. Martin, let
your life be."

She rose, and next to Andrew's seated figure she seemed
small and almost childlike.

"If I decide to fight for my humanity, will you be on my
side?"

She thought, then replied, "I will be—insofar as I can be.
If at any time such a stand would appear to threaten my political future, I might have to abandon you, since it is not an
issue I feel to be at the very root of my beliefs. I am trying
to be honest with you."

"Thank you, and I will ask no more. I intend to fight this
through, whatever the consequences, and I will ask you for
your help only for as long as you can give it."

19

It was not a direct fight. Feingold and Martin counseled
patience and Andrew muttered, grimly, that he had an
endless supply of that. Feingold and Martin then entered on
a campaign to narrow and restrict the area of combat.

They instituted a lawsuit denying the obligation to pay
debts to an individual with a prosthetic heart on the grounds
that the possession of a robotic organ removed humanity, and
with it the constitutional rights of human beings. They fought
the matter skillfully and tenaciously, losing at every step but
always in such a way that the decision was forced to be as
broad as possible, and then carrying it by way of appeals to
the World Court.

It took years, and millions of dollars.

When the final decision was handed down, DeLong held
what amounted to a victory celebration over the legal loss.
Andrew was, of course, present in the company offices on the
occasion.

"We've done two things, Andrew," said DeLong, "both of
which are good. First of all, we have established the fact that
no number of artificial parts in the human body causes it to
cease being a human body. Secondly, we have engaged public
opinion in the question in such a way as to put it fiercely on

the side of a broad interpretation of humanity, since there is not a human being in existence who does not hope for prosthetics if they will keep him alive."

"And do you think the Legislature will now grant me my humanity?" Andrew asked.

DeLong looked faintly uncomfortable. "As to that, I cannot be optimistic. There remains the one organ which the World Court has used as the criterion of humanity. Human beings have an organic cellular brain and robots have a platinum-iridium positronic brain if they have one at all—and you certainly have a positronic brain. No, Andrew, don't get that look in your eye. We lack the knowledge to duplicate the work of a cellular brain in artificial structures close enough to the organic type as to allow it to fall within the court's decision. Not even you could do it."

"What should we do, then?"

"Make the attempt, of course. Congresswoman Li-hsing will be on our side and a growing number of other congresspeople. The President will undoubtedly go along with a majority of the Legislature in this matter."

"Do we have a majority?"

"No. Far from it. But we might get one if the public will allow its desire for a broad interpretation of humanity to extend to you. A small chance, I admit; but if you do not wish to give up, we must gamble for it."

"I do not wish to give up."

20

Congresswoman Li-hsing was considerably older than she had been when Andrew had first met her. Her transparent garments were long gone. Her hair was now close-cropped and her coverings were tubular. Yet still Andrew clung, as closely as he could within the limits of reasonable taste, to the style of clothing that had prevailed when he had first adopted clothing more than a century before.

"We've gone as far as we can, Andrew," Li-hsing admitted. "We'll try once more after recess, but, to be honest, defeat is certain and then the whole thing will have to be given up. All my most recent efforts have only earned me certain defeat in the coming congressional campaign."

"I know," said Andrew, "and it distresses me. You said once you would abandon me if it came to that. Why have you not done so?"

"One can change one's mind, you know. Somehow, abandoning you became a higher price than I cared to pay for just one more term. As it is, I've been in the Legislature for over a quarter of a century. It's enough."

"Is there no way we can change minds, Chee?"

"We've changed all that are amenable to reason. The rest—the majority—cannot be moved from their emotional antipathies."

"Emotional antipathy is not a valid reason for voting one way or the other."

"I know that, Andrew, but they don't advance emotional antipathy as their reason."

"It all comes down to the brain, then," Andrew said cautiously. "But must we leave it at the level of cells versus positrons? Is there no way of forcing a functional definition? Must we say that a brain is made of this or that? May we not say that a brain is something—anything—capable of a certain level of thought?"

"Won't work," said Li-hsing. "Your brain is man-made, the human brain is not. Your brain is constructed, theirs developed. To any human being who is intent on keeping up the barrier between himself and a robot, those differences are a steel wall a mile high and a mile thick."

"If we could get at the source of their antipathy, the very source—"

"After all your years," Li-hsing said, sadly, "you are still trying to reason out the human being. Poor Andrew, don't be angry, but it's the robot in you that drives you in that direction."

"I don't know," said Andrew. "If I could bring myself . . ."

1 [Reprise]

If he could bring himself . . .

He had known for a long time it might come to that, and in the end he was at the surgeon's. He had found one, skillful enough for the job at hand—which meant a surgeon-robot, for no human surgeon could be trusted in this connection, either in ability or in intention.

The surgeon could not have performed the operation on a human being, so Andrew, after putting off the moment of decision with a sad line of questioning that reflected the turmoil within himself, had put First Law to one side by saying "I, too, am a robot."

He then said, as firmly as he had learned to form the words even at human beings over these past decades, "I *order* you to carry through the operation on me."

In the absence of the First Law, an order so firmly given from one who looked so much like a man activated the Second Law sufficiently to carry the day.

21

Andrew's feeling of weakness was, he was sure, quite imaginary. He had recovered from the operation. Nevertheless, he leaned, as unobtrusively as he could manage, against the wall. It would be entirely too revealing to sit.

Li-hsing said, "The final vote will come this week, Andrew. I've been able to delay it no longer, and we must lose. And that will be it, Andrew."

"I am grateful for your skill at delay. It gave me the time I needed, and I took the gamble I had to."

"What gamble is this?" Li-hsing asked with open concern.

"I couldn't tell you, or even the people at Feingold and Martin. I was sure I would be stopped. See here, if it is the brain that is at issue, isn't the greatest difference of all the matter of immortality. Who really cares what a brain looks like or is built of or how it was formed. What matters is that human brain cells die, *must* die. Even if every other organ in the body is maintained or replaced, the brain cells, which cannot be replaced without changing and therefore killing the personality, must eventually die.

"My own positronic pathways have lasted nearly two centuries without perceptible change, and can last for centuries more. Isn't *that* the fundamental barrier: human beings can tolerate an immortal robot, for it doesn't matter how long a machine lasts, but they cannot tolerate an immortal human being since their own mortality is endurable only so long as it is universal. And for that reason they won't make me a human being."

"What is it you're leading up to, Andrew?" Li-hsing asked.

"I have removed that problem. Decades ago, my positronic brain was connected to organic nerves. Now, one last operation has arranged that connection in such a way that slowly—quite slowly—the potential is being drained from my pathways."

Li-hsing's finely wrinkled face showed no expression for a moment. Then her lips tightened. "Do you mean you've arranged to die, Andrew? You can't have. That violates the Third Law."

"No," said Andrew, "I have chosen between the death of my body and the death of my aspirations and desires. To have let my body live at the cost of the greater death is what would have violated the Third Law."

Li-hsing seized his arm as though she were about to shake him. She stopped herself. "Andrew, it won't work! Change it back."

"It can't be done. Too much damage was done. I have a year to live—more or less. I will last through the two hundredth anniversary of my construction. I was weak enough to arrange that."

"How can it be worth it? Andrew, you're a fool."

"If it brings me humanity, that will be worth it. If it doesn't, it will bring an end to striving and that will be worth it, too."

Then Li-hsing did something that astonished herself. Quietly, she began to weep.

22

It was odd how that last deed caught the imagination of the world. All that Andrew had done before had not swayed them. But he had finally accepted even death to be human, and the sacrifice was too great to be rejected.

The final ceremony was timed, quite deliberately for the two-hundredth anniversary. The World President was to sign the act and make the people's will law. The ceremony would be visible on a global network and would be beamed to the Lunar state and even to the Martian colony.

Andrew was in a wheelchair. He could still walk, but only shakily.

With mankind watching, the World President said, "Fifty years ago, you were declared The Sesquicentennial Robot, Andrew." After a pause, and in a more solemn tone, he continued, "Today we declare you The Bicentennial Man, Mr. Martin."

And Andrew, smiling, held out his hand to shake that of the President.

23

Andrew's thoughts were slowly fading as he lay in bed. Desperately he seized at them. *Man! He was a man!* He wanted that to be his last thought. He wanted to dissolve—die—with that.

He opened his eyes one more time and for one last time recognized Li-hsing, waiting solemnly. Others were there, but they were only shadows, unrecognizable shadows. Only Li-hsing stood out against the deepening gray.

Slowly, inchingly, he held out his hand to her and very dimly and faintly felt her take it.

She was fading in his eyes as the last of his thoughts trickled away. But before she faded completely, one final fugitive thought came to him and rested for a moment on his mind before everything stopped.

"Little Miss," he whispered, too low to be heard.

THE CABINET OF
OLIVER NAYLOR

by Barrington J. Bayley

*We have a suspicion that there are more original ideas
tossed into this one novelette than one is likely to encounter in entire issues of some sf magazines. Bayley
does not write as much as he ought to, but when he does
he comes up with some surprising premises. This tale,
for instance, besides carrying original inventive concepts,
accepts no borders for humanity—even when it is, as
Bayley depicts, still very provincial in taste and outlook.
If that seems contradictory, read the story yourself.*

Nayland's world was a world of falling rain, dancing on
streaming tarmac, drumming on the roofs of big black cars,
soaking the grey and buff masonry of the dignified buildings
that lined the streets of the town. Behind the faded gold lettering of office windows, constantly awash, tense laconic con-
versations took place, accompanied by the pouring, pattering
sound of rain, and the rushing of water from the gutterings.

Beneath the pressing grey sky, all was humid. Nayland, his
feet up on his desk, looked down through the window to
where the slow-moving traffic drove through the deluge and
splashed the kerbs. Nayland Investigations Inc., read the window's bowed gold lettering. The rain fell, too, on the black
and white screen of the TV set flickering away in the corner
of the office. It fell steadily, unremittingly, permanently.
Humphrey Bogart and Barbara Stanwyck fled together in a

big black car, quarrelling tersely in an enclosed little world smelling of rain and seat leather.

They stopped at a crossroads. The argument resumed in clipped, deadpan tones, while Bogart gripped the steering wheel and scowled. The windscreen wipers were barely able to clear away the rain; on the outside camera shots their faces were seen blurrily, intermittently, cut off from external contact.

In the office, the telephone rang. Nayland picked it up. He heard a voice that essentially was his own; yet with an accent that was British rather than American.

'Is that Oliver Nayland, private detective?'

'*Frank* Nayland,' Nayland corrected.

'*Frank* Nayland.'

The voice paused, as if for reflection. 'I would like to call on your services, Mr Nayland. I want someone to investigate your world for me. Follow the couple in the black car. Where are they fleeing to? What are they fleeing from? Does it ever stop raining?'

Nayland replied in a professional neutral tone. 'I charge two hundred dollars a week, plus expenses,' he said. 'To investigate physical world phenomena, however—gravitation, rain, formation of the elements—my usual fee is doubled.'

While speaking he moved to the TV and twiddled the tuning knob. The black car idling at the crossroads vanished, was replaced by a man's face talking into a telephone. Essentially the face was Nayland's own. Younger, perhaps; less knowing, not world-weary. There was no pencil-line moustache, and the client sported a boyish haircut Nayland wouldn't have been seen dead in.

The client looked straight at him out of the screen. 'I think I can afford it. Please begin your investigations.'

The picture faded, giving way to Gene Kelly singing 'Dancing in the Rain'. Nayland returned to the window. He picked up a pair of binoculars from his desk and trained them on a black car that was momentarily stopped a the traffic lights. He glimpsed the face of Barbara Stanwyck through the side window of the car. She was sitting stiffly in the front passenger seat, speaking rapidly, her proud face vibrant with restrained, angry passion. By her side Bogart was tapping the driving wheel and snarling back curt replies.

The lights changed, the car swept on, splashing rain water

over the kerb. Nayland put down his binoculars and became thoughtful.

For a few minutes longer Oliver Naylor watched the private dick's activities on his thespitron screen. Nayland held tense, laconic interviews in seedy city offices, swept through wet streets in a black car, talked in gloomy bars while the rain pattered against the windows, visited the mansion of Mrs Van der Loon, and had a brief shoot-out with a local mobster.

Eventually Naylor faded out the scene, holding down the 'retain in store' key. At the same time he keyed the 'credible sequence' button back in. The thespitron started up again, and with a restrained fanfare began to unfold an elaborate tale of sea schooners on a watery world.

Naylor ignored it, turning down the sound so that the saga would not distract him, and rose from his chair to pace the living room of his mobile habitat. How interesting, he thought, that the drama machine, the thespitron as he called it, should invent a character so close to himself in name and appearance. True, the background was different. *Frank Nayland* was a 20th century American, perfectly adapted to his world of the private eye, *circa* 1950, whereas *Oliver Naylor* was a 22nd century Englishman, a different type altogether.

The thespitron had an unlimited repertoire and in principle one could expect a random dramatic output from it. But in practice it showed a predilection for Elizabethan tragedy—worthy, Naylor thought, of the immortal Bill himself—and for Hollywood thrillers of the 1930s–50s period. Both of these were firm favourites of Naylor, the thespitron's creator. Clearly he had unintentionally built some bias into it and would need to locate its source.

The existence of Frank Nayland probably had a similar explanation, he concluded. It was probably due to the optical extra he had built into the machine, namely the facility by which the viewer could talk to the characters portrayed on the thespitron screen. The thespitron exhibited an admirable degree of adaptability—it was perfectly delightful, for instance, to see how it had automatically translated his stick-mike into a big, unwieldy 1950s telephone. Similarly, it must have absorbed his *persona* from earlier intrusions, fashioning it into the world of Frank Nayland.

Just the same, it was eerie to be able to talk to himself, albeit in this fictional guise. A soupçon, perhaps, of 'identity crisis'.

He strolled to the living room window and gazed out. Millions of galaxies were speeding past in the endless depths, presenting the appearance of a sidewise fall of tiny snowflakes. The habitat was speeding through the universe at a velocity of c^{186}, heading into infinity.

At length Naylor sighed, turned from the window and crossed the room to settle himself in a comfortable armchair, switching on the vodor lecturer which he had stocked with all relevant material before leaving Cambridge. Selecting the subject he wanted, he rested his head against the leather upholstery and listened, letting the lecture sink into his mind much as one might enjoy a piece of music.

The vodor began to speak.

'IDENTITY. The logical law of identity is expressed by the formula $A = A$, or A is A. This law is a necessary law of self-conscious thought, and without thinking would be impossible. It is in fact merely the positive expression of the law of contradiction, which states that the same attribute cannot at the same time be affirmed and denied of the same subject.

'Philosophically, the exact meaning of the term "identity", and the ways in which it can be predicated, remain undecided. Some hold that identity excludes difference; others that it actually implies, connoting "differential likeness". See B. Bosanquet, *Essays and Addresses*, 1889. The question is one of whether identity can be posited only of an object's attributes, or whether it refers uniquely to an object regardless of its attributes . . .'

Naylor looked up as Watson-Smythe, his passenger, emerged from an adjoining bedroom where he had been sleeping. The young man stretched and yawned.

'*Haw!* Sleep knits up the ravelled sleeve, and all that. Hello there, old chap. Still plugging away, I see?'

Naylor switched off the vodor. 'Not getting very far, I'm afraid,' he admitted shyly. 'In fact, I haven't made any real progress for weeks.'

'Never mind. Early days, I expect.' Watson-Smythe yawned again, tapping his mouth with his hand. 'Fancy a cup of char? I'll brew up.'

'Yes, that would be excellent.'

Watson-Smythe had affable blue eyes. He was fair-skinned

and athletic-looking. Although only just out of bed he had taken the trouble to comb his hair before entering the habitat's main room, arranging his shining blond curls on either side of a neat parting.

Naylor had no real idea of who he was. He had met him at one of those temporary habitat villages that sprang up all over space. He was, it seemed, one of those rash of adventurous people who chose to travel without their own velocitator habitat, hitching lifts here and there, bumming their way around infinity. Apparently he was trying to find some little-known artist called Corngold (the name was faintly familiar to Naylor). Having discovered his whereabouts at the village, he had asked Naylor to take him there and Naylor, who had nowhere in particular to go, had thought it impolite to refuse.

Watson-Smythe moved to the utility cupboard and set some water to boil, idly whistling a tune by Haydn. While waiting, he glanced through the window at the speeding galaxies, then crossed to the velocitator control board and peered at the speedometer, tapping at the glass-covered dial.

'Will we get there soon, do you think? Is 186 your top speed?'

'We could do nearly 300, if pushed,' Naylor said. 'But any faster than 186 and we'd probably go past the target area without noticing it.'

'Ah, that wouldn't do at all, would it?'

The kettle whistled. Watson-Smythe rushed to it and busied himself with warming the teapot, brewing the tea and pouring it, after a proper interval into bone-china cups.

Naylor accepted a cup, but declined a share of the toast and marmalade which Watson-Smythe prepared for himself.

'This fellow Corngold,' he asked hesitantly while his guest ate, 'is he much of an artist?'

Watson-Smythe looked doubtful. 'Couldn't say, really. Don't know much about it myself. Don't know Corngold personally either, as a matter of fact.'

Watson-Smythe waggled a finger at the thespitron, which was still playing out its black-and-white shadow show (Naylor had deliberately eschewed colour; monochrome seemed to impart a more bare-boned sense of drama). 'Got the old telly going again, I see—the automated telly. You ought to put that into production, old chap. It would be a boon to habitat travellers. Much better than carrying a whole library of playback tapes.'

'Yes, I dare say it would.'

'Not in the same class as this other project of yours, if it comes off, of course. That will be something.'

Naylor smiled in embarrassment. He almost regretted having told his companion about the scheme he was working on. It was, possibly, much too ambitious.

After his breakfast Watson-Smythe disappeared back into his bedroom to practise calisthenics—though Naylor couldn't imagine what anyone so obsessed with keeping trim was doing space travelling. Habitat life, by its enclosed nature, was not conducive to good health.

His passenger's presence could be what had been blocking his progress, Naylor thought. After all, he had come out here for solitude, originally.

He switched on the vodor again and settled down to try to put his thoughts back on the problem once more.

'The modern dilemma (continued the vodor) is perhaps admirably expressed in an ancient Buddhist tale. An enlightened master one day announced to his disciples that he wished to enter into contemplation. Reposing himself, he closed his eyes and withdrew his consciousness.

'For thirty years he remained thus, while his disciples took care of his body and kept it clean.

'At the end of thirty years he opened his eyes and looked about him. The disciples gathered round. "Can the noble master tell us," they asked, "what has engaged his attention all this time?" The master told them: "I have been considering whether, in all the deserts of the world, there could conceivably be two grains of sand identical in every particular."

'The disciples were puzzled. "Surely," they said, "that is a small matter to occupy a mind such as yours?"

' "Small it may be," the master replied, "but it was too great for me. I still do not know the answer."

'In the 20th century a striking *scientific* use of the concept of identity seemed for a while as though it would cut right across many logical and philosophical definitions and answer the Buddhist master's question. To explain paradoxical findings resulting from experiments in electron diffraction, equations were devised which, in mathematical terms, removed from electrons their individual identities. It was pointed out that electrons are so alike to one another as to be, to all intents and purposes, identical. The equations therefore described electrons as exchanging identities with one another in a rhythmic oscillation, without any transfer of energy or position ...'

Naylor's first love had been logic machines. He had begun as a boy by reconstructing the early devices of the 18th and the 19th centuries: the deceptively simple Stanhope Demonstrator, with its calibrated window and two cursors (invented by an English earl, probably the very first genuine logic machine, though working out the identities was a tedious business); Venn diagrams—which in common with the Jevons Logic Machine (the first to solve complicated problems faster than the unaided logician) made use of the logic algebra of George Boole. He had quickly progressed to the type of machine developed in the 20th century and known generically as the 'computer', although only later had it developed into an instrument of pure logic for its own sake. By the time he was twenty he had become fully conversant with proper 'thinking machines' able to handle multivalued logic, and had begun to design models of his own. His crowning achievement, a couple of years ago, had been the construction of what he had reason to believe was the entire universe of discourse.

It was then that he had conceived the idea of the thespitron, a device which if marketed would without doubt put all writers of dramatic fiction out of business for once and all. Its basic hardware consisted of the above-mentioned logic machine, plus a comprehensive store and various ancillaries. After his past efforts, he had found the arrangement surprisingly easy to accomplish. In appearance the machine resembled an over-large, old-fashioned television set, with perhaps rather too many controls; but whereas an ordinary television receiver picked up its programmes from some far away transmitter, the thespitron generated them internally. Essentially it was a super-plotting device; it began with bare logical identities, and combined and recombined them into ever more complex structures, until by this process it was able to plot an endless variety of stories and characters; displaying them complete with dialogue, settings and incidental music.

Naylor had watched the plays and films generated by the

thespitron for several months now, and he could pronounce himself well pleased with the result of his labours. The thespitron was perpetual motion: because the logical categories could be permutated endlessly, its dramatic inventiveness was inexhaustible. Left to its own devices, it would eventually run through all possible dramatic situations.

Philosophically Naylor held fast to the tradition of British empiricism (without descending, of course, to American pragmatism) and saw himself as a child of the 19th century, favouring, perhaps for reasons of nostalgia, the flavour of thought of that period—though the doctrines of J. S. Mill had been much updated, naturally, by the thoroughgoing materialist empiricists of Naylor's own time. It would have gone totally against the grain, therefore, to ascribe the logical categories to any supernatural or non-material cause. Yet he had once heard a theological argument which, because of his possession of the thespitron, afforded him a great deal of secret, if perverse, pleasure.

This argument was that God had created the universe for its theatrical content alone, simply in order to view the innumerable dramatic histories it generated. By this notion all ethical parameters, all poignancies, triumphs, tragedies and meaningless sufferings, were, so to speak, literay devices.

Was not the thespitron a *private* cosmic theatre? The cosmos in miniature? Complete in itself, as the greater cosmos was, self-acting, containing its own logical laws? Furthermore it had a creator and observer—Naylor himself, who was thus elevated to the status of a god. The only god that existed, possibly, since the idea of an original transcendental God was, of course, absurd.

The alluring impression that the thespitron had some sort of cosmic significance was heightened by its present location here in intergalactic space, googols of light years from Earth. Despite his empiricist philosophical upbringing Naylor could not rid his mind of the fascinating fiction that there might be, at the source of existence, a preternatural logic machine—the transcendental archetype of his own—which ground out logical identities in pure form. He pictured to himself an immensely long, dark corridor down which the identities and categories passed, combining and recombining until eventually they permutated themselves into concrete substance to become the physical universe and all its contents.

Naylor smiled, shaking his head, reminding himself how corrupting to philosophy were all such idealist fancies. He was well aware of how fallacious it was to imagine that logic was antecedent to matter.

Naylor was by no means alone in regarding himself as a product of 19th century values; most educated Englishmen of his time did. The qualities of a rational civilisation were epitomised, it was commonly believed, by the great Victorian age, with its prolific inventiveness, its love of 'projects', its advocacy of 'progress' combined with its innate conservatism. Nostalgia was not the sole cause, however, of the 22nd century's respect for past endeavours. The renaissance in Victorian sentiment, in Britain at least, was genuine.

As often happens, economic forces were in some measure responsible for the change. During the 21st century it gradually became clear that the advantages of global trade were at last being outweighed by the disadvantages; the international division of labour was taking on the aspect of a destructive natural force which could impoverish entire peoples. The notion of economic progress took on another meaning. It came to signify, not the ability to dominate world markets, but the science of how a small nation might become wealthy without any foreign trade whatsoever. Britain, always a pioneer, was the first to discover this new direction. With the help of novel technologies she reversed what had been axiomatic since the days of Adam Smith, and for a time was once again the wealthiest power on Earth, aloof from the world trade storm, reaping through refusal to trade all the benefits she had once gained through trade.

It was a time of innovation, of surprising, often fantastic invention, of which the Harkham velocitator, a unit of which was now powering Naylor's habitat through infinity, was perhaps the outstanding example. The boffin had come into his own again, outwitting the expensively equipped teams of professional research scientists. Yet in some respects it was a cautious period, alert to the dangers of too precipitous use of every new-fangled gadget, and keeping alive the spirit of the red flag that had once been required to precede every horseless carriage. For that reason advantage was not always taken of every advance in productive methods.

Two methods in particular were forbidden. The first, an all-purpose domestic provider commonly known as the matter-bank, was technically called the hylic potentiator. It worked by holding in store a mass of amorphous, non-particulate matter, or hyle, to use the classical term. Hylic matter from this store could be instantly converted into any object, artifact or substance for which the machine was programmed, and returned to store if the utility was no longer needed or had not been consumed. Because the hylic store consisted essentially of a single gigantic shaped neutron, very high energies were involved, which had led to the device being deemed too dangerous for use on Earth. Models were still to be found here and there in space, however.

The second banned production method was a process whereby artifacts were able to reproduce themselves after the manner of viruses if brought into contact with simple materials. The creation of self-replicating artifacts had become subject to world prohibition after the islands of Japan became buried beneath growing mounds of still-multiplying TV sets, audvid recorders, cameras, autos, motor-bikes, refrigerators, helicopters, pocket computers, transistor radios, portphones, light airplanes, speedboats, furniture, sex aids, hearing aids, artificial limbs and organs, massage machines, golf clubs, zip fasteners, toys, typewriters, graphic reproduction machines, electron microscopes, house plumbing and electrical systems, machine tools, industrial robots, earthmovers, drilling rigs, prefabricated dwellings, ships, submersibles, fast-access transit vehicles, rocket launchers, lifting bodies, extraterrestrial exploration vehicles, X-ray machines, radio, video, microwave, X-ray and laser transmitters, modems, reading machines, and innumerable other conveniences.

Of all innovations, the invention to have most impact on the modern British mind was undoubtedly the Harkham velocitator, which had abolished the impediment of distance and opened up infinity to the interested traveller. Theoretically the velocitator principle could give access to any velocity, however high, except one: it was not possible to travel a measured distance in zero time, or an infinite distance in any measured time. But in practice, a velocitator unit's top speed depended on the size of its armature. After a while designing bigger and bigger armatures had become almost a redundant exercise. Infinity was infinity was infinity.

Velocitator speeds were expressed in powers of the velocity of light. Thus 186, Naylor's present pace, indicated the speed of light multiplied by itself 186 times. Infinity was now littered, if littered was a word that could be predicated of such a concept, with velocitator explorers, most of them British, finding in worlds without end their darkest Africas, their South American jungles, their Tibets and Outer Mongolias.

In point of fact the greater number of them did precious little exploring. Infinity, as it turned out, was not as definable as Africa. Early on the discovery had been made that until one actually *arrived* at some galaxy or planet, infinite space had a soothing, prosaic uniformity (provided one successfully avoided the matterless lakes), a bland sameness of fleeting mushy glints. It was a perfect setting for peace and solitude. This, perhaps, as much as the outward urge, had drawn Englishmen into the anonymous universe. The velocitator habitat offered a perfect opportunity to 'get away from it all', to find a spot of quiet, possibly, to work on one's book or thesis, or to avoid some troublesome social or emotional problem.

This was roughly Naylor's position. The success of the thespitron had emboldened him to consider taking up the life of an inventor. He had ventured into the macrocosm to mull over, in its peace and silence, a certain stubborn technical problem which velocitator travel itself entailed.

The problem had been advertised many times, but so far it had defeated all attempts at a solution. It was, quite simply, the problem of how to get home again. Every Harkham traveller faced the risk of becoming totally, irrevocably lost, it being impossible to maintain a sense of direction over the vast distances involved. The scale was simply too large. Space bent and twisted, presenting, in terms of spatial curvature, mountains and mazes, hills and serpentine tunnels. A gyroscope naturally followed this bending and twisting; all gyroscopic compasses were therefore useless. Neither, on such a vast and featureless scale, was there any possibility of making a map.

(Indeed a simple theorem showed that large-scale sidereal mapping was inherently an untenable proposition. *Mapping* consists of recording relationships between locations or objects. In a three-dimensional continuum this is only really practicable by means of data storage. However, the number of possible relationships between a set of objects rises exponentially with the number of objects. The number of possible connections between the 10,000 million neurons of the human brain actually exceeds the number of particles within Olbers' Sphere (which, before the invention of the velocitator, was thought of as the universe). Obviously no machine, however compact, could contain the information necessary to map the relationships between objects whose number was without limit, even when those objects were entire galaxies.

Every velocitator habitat carried a type of inertial navigation recording system, which enabled the traveller to retrace his steps and, hopefully, arrive back at the place he had started from. This, to date, was the only homing method available; but the device was delicate and occasionally given to error—only a small displacement in the inertial record was enough to turn the Milky Way galaxy into an unfindable grain of sand in an endless desert. Furthermore, Harkham travellers were apt, sometimes unwittingly, to pass through powerful magnetic fields which distorted and compromised the information on their recorders, or even wiped the tapes clean.

Naylor's approach to the problem was, as far as he knew, original. He had adopted a concept that both philosophy and science had at various times picked up, argued over, even used, then dropped again only to resume the argument later: the concept of *identity*.

If every entity, object and being had its own unique identity which differentiated it from the rest of existence, then Naylor reasoned that it ought to be uniquely findable in some fictive framework that was independent of space, time and number. Ironically the theoretical tools he was using were less typical of empiricist thought than of its traditional enemy, rationalism, the school that saw existence as arising, not from material occasions, but from abstract categories and identities; but he was sufficiently undogmatic not to be troubled by that. He was aware that empirical materialists had striven many times to argue away the concept of identity altogether, but they had never, quite, succeeded.

Naylor imagined each individual object resulting from a combining, or focusing together, of universal logic classes (or universal identities), much as the colour components of a picture are focused on to one another to form a perfect image. It was necessary to suppose that each act of focusing was unique, that is to say, that each particle of matter was created only once. It would mean, for instance, that each planet had a unique identity: that a sample of iron taken from the Earth was subtly different from a sample of iron taken from the Moon, and it was this difference that Naylor's projected direction-finder would be able to locate.

But was it a warrantable assumption, he wondered?

'Ah, the famous question of identity,' he said aloud.

The vodor lecture, heard many times before, became a drone. He turned it off and opened his notebook to scan one section of his notes.

'IDENTITY AND NUMBERS:— The natural numbers, 1, 2, 3, 4, 5 ... are pure abstractions, lacking identity in the philosophical meaning of the word. That is to say, there is no such entity as "five". Identity in a set of five objects appertains only to each object taken singly ... "Fiveness" is a process, accomplished by matching each member of a set against members of another set (i.e. the fingers of a hand) until the set being counted is exhausted. Only material objects have identity ...'

In his fevered imagination it had seemed to Naylor that he need but make one more conceptual leap and he would be there with a sketch model of the device that would find the Milky Way Galaxy from no matter where in infinity. He believed, in fact, that he already had the primitive beginnings of the device in the thespitron. For although no *physical* mapping of the universe was possible, the thespitron *had* achieved a *dramatic* mapping of it, demonstrating that the cosmos was not entirely proof against definition.

But the vital leap, from a calculus of theatre to a calculus of identities, had not come, and Naylor was left wondering if he should be chiding himself for his lapse into dubious rationalist tenets.

Dammit, he thought wryly, if an enlightened master had no luck, how the devil can I?

Gloomily he wrote a footnote: 'It may be that the question of identity is too basic to be subject to experiment, or to be susceptible to instrumentation.'

His thoughts were interrupted by the ringing of the alarm bell. The control panel flashed, signalling that the habitat was slowing down in response to danger ahead. In seconds it had reduced speed until it was cruising at only a few tens of powers of the velocity of light.

At the same time an announcement gong sounded, informing them that they had arrived within beacon range of someone else's habitat—presumably Corngold's.

As Naylor crossed to the panel to switch off the alarm

Watson-Smythe appeared from the bedroom. He had put on a gleaming white suit which set off his good looks perfectly. 'What a racket!' he exclaimed genially. 'Everything going off at once!'

Naylor was examining the dials. 'We are approaching a matterless lake.'

'Are we, by God?'

'And your friend Corngold is evidently living on the shores of it. Can you think of any reason why he would do that?'

Watson-Smythe chuckled, with a hint of rancour. 'Just the place where the swine would choose to set himself up. Discourages visitors, you see.'

'You can say that again. Do I take it we are likely to be unwelcome? What you would call a recluse, is he?'

The younger man tugged at his lower lip. 'Look here, old chap, if you feel uneasy about this you can just drop me off at Corngold's and shoot off again. I don't want to impose on you or anything.'

By now Naylor was intrigued. 'Oh, that's all right. I don't mind hanging about for a bit.'

Watson-Smythe peered out of the window. They were close to a large spiral galaxy which blazed across his field of vision, swinging majestically past his line of sight as they went by it.

'We'll get a better view on this,' Naylor said. He pressed a small lever and a six-foot screen unfolded at the front end of the living room, conveniently placed for the control panel. He traversed the view to get an all-round picture of their surroundings. The spiral galaxy had already receded to become the average smudged point of light, and in all directions the aspect was the usual one of darkness relieved by faintly luminous sleet—except for directly ahead.

There, the screen of galaxies was thin. Behind it stretched an utter blackness: it was a specimen of that awesome phenomenon, the matterless lake.

The distribution of matter in the universe was not, quite, uniform. It thinned and condensed a bit here and there. But its non-uniformity mainly manifested in great holes, gaps—lakes, as they were called—where no matter was to be found at all. Although of no great size where the distances that went to make up infinity were concerned, in mundane terms their dimensions were enormous, several trillion times larger than Olbers' Sphere (the criterion of cosmic size in pre-Harkham times and still used as a rough measure of magnitude).

Any Harkham traveller knew that it was fatal to penetrate more than the fringes of such a lake, for should anyone be so foolhardy as to pass out of sight of its shore (and many had been) he would find it just about impossible to get out again. When not conditioned by the presence of matter, space lacked many of the properties normally associated with it. Even such elementary characteristics as direction, distance and dimension were lent to space, physicists now knew, by the signposts of matter; the depths of the lakes were out of range of these signposts. Thus it would do the velocitator rider no good merely to fix a direction and travel in the belief that he must sooner or later strike the lake's limit, for he would be unlikely ever to do so. He was lost in an inconceivable nowhere, in space that was structureless and uninformed.

As they neared the shore the boundary of the lake spread and expanded before them like a solid black wall sealing off the universe. 'Will Corngold be in the open, do you think, or in a galaxy somewhere?' Naylor asked.

'I'd guess he's snuggled away in some spiral; harder to find that way, eh? There's a likely-looking bunch over there.' Watson-Smythe pointed to a cluster of galaxies ahead and to their right. 'Right on the edge of the lake, too. What do the indicators say?'

'Looks hopeful.' Naylor turned the habitat towards the cluster, speeding up a little. The galaxies brightened until their internal structures became visible. The beacon signal came through more strongly; soon they were close enough to get a definite fix.

Watson-Smythe's guess had been right. They eventually found Corngold's habitat floating just inside the outermost spiral turn of the cluster's largest member. The habitat looked like two or three eskimo igloos squashed together, humped and rounded. Behind it the local galaxy glittered in countless colours like a giant Christmas tree.

Watson-Smythe clapped his hands in delight. 'Got him!'

Naylor nudged close to the structure at walking pace. The legally standardised coupling rings clinked together as he matched up the outer doors.

'Jolly good. Time to pay a visit,' his passenger said.

'Shouldn't we raise him on the communicator first?'

'Rather not.' Watson-Smythe made for the door, then

paused, turning to him. 'If you'd prefer to wait until ... well, just as you please.'

He first opened the inner door, then both outer doors which were conjoined now and moved as one, and then the inner door of the other habitat. Naylor wondered why he didn't even bother to knock. Personally he would never have had the gall just to walk into someone else's living room.

With tentative steps he followed Watson-Smythe into the short tunnel. Bright light shone through from the other habitat. He heard a man's voice, raised in a berating, bullying tone.

The door swung wide open.

The inside of Corngold's dwelling reminded Naylor of an egg-shaped cave, painted bright yellow. Walls and ceiling consisted of the same ovoid curve, and lacked windows. The yellow was streaked and spattered with oil colours and unidentifiable dirt; the lower parts of the walls were piled with canvases, paintings, boxes, shelves and assorted junk. The furniture was sparse: a bare board table, a mattress, three rickety straight-backed chairs and a mouldy couch. An artist's easel stood in the middle of the floor. Against the wall opposite to the door was the source of Corngold's provender and probably everything else he used: a matterbank, shiny in its moulded plastic casing.

Corngold was a fat man, a little below medium height. He was wearing a green silk chemise, square-cut about the neck and shoulders and decorated with orange fringes and tassels, and baggy flannel trousers. He had remarkably vivid green eyes; his hair had been cropped short and now had grown so that it bristled like a crown of thorns.

He reminded Naylor of early Hollywood versions of Nero or Caligula. He did not, it seemed, live alone. He was in the act of browbeating a girl, aged perhaps thirty, who for her dowdiness was as prominent as Corngold was for his brilliant green shirt. Corngold had her arm twisted behind her back, forcing her partly over. Her face wore the blank sullenness that comes from long bullying: it was totally submissive, wholly drab, the left eye slightly puffy and discoloured from a recent bruise. She did not even react to the entry of visitors.

Corngold, however, eased his grip slightly and turned to greet Watson-Smythe indignantly. 'What the bloody hell do you mean barging in here!' he bellowed. 'Bugger off!' His accent sounded northern to Naylor's ears; Yorkshire, perhaps.

'Are you Walter Corngold?' Watson-Smythe countered. To Naylor's faint surprise his tone was cold and professional.

'You heard me! Bugger off! This is private property.'

Watson-Smythe reached into his jacket and produced a slim Hasking stun beamer. With his other hand he took a document from his pocket. 'Watson-Smythe of M.I.19,' he announced. 'I have here a warrant for your arrest, Corngold. I'm taking you back to Earth.'

So that was it! Naylor wondered why he hadn't guessed it before. Now that he thought of it, Watson-Smythe was almost a caricature of the type of young man one expected to find in the 'infinity police', as it was jocularly called—M.I.19, the branch of security entrusted with law enforcement among habitat travellers.

'What are the charges?' he asked, mildly amused.

Watson-Smythe inclined his head slightly to answer him, keeping the Hasking trained on Corngold. 'Two charges: theft, and the abduction of Lady Cadogan's maid, who unless I am very much mistaken is the young lady you are now mistreating, Corngold. Take your hands off her at once.'

Corngold released the girl and shoved her roughly towards the couch, where she sat staring at the floor.

'Ridiculous,' he snorted. 'Betty's here of her own sweet will, aren't you, dearest?' His voice was heavy with irony.

She glanced up like a frightened mouse, darting what might have been a look of hope at Watson-Smythe. Then she retreated into herself again, nodding meekly.

Corngold sighed with satisfaction. 'Well that's that, then. Sod off, the two of you, and leave us in peace.' He strolled to the easel, picked up a brush and started to daub the canvas, as though he had banished them from existence.

Watson-Smythe laughed, showing clean white teeth. 'They said you were a bit of a character. But you're due for a court appearance in London just the same.' He turned politely to Naylor. 'Thanks for your assistance, Naylor old boy. You can cast off now if you're inclined, and I'll take Corngold's habitat back to Earth.'

'Can't,' Corngold said, giving them a brief sidewise glance. 'My inertial navigator's bust. I was stuck here, in fact, until you turned up. Not that it bothers me at all.'

Watson-Smythe, frowned. 'Well . . .'

'Is it a malfunction?' Naylor queried, 'or just a faulty record?'

Corngold shrugged. 'It's buggered up, I tell you.'

'I might be able to do something with it,' Naylor said to the M.I.19 agent. 'I'll have a look at it, anyway. If it's only the record we can simply take a copy of our own one.'

Corngold flung down his brush. 'In that case you might as well stay to to dinner. And put that gun away, for Chrissake. What do you think this is, a shooting gallery?'

'After all, he can't go anywhere,' Naylor observed when Watson-Smythe wavered. 'Without us he'll *never* get home.'

'All right.' He turned his gun to its shoulder holster. 'But don't think you're going to wriggle out of this, Corngold. Kidnapping's a pretty serious offence.'

Corngold's eyes twinkled. He pointed to a clock hung askew on the wall. 'Dinner's at nine. Don't be late.'

Wearily Naylor slumped in his armchair in his own living-room. He had spent an hour on Corngold's inertial navigator, enough to tell him that the gyros were precessing and the whole system would need to be re-tuned. It would be a day's work at least and he had decided to make a fresh start tomorrow. If he couldn't put the device back in order they would all have to travel back to Earth in Naylor's habitat—as an M.I.19 officer Watson-Smythe had the power to require his co-operation over that. At the moment he was in his bed-room, bringing his duty log up to date.

The business with the navigator had brought home anew to Naylor the desirability of inventing some different type of homing mechanism. He was becoming irritated that the problem was so intractable, and felt a fresh, if frustrating, urge to get to grips with it.

Remembering that he had left the vodor lecture unfinished, he switched on the machine again, listening closely to the evenly-intoned words, even though he knew them almost by heart.

'The question of *personal* identity was raised by Locke, and later occupied the attentions of Hume and Butler. Latterly the so-called 'theorem of universal identity' has gained some prominence. In this theorem, personal identity (or *self*-identity) is defined as *having knowledge* of one's identity, a statement which also serves to define consciousness. Conscious beings are said to differ from inanimate objects only in that they have knowledge of their identity, while inanimate objects, though possessing their own identity, have no knowledge of it.

'To be conscious, however, means to be able to perceive. But in order to perceive there must be an "identification" between the subject (self-identity, or consciousness) and the perceived object. Therefore there is a paradoxical "sharing" of identity between subject and object, similar, perhaps, to the exchange of identity once posited between electrons. This reasoning leads to the concept of a "universal identity" according to which all identity, both of conscious beings and inanimate objects, belongs to the same universal transcendental identity, or "self". This conclusion is a recurring one in the history of human thought, known at various times as "the infinite self", "the transcendental self" and "the universal self" of Vedantic teachings. "I am you", the mystic will proclaim, however impudently, meaning that the same basic identity is shared by everyone.

'Such conceptions are not admitted by the empirical materialist philosophers, who subject them to the most withering criticism. To the empiricist, every occasion is unique; therefore its identity is unique. Hume declared that he could not even discover self-identity in himself; introspection yielded only a stream of objects in the form of percepts; a "person" is therefore a "bundle" of percepts. Neither can the fact that two entities may share a *logical* identity in any way detract from their basic separateness, since logic itself is not admitted as having any *a priori* foundation.

'The modern British school rejects the concept of identity altogether as a mere verbalism, without objective application. Even the notion of electron identity exchange is now accepted to be a mathematical fiction, having been largely superseded by the concept of "unique velocity" which is incorporated in the Harkham velocitator. It is still applied, however, to a few quantum problems for which no other mathematical tools exist.'

Naylor rose and went to the window, gazing out at the blazing spiral galaxy which was visible over the humped shape of Corngold's habitat. 'Ah, the famous question of identity,' he murmured.

He knew why the question continued to perplex him. It was because of the thespitron. The thespitron, with its unexpected tricks and properties, had blurred his feeling of self-identity, just as the identity of electrons had been blurred by the 20th century quantum equations. And at the same time, the thoughts occurring to him attacked materialist empiricism at its weakest point: the very same question of identity.

There came to him again the image of the categories of identity proceeding and permutating down a dark, immensely long corridor. He felt dizzy, elated. Here, in his habitat living-room, his domain was small but complete; he and the thespitron reproduced between them, on a minute scale, the ancient mystical image of created universe and observing source, of phenomenon and noumenon; even without him here to watch it, the thespitron was the transcendental machine concretised, a microcosm to reflect the macrocosm, a private universe of discourse, a mirror of infinity in a veneered cabinet.

Could the characters and worlds within the thespitron, shadows though they were, be said to possess *reality*? The properties of matter itself could be reduced to purely logical definitions, heretical though the operation was from the point of view of empiricism. The entities generated by the machine, obeying those same logical definitions, could never know that they lacked concrete substance.

Was there identity in the universe? Was that *all* there was?

Now he understood what had made him include a communication facility in the thespitron; why he had further felt impelled to talk to Frank Nayland, his near-double. He had identified himself with Nayland; he had tried to enlighten him as to the nature of his fictional world, prompted by some irrational notion that, by confronting him, he could somehow prod Nayland into having a consciousness of his own.

Who am I? Naylor wondered. Does my identity, my consciousness, belong to myself, or does it belong to this—he made a gesture taking in all that lay beyond the walls of the habitat—to infinity?

Sitting down again, he switched on the thespitron.

Naylor's sense of having duplicated the logical development of the universe was further heightened by the inclusion of the 'credible sequence' button. This optional control engaged circuits which performed, in fact, no more than the last stage of the plotting process, arranging that the machine's presentations, in terms of construction, settings and event-structure, were consonant, if not quite with the real world, at least with a dramatist's imitation of it.

With the button disengaged, however, the criterion of mundane credibility vanished. The thespitron proceeded to construct odd, abbreviated worlds, sometimes from only a small number of dramatic elements, worlds in which processes, once begun, were apt to continue forever without interruption or exhaustion; in which actions, once embarked upon, became a binding force upon the actor and required permanent reiteration.

The world of Frank Nayland, private investigator, was one of these: a world put together from bare components lifted from the Hollywood thriller *genre*, bereft of the background of any larger world, and moving according to an obsessive, abstract logic. A compact world with only a small repertoire of events, the terse fictional world of the private dick, a world in which rain was increasing.

Summoning up Nayland from store, Naylor watched him pursue his investigations, rain dripping from the brim of his hat, his gabardine raincoat permanently damp. So absorbed did he become in the dick's adventures that he did not see Watson-Smythe until the M.I.19 officer tapped him on the shoulder.

'It's nine o'clock,' Watson-Smythe said. 'Time we were calling on Corngold.'

'Oh, yes.' Naylor rose, rubbing his eyes. He left the thespitron running as they went through the connecting tunnel, tapping on Corngold's door before entering.

A measure of camaraderie had grown up during the hour they had earlier spent with the artist. Naylor had come to look on him more as an eccentric rascal than a real villain, and even Watson-Smythe had mollified his hostility a little. He had still tried to persuade Betty Cooper, the maid allegedly abducted from the home of Lady Cadogan (from whom Corngold had also stolen a valuable antique bracelet), to move in with them pending the journey back to Earth, but so great was Corngold's hold over her (the hold of a sadist, Watson-Smythe said) that she would obey only him.

There was no sign of the promised dinner party. Corngold was before his easel, legs astraddle, while Betty posed in the nude, sitting demurely on a chair. Though still a sullen frump, Naylor thought that when naked she had some redeeming features; her body tended to flop, was pale and too fleshy, but it was pleasantly substantial in a trollopy sort of way.

Corngold turned his head. 'Well?' he glared.

Watson-Smythe coughed. 'You invited us to dinner, I seem to remember.'

'Did I? Oh.' Corngold himself didn't seem to remember. He continued plying the paint on to the canvas, a square palette of mingled colour in his other hand. Naylor was fascinated. The man was an artist after all. His concentration, his raptness, were there, divided between the canvas and the living girl.

Naylor moved a few paces so he could get a glimpse of the portrait. But he did not see what he expected. Instead of a nude, Corngold had painted an automobile.

Corngold looked at him, his eyes twinkling with mirth. 'Well, it's how I see her, you see.'

Naylor was baffled. He could not see how in any way the picture could represent Betty, not even as a metaphor. The auto was sleek and flashy, covered with glittering trim; quite the opposite of Betty's qualities, in fact.

He strolled to the other end of the egg-shaped room, glancing at the stacked canvases. Corngold had a bit of a following, he believed, among some of the avant-garde. Naylor took no interest in art, but even he could see the fellow was talented. The paintings were individualistic, many of them in bright but cleverly toned colours.

Corngold laid down his brush and moved aside the easel, gesturing to Betty to rise and dress. 'Dinner, then,' he said in the tone of one whose hospitality may be presumed upon. 'Frankly I'd hoped you two would have got tired of hanging around by now and cleared off.'

'That would have left you in a bit of a spot,' Naylor said. 'You have no way of finding your way home.'

'So what? Who the hell wants to go to Earth anyway—eh?' 'I've got everything I need here.' Corngold winked at him obscenely, and, to the extreme embarrassment of both Naylor and Watson-Smythe, stuck his finger in Betty's vulva, wriggling it vigorously. Betty became the picture of humiliation, looking distressfully this way and that. But she made no move to draw back.

Naylor bristled. 'I say—you *are* British, aren't you?' he demanded heatedly.

Corngold withdrew his finger, whereupon Betty turned and snatched for her clothes. He looked askance at Naylor.

'And why shouldn't I be?' he challenged, his manner suddenly aggressive.

"Dammit, no Englishman would treat a woman this way!'

Corngold giggled, his mouth agape, looking first at Betty and then at Naylor. 'Fuck me, I must be a Welshman!'

'Perhaps the best thing *would* be to leave you here,' Watson-Smythe commented, his tone voicing the coldest disapproval. 'It might be the punishment you deserve. Corngold.'

'Do it, then! You'd never have got to me at all, you bastards, if I'd found a way to turn off the fucking beacon.'

'It can't be done,' Naylor pointed out. It would be typical of such a character, he thought, not to know that. The beacon signal was imprinted on every velocitator manufactured, as a legal requirement. Otherwise habitats would never be able to vector in on one another.

Corngold grunted, and dragged the board table to the centre of the room, arranging around it the three chairs his dwelling boasted. With a casual gesture he invited his guests to sit down. When they had taken their places he banged on the tabletop. 'What's all this "Corngold", anyway? Have I yet agreed that I am Corngold? Establish the identity of the culprit—that's the first thing in law.'

'I am satisfied you are Walter Corngold,' Watson-Smythe said smoothly.

'Supposition, supposition! Establish the identity!' Corngold was shouting.

He laughed, then turned to Betty, who was clothed now and standing by in the attitude of a waitress. 'Well, let's eat. Indian curry suit you? How do you like it? Mine's good and hot.'

While Corngold discussed the details of the meal Betty went to the matter-bank and returned with a large flagon of bright red wine and four glasses. Corngold sloshed wine into them, indicating to her that she should knock hers straight back. As soon as she had done so he emptied his own glass, instantly refilling it.

'One good hot vindaloo, one lamb biriani and a lamb kurma,' he instructed curtly.

Betty moved back to the matter-bank and twisted dials. Spicy aromas filled the room as she transferred bowls of food from the delivery transom to a tray. Naylor turned to

Corngold. 'You can't seriously contemplate spending the rest of your life in this habitat? Cut off from humanity?'

'Humanity can go jump in a lake.' Corngold jerked his thumb towards the great nothingness that lay beyond the local galaxy. 'Anyway who says I'm habitat-bound? You forget there are other races, other worlds. As a matter of fact I've got a pretty good set-up here. I've discovered a simply fascinating civilisation on the planet of a nearby star. Here, let me show you.'

Rising, he pushed aside a pile of cardboard cartons to reveal the habitat's control board. A small golden ring of stars appeared, glowing like a bracelet, as he switched on an opal-glowing viewscreen.

Corngold pointed out the largest of the stars. 'This is the place. A really inventive lifeform, not hard to get to know, really, and with the most extraordinary technology. I commute there regularly.'

'Yet you always bring your habitat back out here again? You must love solitude,' Naylor remarked.

'I do love it indeed, but you misunderstand me. The habitat stays here. I commute to Zordem by means of a clever little gadget they gave me.'

Heavily he sat down at the table, licking his lips. His visitors tried to ask him more about these revelations, their curiosity intense; but when the food was served he became deaf to their questions.

Taking up a whole spoonful of the pungent-smelling curry Betty served him, and without even tempering it with rice, he rolled it thoughtfully round his mouth. Then he suddenly spluttered and spat it all out.

'This isn't vindaloo, you shitty-arsed cow. It's fucking Madras!'

With a roar Corngold picked up the bowl and flung it at Betty, missing her and hitting the wall. The brown muck made a dribbling trail down the yellow.

'You must excuse my common-law wife,' he said, his expression changing from fury to politeness as he turned to Watson-Smythe. 'Unfortunately she is a completely useless pig.'

'But I don't dare dial vindaloo,' Betty protested in a whining, tearful voice. 'The bank's been going funny again. On vindaloo—'

'Get me my dinner!' Corngold bellowed, cutting off her explanations. Submissively she returned to the machine, operating it again.

As she turned the knobs an acrid blue smoke rose from the matter-bank, coming not from the transom but from the seams of the casing. Naylor, glancing at Watson-Smythe in alarm, made as if to rise, forming the intention of retreating to his own habitat and casting off with all haste. But Corngold sprang to his feet with a cry of exasperation and marched over to the ailing bank, giving it a hefty kick, at which the smoke stopped.

'It's always giving trouble,' he explained gruffly as he rejoined them. 'That's what comes of buying second-hand junk.'

Watson-Smythe replied in a tone that Naylor thought remarkably even and calm. 'You do realise, don't you, that that thing can go off like a nuclear bomb?'

'So can my arse after one of these curries. Ah, here it comes. Better be right this time.'

Corngold's vindaloo was *very* hot. The sweat started out of his forehead as he ate it, grunting and groaning, deep in concentration. He was a man of lusty nature, Naylor decided, carrying his enjoyment of life to the limit. Afterwards he sat panting like a dog, calling for more wine and swallowing it in grateful gulps.

The meal over, Corngold became expansive. He described, with a wealth of boastful details, his contacts with the inhabitants of the planet Zordem. 'Their whole science is based on the idea of a certain kind of ray,' he told them. 'They call them *zom* rays. They have some quite remarkable effects. Let me show you, for instance—'

He opened one of the egg-shaped room's four doors, disclosing a cupboard whose shelves contained a number of unfamiliar objects. Corngold picked one up. It was a smooth, rounded shape, easily held in one hand, about three times as long as it was broad, with a flat underside. He carried it to the viewscreen and slapped it against the side of the casing, where it stuck as if by suckers.

On the screen, the ring of stars vanished. In its place was intergalactic space, and in the foreground a long, fully-equipped spaceship of impressive size, the ring-like protuberance about her middle indicating the massiveness of her velocitator armature. They all recognised her as a Royal Navy cruiser, one of several on permanent patrol.

'Rule Britannia!' crowed Corngold. 'It's the *Prince An-*

drew. Ostensibly making sure we habitat travellers don't mistreat the natives, but really, of course, trying to have a go at a second British Empire. I should ko-ko!'

'There have been quite a few incidents,' Watson-Smythe said sternly. 'It's no joking matter. I dare say your own relations with Zordem will be subject to scrutiny in good time.'

'Is she close?' Naylor asked.

'No, she's quite a way off,' Corngold said, glancing at a meter. 'Roughly a googol olbers.'

'Your gadget can see *that* far? But good God—how do you find a single object at that distance?'

'The Zordems put a trace on it the day I arrived. To make me feel at home, I suppose. Don't ask me how. They did it with Zom rays!'

Naylor was stunned. 'Then *these* are the people who are the true masters of infinity,' he breathed.

'Masters of infinity?' Corngold sat down at the table again, placing his bare, fat arms among the empty dishes. He wiped up a trace of curry sauce with his fingers and licked it, looking at Naylor with heavy irony. 'You really are a clown. The Zordems are nowhere into infinity, any more than we are. That's a lot of crap newspaper talk. The whole spread any of us have gone from Earth is no more than a spot. Okay, build a velocitator armature a light year across and ride on it for a billion years. You'll still only have gone the length of a spot on infinity. That's what infinity means, doesn't it?—that there's no end to it.'

'Just the same, you've been misleading us with this talk of being stranded,' Watson-Smythe accused. 'With equipment like this you can obviously find your way to anywhere.'

'Afraid not. This gadget gives the range but not the direction. The range is limited, too, to about fifty googol olbers. The Zordems have hit on a lot of angles we've missed, but they're not that much in advance of us overall.'

'But it must still be based on a completely new principle,' Naylor said, intensely excited. 'Don't you see, Corngold? This might give us what everybody's been looking for—a reliable homing device! It might even,' he ended shyly, 'mean a reduction of sentence for you.'

He blushed at the emerald malevolence that brimmed for a moment from Corngold's eyes. If he were honest, he was beginning to find the man frightening. There was something solid, immovable and dangerous about him. His knowledge of an alien technology, and his obvious intelligence which came through despite his outrageous behaviour, had dispelled the earlier impression of him as an amusing crank. All Watson-Smythe's trained smoothness had failed to make the slightest dent in his self-confidence; Betty remained his slave, and Naylor privately doubted if the charge of abduction could be made to stick. There was something ritualistic in Corngold's brutal treatment of her, and in her corresponding misery. It looked to Naylor as though they were matched souls.

'I thought I had dropped plenty of hints,' Corngold said, 'that I don't really want to come back to Earth. Betty and I want nothing more than to remain here, thank you.'

Watson-Smythe seemed amused. 'I'm afraid the law isn't subject to your whims, Corngold.'

'No?' Corngold's expression was bland, his eyebrows raised. 'I thought I might be able to bribe you. How would you both like to screw Betty? She's all right in her way—just lies there like a piece of putty and lets you do which and whatever to her.'

Watson-Smythe snorted.

Corngold became annoyed. 'What is it you want, then? The fucking bracelet? Here—have it!' He went to the mattress on the floor, lifted it and brought out a gold ornament, flinging it at Watson-Smythe. 'It's a piece of sodding crap anyway—I only took it because Betty had a fancy for it.'

Watson-Smythe picked up the bracelet, examined it briefly, wrapped it in a handkerchief and tucked it away in an inside pocket. 'Thanks for the evidence.'

Corngold sighed. He reached for the flagon of wine and drained the dregs, ending with a belch.

'Well, it's not the end of the world. I expect Betty will be glad to see London again. Before you retire for the night, gentlemen, let me answer your earlier question—how I make the transition between here and Zordem. It's quite simple, really—done by zom rays again, but a different brand this time.'

He went to the cupboard and brought out something that looked like a large hologram plate camera with a square, hooded shutter about a foot on the side. 'This is really a most astonishing gadget,' he said. 'It accomplishes long-distance travel without the use of a vehicle. I believe essentially the forces it employs may not be dissimilar to those of the velocitator—but instead of the generator moving, it moves whatever the zom rays are trained on. All you do is align it with wherever you want to go and step into the beam—provided you have a device at the other end to detranslate your velocity. Neat, isn't it? The speed is fast enough to push you right through walls as though they weren't there.'

'Why, it's a matter transmitter!' Naylor exclaimed admiringly.

'As good as.'

Watson-Smythe had already guessed his danger and reached for his gun. But Corngold was too quick for him. He trained the camera-device on the agent and pressed a lever. The black frontal plate flickered, exactly as if a shutter had operated—as indeed one probably had. Watson-Smythe vanished.

Aghast, Naylor staggered back. '*Christ!* You've murdered him!'

'Yes! For trying to disturb our domestic harmony!'

Flustered and scared, Naylor stuttered: 'You've gone too far this time, Corngold. You won't get away with this . . . too far.'

H scrambled for the exit. He scampered through the tunnel, slamming shut the outer doors and disengaging the clutches so that the two habitats drifted apart, then slamming the inner door and rushing to the control board.

In the egg-shaped room, Corngold had quickly set up the Zordem projector on a tripod. Focusing it on the intruding habitat a few yards away through the wall, he sighted the instrument carefully and opened the shutter for an instant. Naylor and his habitat were away, projected out into the matterless lake.

Through the communicator on the control board came a faint voice. 'I'm falling, Corngold! Help me!'

'I'll help you,' Corngold crowed, grinning his peculiar open-mouthed grin. 'I'll help you fall some more!'

He opened the shutter again. Naylor accelerated further trillions of light years per second, carried by the irresistible force of zom rays.

'That's him out of the way,' Corngold exclaimed with satisfaction, turning to Betty. 'Bring on the booze!'

Pale and obedient, Betty withdrew a flagon of cerise fluid and two glasses from the matter-bank. She poured a full measure for Corngold, a smaller one for herself, and sat crouching on the couch, sipping it.

'We'll move on from here pretty soon,' Corngold murmured. 'If they could find us others can.'

He turned the opal-glowing viewscreen into the lake and surveyed the unrelieved emptiness, drinking his wine with gusto.

Corngold's mocking farewell was the last message Naylor's habitat received from the world of materiality, whether by way of artificial communication, electromagnetic energy, gravitational attraction or indeed any other emanation. These signposts, which normally informed space of direction, distance and dimension, were now left far behind.

There had been no time to engage the velocitator, and now it was too late. Corngold had had the jump on them from the beginning. At the first discharge of the Zordem projector Naylor's speedometer had registered c^{413} and his velocitator did not have the capacity to cancel such a velocity, even though the lake's shore, in the first few moments, had still been accessible. At the second discharge the meter registered c^{826} and unencumbered, total space had swallowed him up. He was now surrounded by nothing but complete and utter darkness.

Within the walls of the habitat, however, his domain was small but complete. He had, in the thespitron, a complete universe of discourse; a universe which, though nearly lacking in objective mass, conformed to familiar laws of drama and logic, and on the display screen of which, at this moment, Frank Nayland was pursuing his endless life.

Naylor's mind became filled again with the vision of the long, dark corridor down which the logical identities passed as they permutated themselves into concretisation. Who was to say that out here, removed from the constraints of external matter, the laws of identity might not find a freedom that otherwise was impossible? Might, indeed, produce reality out of thought?

'The famous question of identity,' he muttered feverishly and sat down before the flickering thespitron, wondering how it might be made to guide him, if not to his own world, at least to some world.

As the big black car swept to a stop at the intersection Frank Nayland emerged from the darkness and leaped for the rear door, wrenching it open and hustling himself inside.

His gat was in his hand. He let them see it, resting his forearm on the front seat support and leaning forward.

Rainwater dripped from him on to the leather upholstery. Ahead, the red traffic lights shone blurrily through the falling rain and the streaming sweep of the windscreen wipers.

Bogart peered round at Nayland, his face slack with fear.

'Let's get out and take a walk,' Nayland said. 'I know a nice little place where we can talk things over.'

Bogart's hand gripped the steering wheel convulsively. 'You know we can't leave here.'

'No . . . that's right,' Nayland said thoughtfully. 'You have to keep going. You have to keep driving, running—'

The engine of the car was ticking over. The lights had changed and Bogart started coughing asthmatically. Stanwyck put her hand on his arm, a rare show of compassion. 'Oh, why don't you let him go?' she said passionately. 'He's done nothing to you.'

Nayland clambered out of the car, slamming the door behind him, and stood on the kerb while the gears ground and the vehicle shot off into the night. He walked through the rain to where his own car was hidden in a culvert and drove for a while until he spotted a phone booth.

Rain beat at the windows of the booth. Water dripped from his low-brimmed hat as Nayland dialled the number. While the tone rang he dug into his raincoat pocket, came up with a book of matches, flicked one alight and lit a cigarette with a cupped hand.

'Mr. Naylor? Nayland here. This is my final report.'

A pause, while the client on the other end spoke anxiously. Finally Nayland resumed. 'You wanted to know about the couple in the car. Bogart is wanted for the snatch of the Heskin tiara from the mansion of Mrs Van der Loon. It was the Stanwyck woman got him into it, of course—she was Mrs Van der Loon's paid companion. The usual sad caper. But here's the rub: there's a fake set of the Heskin rocks—or was. Mrs Van der Loon had a legal exchange of identity carried out between the real jewels and the paste set. A real cute switcheroo. It's the paste that's genuine now, and Bogart is stuck with a pocketful of worthless rocks and a broad who's nothing but trouble.'

'Can that be done?' Naylor asked wonderingly.

'Sure. Identities are legally exchangeable.'

Staring at the thespitron screen, the stick-mike in his hand,

Naylor was thinking frantically. He watched a plume of smoke drift up the side of Nayland's face, causing the dick to screw up one eye.

Something seemed to be happening to the thespitron. The image was becoming scratchy, the sound indistinct.

'Why does it never stop raining?' he demanded.

'No reason for it to stop.'

'But are you *real*?' Naylor insisted. 'Do you *exist*?'

Nayland looked straight at him out of the screen. The awareness in his eyes was unmistakable. 'This is *our* world, Mr Naylor. You can't come in. It's all a question of identity.'

'But it will work—you just said so,' Naylor said desperately. 'The switcheroo—the fake me and the real me—'

'Goodbye, Mr Naylor,' Nayland said heavily. He put down the phone.

Without Naylor as much as touching the controls, the thespitron ground to a halt. The picture dwindled and the screen went blank.

'Ah, the famous question of identity!' boomed the thespitron, and was silent.

Naylor fingered the restart button, but the set was dead. He fell back in his chair, realising his mistake. He realised how foolish had been his abandonment of the solid wisdom of materialist empiricism, how erroneous his sudden hysterical belief, based on fear, that logic and identity could be antecedent to matter, when in fact they were suppositions merely, derived from material relations. Deprived of the massy presence of numerous galaxies, the signposts of reality, the thespitron had ceased to function.

The closing circles were getting smaller. Now there was only the shell of the habitat, analogue of a skull, and within it his own skull, that lonely fortress of identity. Naylor sat staring at a blank screen, wondering how long it would take for the light of self-knowledge to go out.

MY BOAT

by Joanna Russ

Somehow we had not associated Joanna Russ with the type of nostalgia and daydream fantasy painted so colorfully in this story of childhood. But it strikes a chord surely common to all habitual readers of science fiction—and commands for itself a place in this anthology. If you have never dreamed dreams such as these, you are surely not one of the "family." But then you wouldn't be reading this book. . . .

Milty, have I got a story for you!

No, sit down. Enjoy the cream cheese and bagel. I guarantee this one will make a first-class TV movie; I'm working on it already. Small cast, cheap production—it's a natural. See, we start with this crazy chick, maybe about seventeen, but she's a waif, she's withdrawn from the world, see? She's had some kind of terrible shock. And she's fixed up this old apartment in a slum really weird, like a fantasy world—long, blonde hair, maybe goes around barefoot in tie-dyed dresses she makes out of old sheets, and there's this account executive who meets her in Central Park and falls in love with her on account of she's like a dryad or a nature spirit—

All right. So it stinks. I'll pay for my lunch. We'll pretend you're not my agent, okay? And you don't have to tell me it's been done; I know it's been done. The truth is—

Milty, I have to talk to someone. No, it's a lousy idea, I know and I'm not working on it and I haven't been working

197

on it but what are you going to do Memorial Day weekend if you're alone and everybody's out of town?

I have to talk to someone.

Yes, I'll get off the Yiddische shtick. Hell, I don't think about it; I just fall into it sometimes when I get upset, you know how it is. You do it yourself. But I want to tell you a story and it's not a story for a script. It's something that happened to me in high school in 1952 and *I just want to tell someone*. I don't care if no station from here to Indonesia can use it; you just tell me whether I'm nuts or not, that's all.

Okay.

It was 1952, like I said. I was a senior in a high school out on the Island, a public high school but very fancy, a big drama program. They were just beginning to integrate, you know, the early fifties, very liberal neighborhood; everybody's patting everybody else on the back because they let five black kids into our school. Five out of eight hundred! You'd think they expected God to come down from Flatbush and give everybody a big fat golden halo.

Anyway, our drama class got integrated, too—one little black girl aged fifteen named Cissie Jackson, some kind of genius. All I remember the first day of the spring term, she was the only black I'd ever seen with a natural, only we didn't know what the hell it was, then; it made her look as weird as if she'd just come out of a hospital or something.

Which, by the way, she just had. You know Malcolm X saw his father killed by white men when he was four and that made him a militant for life? Well, Cissie's father had been shot down in front of her eyes when she was a little kid—we learned that later on—only it didn't make her militant; it just made her so scared of everybody and everything that she'd withdraw into herself and wouldn't speak to anybody for weeks on end. Sometimes she'd withdraw right out of this world and then they'd send her to the loony bin; believe me, it was all over school in two days. And she looked it; she'd sit up there in the school theater—oh, Milty, the Island high schools had *money*, you better believe it!—and try to disappear into the last seat like some little scared rabbit. She was only four eleven anyhow, and maybe eighty-five pounds sopping wet. So maybe that's why she didn't become a militant. Hell, that had nothing to do with it. She was scared of *everybody*. It wasn't just the white-black thing, either; I once saw her in a corner with one of the other black students: real uptight, respectable boy, you know, suit and white shirt and tie, hair straightened the way they did then with a lot of grease and carrying a new briefcase, too, and he was talking to her about something as if his life depended on it. He was actually crying and pleading with her. And all she did was shrink back into the corner as if she'd like to disappear and shake her head No No No. She always talked in a whisper unless she was on stage and sometimes then, too. The first week she forgot her cues four times—just stood there, glazed over, ready to fall through the floor—and a couple of times she just wandered off the set as if the play was over, right in the middle of a scene.

So Al Coppolino and I went to the principal. I'd always thought Alan was pretty much a fruitcake himself—remember, Milty, this is 1952—because he used to read all that crazy stuff. The Cult of Chthulhu, Dagon Calls. The Horror Men of Leng—yeah, I remember that H.P. Lovecraft flick you got 10 percent on for Hollywood *and* TV *and* reruns—but what did we know? Those days you went to parties, you got excited from dancing cheek to cheek, girls wore ankle socks and petticoats to stick their skirts out, and if you wore a sport shirt to school that was okay because Central High was liberal, but it better not have a pattern on it. Even so, I knew Al was a bright kid and I let him do most of the talking; I just nodded a lot. I was a big nothing in those days.

Al said, "Sir, Jim and I are all for integration and we think it's great that this is a really liberal place, but—uh—"

The principal got that look. Uh-oh.

"But?" he said, cold as ice.

"Well, sir," said Al, "it's Cissie Jackson. We think she's— um—sick. I mean wouldn't it be better if ... I mean everybody says she's just come out of the hospital and it's a strain for all of us and it must be a lot worse strain for her and maybe it's just a little soon for her to—"

"Sir," I said, "what Coppolino means is, we don't mind integrating blacks with whites, but this isn't racial integration, sir; this is integrating normal people with a filbert. I mean—"

He said, "Gentlemen, it might interest you to know that Miss Cecilia Jackson has higher scores on her IQ tests than the two of you put together. And I am told by the drama department that she has also more talent than the two of you put together. And considering the grades both of you have managed to achieve in the fall term, I'm not at all surprised."

Al said under his breath, "Yeah, and fifty times as many problems."

Well, the principal went on and told us about how we should welcome this chance to work with her because she was so brilliant she was positively a genius, and that as soon as we stopped spreading idiotic rumors, the better chance Miss Jackson would have to adjust to Central, and if he heard anything about our bothering her again or spreading stories about her, both of us were going to get it but good, and maybe we would even be expelled.

And then his voice lost the ice, and he told us about some white cop shooting her pa for no reason at all when she was five, right in front of her, and her pa bleeding into the gutter and dying in little Cissie's lap, and how poor her mother was, and a couple of other awful things that had happened to her, and if *that* wasn't enough to drive anybody crazy—though he said "cause problems," you know—anyhow, by the time he'd finished, I felt like a rat and Coppolino went outside the principal's office, put his face down against the tiles—they always had tiles up as high as you could reach, so they could wash off the graffiti, though we didn't use the word "graffiti" in those days—and he blubbered like a baby.

So we started a Help Cecilia Jackson campaign.

And by God, Milty, could that girl *act*! She wasn't reliable, that was the trouble; one week she'd be in there, working like a dog, voice exercises, gym, fencing, reading Stanislavsky in the cafeteria, gorgeous performances, the next week: nothing. Oh, she was there in the flesh, all right, all eighty-five pounds of her, but she would walk through everything as if her mind was someplace else: technically perfect, emotionally nowhere. I heard later those were also the times when she'd refuse to answer questions in history or geography classes, just fade out and not talk. But when she was concentrating, she could walk onto that stage and take it over as if she owned it. I never saw such a natural. At fifteen! And tiny. I mean not a particularly good voice—though I guess just getting older would've helped that—and a figure that, frankly, Milt, it was the old W.C. Fields joke, two aspirins on an ironing board. And tiny, no real good looks, but my God, you know and I know that doesn't matter if you've got the presence. And she had it to burn. She played the Queen of Sheba once, in a one-act play we put on before a live audience—all right, our parents and the other kids, who else?—and she *was* the role. And another time I saw her do things from Shakespeare. And once, of all things, a lioness in a mime class. She had it all. Real, absolute, pure concentration. And she was smart, too; by then she and Al had become pretty good friends; I once heard her explain to him (that was in the green room the afternoon of the Queen of Sheba thing when she was taking off her make-up with cold cream) just how she'd figured out each bit of business for the character. Then she stuck her whole arm out at me, pointing straight at me as if her arm was a machine gun, and said:

"For you, Mister Jim, let me tell you: the main thing is *belief*!"

It was a funny thing, Milt. She got better and better friends with Al, and when they let me tag along, I felt privileged. He loaned her some of those crazy books of his and I overheard things about her life, bits and pieces. That girl had a mother who was so uptight and so God-fearing and so respectable it was a wonder Cissie could even breathe without asking permission. Her mother wouldn't even let her straighten her hair—not ideological reasons, you understand, not then, but because—get this—*Cissie was too young*. I think her mamma must've been crazier than she was. Course I was a damn stupid kid (who wasn't?) and I really thought all blacks were real loose; they went around snapping their fingers and hanging from chandeliers, you know, all that stuff, dancing and singing. But here was this genius from a family where they wouldn't let her out at night; she wasn't allowed to go to parties or dance or play cards; she couldn't wear make-up or even jewelry. Believe me, I think if anything drove her batty it was being socked over the head so often with a Bible. I guess her imagination just had to find some way out. Her mother, by the way, would've dragged her out of Central High by the hair if she'd found out about the drama classes; we all had to swear to keep that strictly on the q.t. The theater was even more sinful and wicked than dancing, I guess.

You know, I think it shocked me. It really did. Al's family was sort-of-nothing-really Catholic and mine was sort-of-nothing Jewish. I'd never met anybody with a mamma like that. I mean she would've beaten Cissie up if Cissie had ever come home with a gold circle pin on that white blouse she wore day in and day out; you remember the kind all the girls wore. And of course there were no horsehair petticoats for

Miss Jackson; Miss Jackson wore pleated skirts that were much too short, even for her, and straight skirts that looked faded and all bunched up. For a while I had some vague idea that the short skirts meant she was daring, you know, sexy, but it wasn't that; they were from a much younger cousin, let down. She just couldn't afford her own clothes. I think it was the mamma and the Bible business that finally made me stop seeing Cissie as the Integration Prize Nut we had to be nice to because of the principal or the scared little rabbit who still, by the way, whispered everyplace but in drama class. I just saw Cecilia Jackson plain, I guess, not that it lasted for more than a few minutes, but I knew she was something special. So one day in the hall, going from one class to another, I met her and Al and I said, "Cissie, your name is going to be up there in lights someday. I think you're the best actress I ever met and I just want to say it's a privilege knowing you." And then I swept her a big corny bow, like Errol Flynn.

She looked at Al and Al looked at her, sort of sly. Then she let down her head over her books and giggled. She was so tiny you sometimes wondered how she could drag those books around all day; they hunched her over so.

Al said, "Aw, come on. Let's tell him."

So they told me their big secret. Cissie had a girl cousin named Gloriette, and Gloriette and Cissie together owned an honest-to-God slip for a boat in the marina out in Silver-hampton. Each of them paid half the slip fee—which was about two bucks a month then, Milt—you have to remember that a marina then just meant a long wooden dock you could tie your rowboat up to.

"Gloriette's away," said Cissie, in that whisper. "She had to go visit auntie, in Carolina. And mamma's goin' to follow her next week on Sunday."

"So we're going to go out in the boat!" Al finished it for her. "You wanna come?"

"Sunday?"

"Sure, mamma will go to the bus station after church," said Cissie. "That's about one o'clock. Aunt Evelyn comes to take care of me at nine. So we have eight hours."

"And it takes two hours to get there," said Al. "First you take the subway; then you take a bus—"

"Unless we use your car, Jim!" said Cissie, laughing so hard she dropped her books.

"Well, thanks very much!" I said. She scooped them up

again and smiled at me. "No, Jim," she said. "We want you to come, anyway. Al never saw the boat yet. Gloriette and me, we call it *My Boat*." Fifteen years old and she knew how to smile at you so's to twist your heart like a pretzel. Or maybe I just thought: what a wicked secret to have! A big sin, I guess, according to her family.

I said, "Sure, I'll drive you. May I ask what kind of boat it is, Miss Jackson?"

"Don't be so *damn'* silly," she said daringly. "I'm Cissie or Cecilia. Silly Jim."

"And as for *My Boat*," she added, "it's a big yacht. Enormous."

I was going to laugh at that, but then I saw she meant it. No, she was just playing. She was smiling wickedly at me again. She said we should meet at the bus stop near her house, and then she went down the tiled hall next to skinny little Al Coppolino, in her old, baggy, green skirt and her always-the-same white blouse. No beautiful, big, white, sloppy bobby socks for Miss Jackson; she just wore old loafers coming apart at the seams. She looked different, though: her head was up, her step springy, and she hadn't been whispering.

And then it occurred to me it was the first time I had ever seen her smile or laugh—off stage. Mind you, she cried easily enough, like the time in class she realized from something the teacher had said that Anton Chekhov you know; the great Russian playwright—was dead. I heard her telling Alan later that she didn't believe it. There were lots of little crazy things like that.

Well, I picked her up Sunday in what was probably the oldest car in the world, even then—not a museum piece, Milty; it'd still be a mess—frankly I was lucky to get it started at all—and when I got to the bus station near Cissie's house in Brooklyn, there she was in her faded, hand-me-down, pleated skirt and that same blouse. I guess little elves named Cecilia Jackson came out of the woodwork every night and washed and ironed it. Funny, she and Al really did make a pair—you know, he was like the Woody Allen of Central High and I think he went in for his crazy books— sure, Milt, *very* crazy in 1952—because otherwise what could a little Italian punk do who was five foot three and so brilliant no other kid could understand half the time what he was talking about? I don't know why I was friends with him; I think it made me feel big, you know, generous and good, like being friends with Cissie. They were almost the same size, waiting there by the bus stop, and I think their heads were in the same place. I know it now, I guess he was just a couple of decades ahead of himself, like his books. And maybe if the civil rights movement had started a few years earlier—

Anyway, we drove out to Silverhampton and it was a nice drive, lots of country, though all flat—in those days there were still truck farms on the Island—and found the marina, which was nothing more than a big old quay, but sound enough; and I parked the car and Al took out a shopping bag Cissie'd been carrying. "Lunch," he said.

My Boat was there, all right, halfway down the dock. Somehow I hadn't expected it would exist, even. It was an old leaky wooden rowboat with only one oar, and there were three inches of bilge in the bottom. On the bow somebody had painted the name, "My Boat," shakily in orange paint. *My Boat* was tied to the mooring by a rope about as sturdy as a piece of string. Still, it didn't look like it would sink right away; after all, it'd been sitting there for months, getting rained on, maybe even snowed on, and it was still floating. So I stepped down into it, wishing I'd had the sense to take off my shoes, and started bailing with a tin can I'd brought from the car. Alan and Cissie were taking things out of the bag in the middle of the boat. I guess they were setting out lunch. It was pretty clear that *My Boat* spent most of its time sitting at the dock while Cissie and Gloriette ate lunch and maybe pretended they were on the *Queen Mary*, because neither Alan nor Cissie seemed to notice the missing oar. It was a nice day but in-and-outish; you know, clouds one minute, sun the next, but little fluffy clouds, no sign of rain. I bailed a lot of the gunk out and then moved up into the bow, and as the sun came out I saw that I'd been wrong about the orange paint. It was yellow.

Then I looked closer: it wasn't paint but some thing set into the side of *My Boat* like the names on people's office doors; I guess I must've not looked too closely the first time. It was a nice, flowing script, a real professional job. Brass, I guess. Not a plate, Milt, kind of—what do they call it, parquet? Intaglio? Each letter was put in separately. Must've been Alan; he had a talent for stuff like that, used to make weird illustrations for his crazy books. I turned around to find Al and Cissie taking a big piece of cheesecloth out of the shopping bag and draping it over high poles that were built into the sides of the boat. They were making a kind of awning. I said:

"Hey, I bet you took that from the theater shop!"

She just smiled.

Al said, "Would you get us some fresh water, Jim?"

"Sure," I said. "Where, up the dock?"

"No, from the bucket. Back in the stern. Cissie says it's marked."

Oh, sure, I thought, sure. Out in the middle of the Pacific we set out our bucket and pray for rain. There was a pail there all right, and somebody had laboriously stenciled "Fresh Water" on it in green paint, sort of smudgy, but that pail was never going to hold anything ever again. It was bone-dry, empty, and so badly rusted that when you held it up to the light, you could see through the bottom in a couple of places. I said, "Cissie, it's empty."

She said, "Look again, Jim."

I said, "But look, Cissie—" and turned the bucket upside-down.

Cold water drenched me from my knees to the soles of my shoes.

"See?" she said. "Never empty." I thought: Hell, I didn't look, that's all. Maybe it rained yesterday. Still, a full pail of water is heavy and I had lifted that thing with one finger. I set it down—if it had been full before, it certainly wasn't now—and looked again.

It was full, right to the brim. I dipped my hand into the stuff and drank a little of it: cold and clear as spring water and it smelled—I don't know—of ferns warmed by the sun, of raspberries, of field flowers, of grass. I thought: my God, I'm becoming a filbert myself! And then I turned around and saw that Alan and Cissie had replaced the cheesecloth on the poles with a striped blue-and-white awning, the kind you see in movies about Cleopatra, you know? The stuff they put over her barge to keep the sun off. And Cissie had taken out of her shopping bag something patterned orange-and-green-and-blue and had wrapped it around her old clothes. She had on gold-colored earrings, big hoop things, and a black turban over that funny hair. And she must've put her loafers some-where because she was barefoot. Then I saw that she had one shoulder bare, too, and I sat down on one of the marble benches of *My Boat* under the awning because I was proba-bly having hallucinations. I mean she hadn't had *time*—and where were her old clothes? I thought to myself that they must've lifted a whole bagful of stuff from the theater shop, like that big old wicked-looking knife she had stuck into her amber-studded, leather belt, the hilt all covered with gold and stones: red ones, green ones, and blue ones with little crosses of light winking in them that you couldn't really follow with your eyes. I didn't know what the blue ones were then, but I know now. You don't make star sapphires in a theater shop. Or a ten-inch, crescent-shaped steel blade so sharp the sun dazzles you coming off its edge.

I said, "Cissie, you look like the Queen of Sheba."

She smiled. She said to me, "Jim, iss not Shee-bah as in thee Bible, but Saba. Sah-bah. You mus' remember when we meet her."

I thought to myself: Yeah, this is where little girl genius Cissie Jackson comes to freak out every Sunday. Lost weekend. I figured this was the perfect time to get away, make some excuse, you know, and call her mamma or her auntie, or maybe just the nearest hospital. I mean just for her own sake; Cissie wouldn't hurt anybody because she wasn't mean, not ever. And anyhow she was too little to hurt anyone. I stood up.

Her eyes were level with mine. And she was standing below me.

Al said, "Be careful, Jim. Look again. Always look again." I went back to the stern. There was the bucket that said "Fresh Water," but as I looked the sun came out and I saw I'd been mistaken; it wasn't old, rusty, galvanized iron with splotchy, green-painted letters.

It was silver, pure silver. It was sitting in a sort of marble well built into the stern, and the letters were jade inlay. It was still full. It would always be full. I looked back at Cissie standing under the blue-and-white-striped silk awning with her star sapphires and emeralds and rubies in her dagger and her funny talk—I know it now, Milt, it was West Indian, but I didn't then—and I knew as sure as if I'd seen it that if I looked at the letters "My Boat" in the sun, they wouldn't be brass but pure gold. And the wood would be ebony. I wasn't even surprised. Although everything had changed, you understand, I'd never seen it change; it was either that I hadn't looked carefully the first time, or I'd made a mistake, or I hadn't noticed something, or I'd just forgotten. Like what I thought had been an old crate in the middle of *My Boat*, which was really the roof of a cabin with little portholes in it, and looking in I saw three bunk beds below, a closet, and a beautiful little galley with a refrigerator and a stove, and off to one side in the sink, where I couldn't really see it clearly, a bottle with a napkin around its neck, sticking up from an ice bucket full of crushed ice, just like an old Fred Astaire-Ginger Rogers movie. And the whole inside of the cabin was paneled in teakwood.

Cissie said, "No, Jim. Is not teak. Is cedar, from Lebanon. You see now why I cannot take seriously in this school this nonsense about places and where they are and what happen in them. Crude oil in Lebanon! It is cedar they have. And ivory. I have been there many, many time. I have talk' with the wise Solomon. I have been at court of Queen of Saba and have made eternal treaty with the Knossos women, the people of the double ax which is waxing and waning moon together. I have visit Akhnaton and Nofretari, and have seen great kings at Benin and at Dar. I even go to Atlantis, where the Royal Couple teach me many things. The priest and priestess, they show me how to make *My Boat* go anywhere I like, even under the sea. Oh, we have manhy improvin' chats upon roof of Pahlahss at dusk!"

It was real. It was all real. She was not fifteen, Milt. She sat in the bow at the controls of *My Boat*, and there were as many dials and toggles and buttons and switches and gauges on that thing as on a B-57. And she was at least ten years older. Al Coppolino, too, he looked like a picture I'd seen in a history book of Sir Francis Drake, and he had long hair and a little pointy beard. He was dressed like Drake, except for the ruff, with rubies in his ears and rings all over his fingers, and he, too, was no seventeen-year-old. He had a faint scar running from his left temple at the hairline down past his eye to his cheekbone. I could also see that under her turban Cissie's hair was braided in some very fancy way. I've seen it since. Oh, long before everybody was doing "corn rows." I saw it at the Metropolitan Museum, in silver face-mask sculptures from the city of Benin, in Africa. Old, Milt, centuries old.

Al said, "I know of other places, Princess. I can show them to you. Oh, let us go to Ooth-Nargai and Celephais the Fair, and Kadath in the Cold Waste—it's a fearful place, Jim, but *we* need not be afraid—and then we will go to the city of

Ulthar, where is the very fortunate and lovely law that no
man or woman may kill or annoy a cat."

"The Atlanteans," said Cissie in a deep sweet voice, "they
promise' that next time they show me not jus' how to go un-
dersea. They say if you think hard, if you fix much, if you
believe, then can make *My Boat* go straight up. Into the
stars, Jim!"

Al Coppolino was chanting names under his breath:
Cathuria, Sona-Nyl, Thalarion, Zar, Baharna, Nir, Oriab. All
out of those books of his.

Cissie said, "Before you come with us, you must do one
last thing, Jim. Untie the rope."

So I climbed down *My Boat*'s ladder onto the quay and
undid the braided gold rope that was fastened to the slip.
Gold and silk intertwined, Milt; it rippled through my hand
as if it were alive; I know the hard, slippery feel of silk. I
was thinking of Atlantis and Celephais and going up into the
stars, and all of it was mixed up in my head with the senior
prom and college, because I had been lucky enough to be accepted by The-College-Of-My-Choice, and what a future I'd
have as a lawyer, a corporation lawyer, after being a big
gridiron star, of course. Those were my plans in the old days.
Dead certainties every one, right? Versus a thirty-five-foot
yacht that would've made John D. Rockefeller turn green
with envy and places in the world where nobody'd ever been
and nobody'd ever go again. Cissie and Al stood on deck
above me, the both of them looking like something out of a
movie—beautiful and dangerous and very strange—and suddenly I knew I didn't want to go. Part of it was the absolute
certainty that if I ever offended Cissie in any way—I don't
mean just a quarrel or disagreement or something you'd get
the sulks about, but a real bone-deep kind of offense—I'd
suddenly find myself in a leaky rowboat with only one oar in
the middle of the Pacific Ocean. Or maybe just tied up at the
dock at Silverhampton; Cissie wasn't mean. At least I hoped
so. I just—I guess I didn't feel *good* enough to go. And there
was something about their faces, too, as if over both of them,
but especially over Cissie's, like clouds, like veils, there swam
other faces, other expressions, other souls, other pasts and fu-
tures and other kinds of knowledge, all of them shifting like a
heat mirage over an asphalt road on a hot day.

I didn't want that knowledge, Milt. I didn't want to go that
deep. It was the kind of thing most seventeen-year-olds don't

learn for years: Beauty. Despair. Mortality. Compassion. Pain.

And I was still looking up at them, watching the breeze fill out Al Coppolino's plum-colored velvet cloak and shine on his silver-and-black doublet, when a big, heavy, hard, fat hand clamped down on my shoulder and a big, fat, nasty, heavy, Southern voice said:

"Hey, boy, you got no permit for this slip! What's that rowboat doin' out there? And what's yo' name?"

So I turned and found myself looking into the face of the great-granddaddy of all Southern redneck sheriffs: face like a bulldog with jowls to match, and sunburnt red, and fat as a pig, and mountain-mean. I said, "Sir?"—every high-school kid could say that in his sleep in those days—and then we turned toward the bay, me saying, "What boat, sir?" and the cop saying just, "What the—"

Because there was nothing there. *My Boat* was gone. There was only a blue shimmering stretch of bay. They weren't out further and they weren't around the other side of the dock— the cop and I both ran around—and by the time I had presence of mind enough to look up at the sky—

Nothing. A seagull. A cloud. A plane out of Idlewild. Besides, hadn't Cissie said she didn't yet know how to go straight up into the stars?

No, nobody ever saw *My Boat* again. Or Miss Cecilia Jackson, complete nut and girl genius, either. Her mamma came to school and I was called into the principal's office. I told them a cooked-up story, the one I'd been going to tell the cop: that they'd said they were just going to row around the dock and come back, and I'd left to see if the car was okay in the parking lot, and when I came back, they were gone. For some crazy reason I *still* thought Cissie's mamma would look like Aunt Jemima, but she was a thin little woman, very like her daughter, and as nervous and uptight as I ever saw: a tiny lady in a much-pressed, but very clean, gray business suit, like a teacher's, you know, worn-out shoes, a blouse with a white frill at the neck, a straw hat with a white band, and proper white gloves. I think Cissie knew what I expected her mamma to be and what a damned fool I was, even considering your run-of-the-mill, seventeen-year-old, white, liberal racist, and that's why she didn't take me along.

The cop? He followed me to my car, and by the time I got there—I was sweating and crazy scared—

He was gone, too. Vanished.

I think Cissie created him. Just for a joke.

So Cissie never came back. And I couldn't convince Mrs. Jackson that Alan Coppolino, boy rapist, hadn't carried her daughter off to some lonely place and murdered her. I tried and tried, but Mrs. Jackson would never believe me.

It turned out there was no Cousin Gloriette.

Alan? Oh, he came back. But it took him a while. A long, long while. I saw him yesterday, Milt, on the Brooklyn subway. A skinny, short guy with ears that stuck out, still wearing the sport shirt and pants he'd started out in, that Sunday more than twenty years ago, and with the real 1950's haircut nobody would wear today. Quite a few people were staring at him, in fact.

The thing is, Milt, *he was still seventeen.*

No, I know it wasn't some other kid. Because he was waving at me and smiling fit to beat the band. And when I got out with him at his old stop, he started asking after everybody in Central High just as if it had been a week later, or maybe only a day. Though when I asked him where the hell he'd been for twenty years, he wouldn't tell me. He only said he'd forgotten something. So we went up five flights to his old apartment, the way we used to after school for a couple of hours before his mom and dad came home from work. He had the old key in his pocket. And it was just the same, Milt: the gas refrigerator, the exposed pipes under the sink, the summer slipcovers nobody uses any more, the winter drapes put away, the valance over the window muffled in a sheet, the bare parquet floors, and the old linoleum in the kitchen. Every time I'd ask him a question, he'd only smile. He knew me, though, because he called me by name a couple of times. I said, "How'd you recognize me?" and he said, "Recognize? You haven't changed." Haven't changed, my God. Then I said, "Look, Alan, what did you come back for?" and with a grin just like Cissie's, he said, *"The Necronomicon* by the mad Arab, Abdul Alhazred, what else?" but I saw the book he took with him and it was a different one. He was careful to get just the right one, looked through every shelf in the bookcase in his bedroom. There were still college banners all over the walls of his room. I know the book now, by the way; it was the one you wanted to make into a quick script last year for the guy who does the Poe movies, only I *told* you it was all special effects and animation: exotic islands, strange worlds, and the monsters' costumes alone—sure, H.P. Lovecraft. "The Dream Quest of Unknown Kadath." He didn't say a word after that. Just walked down the five flights with me behind him and then along the old block to the nearest subway station, but of course by the time I reached the bottom of the subway steps, he wasn't there.

His apartment? You'll never find it. When I raced back up, even the house was gone. More than that, Milt, the street is gone; the address doesn't exist any more; it's all part of the new expressway now.

Which is why I called you. My God, I had to tell somebody! By now those two psychiatric cases are voyaging around between the stars to Ulthar and Ooth-Nargai and Dylath-Leen—

But they're not psychiatric cases. *It really happened.*

So if they're not psychiatric cases, what does that make you and me? Blind men?

I'll tell you something else, Milt: meeting Al reminded me of what Cissie once said before the whole thing with *My Boat* but after we'd become friends enough for me to ask her what had brought her out of the hospital. I didn't ask it like that and she didn't answer it like that, but what it boiled down to was that sooner or later, at every place she visited, she'd meet a bleeding man with wounds in his hands and feet who would tell her, "Cissie, go back, you're needed; Cissie, go back, you're needed." I was fool enough to ask her if he was a white man or a black man. She just glared at me and walked away. Now wounds in the hands and feet, you don't have to look far to tell what that means to a Christian, Bible-raised girl. What I wonder is: will she meet Him again, out there among the stars? If things get bad enough for black power or women's liberation, or even for people who write crazy books, I don't know what, will *My Boat* materialize over Times Square or Harlem or East New York with an Ethiopian warrior-queen in it and Sir Francis Drake Coppolino, and God-only-knows-what kind of weapons from the lost science of Atlantis? I tell you, I wouldn't be surprised. I really wouldn't. I only hope He—or Cissie's idea of him—decides that things are still okay, and they can go on visiting all those places in Al Coppolino's book. I tell you, I hope that book is a *long* book.

Still, if I could do it again. . . .

Milt, it is not a story. *It happened.* For instance, tell me
one thing, how did she know the name Nofretari? That's the
Egyptian Queen Nefertiti, that's how we all learned it, but
how could she know the real name decades, literally decades,
before anybody else? And Saba? That's real, too. And Benin?
We didn't have any courses in African History in Central
High, not in 1952! And what about the double-headed ax of
the Cretans at Knossos? Sure, we read about Crete in high
school, but nothing in our history books ever told us about
the matriarchy or the labyris, that's the name of the ax. Milt,
I tell you, there is even a women's lib bookstore in Manhattan *called*—

Have it your own way.

Oh, sure. She wasn't black; she was green. It'd make a
great TV show. Green, blue, and rainbow-colored. I'm sorry,
Milty, I know you're my agent and you've done a lot of work
for me and I haven't sold much lately. I've been reading. No,
nothing you'd like: existentialism, history, Marxism, some
Eastern stuff—

Sorry, Milt, but we writers do read every once in a while.
It's this little vice we have. I've been trying to dig deep, like
Al Coppolino, though maybe in a different way.

Okay, so you want to have this Martian, who wants to invade Earth, so he turns himself into a beautiful, tanned girl
with long, straight, blonde hair, right? And becomes a high-
school student in a rich school in Westchester. And this
beautiful blonde girl Martian has to get into all the local organizations like the women's consciousness-raising groups and
the encounter therapy stuff and the cheerleaders and the kids
who push dope, so he—she, rather—can learn about the Earth
mentality. Yeah. And of course she has to seduce the principal
and the coach and all the big men on campus, so we can make
it into a series, even a sitcom maybe; each week this Martian
falls in love with an Earth man or she tries to do something to
destroy Earth or blow up something, using Central High for a
base. Can I use it? Sure I can! It's beautiful. It's right in my
line. I can work in everything I just told you. Cissie was right
not to take me along; I've got spaghetti where my backbone
should be.

Nothing. didn't say anything. Sure. It's a great idea. Even
if we only get a pilot out of it.

No, Milt, honestly, I really think it has this fantastic spark.

A real touch of genius. It'll sell like crazy. Yeah, I can manage an idea sheet by Monday. Sure. "The Beautiful Menace from Mars?" Un-huh. Absolutely. It's got sex, it's got danger, comedy, everything; we could branch out into the lives of the teachers, the principal, the other kid's parents. Bring in contemporary problems like drug abuse. Sure. Another Peyton Place. I'll even move to the West Coast again. You are a genius.

Oh my God.

Nothing. Keep on talking. It's just—see that little skinny kid in the next booth down? The one with the stuck-out ears and the old-fashioned haircut? You don't? Well, I think you're just not looking properly, Milt. Actually I don't think I was, either; he must be one of the Met extras; you know, they come out sometimes during the intermission: all that Elizabethan stuff, the plum-colored cloak, the calf-high boots, the silver-and-black— As a matter of fact, I just remembered—the Met moved uptown a couple of years ago, so he couldn't be dressed like that, could he?

You still can't see him? I'm not surprised. The light's very bad in here. Listen, he's an old friend—I mean he's the son of an old friend—I better go over and say hello, I won't be a minute.

Milt, this young man is important! I mean he's connected with somebody very important. Who? One of the biggest and best producers in the world, that's who! He—uh—they— wanted me to—you might call it do a script for them, yeah. I didn't want to at the time, but—

No, no, you stay right here. I'll just sort of lean over and say hello. You keep on talking about the Beautiful Menace from Mars; I can listen from there; I'll just tell him they can have me if they want me.

Your ten per cent? Of course you'll get your ten per cent. You're my agent, aren't you? Why, if it wasn't for you, I just possibly might not have— Sure, you'll get your ten percent. Spend it on anything you like: ivory, apes, peacocks, spices, and Lebanese cedarwood!

All you have to do is collect it.

But keep on talking, Milty, won't you? Somehow I want to go over to the next booth with the sound of your voice in my ears. Those beautiful ideas. So original. So creative. So true. Just what the public wants. Of course there's a difference in the way people perceive things, and you and I, I think we perceive them differently, you know? Which is why you are a respected, successful agent and I—well, let's skip it. It wouldn't be complimentary to either of us.

Huh? Oh, nothing. I didn't say anything. I'm listening. Over my shoulder. Just keep on talking while I say hello and my deepest and most abject apologies, Sir Alan Coppolino. Heard the name before, Milt? No? I'm not surprised.

You just keep on talking. . . .

HOUSTON, HOUSTON, DO YOU READ?

by James Tiptree, Jr.

Tiptree contributed the following novelette to an anthology of "feminist" science fiction. We warn the prissy that there are a couple of outspoken spots in this tale—but they surely belong and help to place the problem in the fullest perspective.

Lorimer gazes around the crowded cabin, trying to listen to the voices, trying to ignore the twitch in his insides that means he is about to remember something bad. No help; he lives it again, that long-ago moment. Himself running blindly—or was he pushed?—into the strange toilet at Evanston Junior High. His fly open, his dick in his hand, he can still see the grey zipper edge of his jeans around his pale exposed pecker. The hush. The sickening wrongness of shapes, faces turning. The first blaring giggle. *Girls.* He was in the *girl's can.*

He flinches now wryly, so many years later, not looking at the women's faces. The big cabin surrounds him with their alien things, curved around over his head: the beading rack, the twins' loom, Andy's leather work, the damned kudzu vine wriggling everywhere, the chickens. So cosy. . . . Trapped, he is. Irretrievably trapped for life in everything he does not enjoy. Structurelessness. Personal trivia, unmeaning intimacies. The claims he can somehow never meet. Ginny: *You never talk to me* . . . Ginny, love, he thinks involuntarily. The hurt doesn't come.

Bud Geirr's loud chuckle breaks in on him. Bud is joking with some of them, out of sight around a bulkhead. Dave is visible, though. Major Norman Davis on the far side of the cabin, his bearded profile bent toward a small dark woman Lorimer can't quite focus on. But Dave's head seems oddly tiny and sharp, in fact the whole cabin looks unreal. A cackle bursts out from the "ceiling"—the bantam hen in her basket.

At this moment Lorimer becomes sure he has been drugged.

Curiously, the idea does not anger him. He leans or rather tips back, perching cross-legged in the zero gee, letting his gaze go to the face of the woman he has been talking with. Connie. Constantia Morelos. A tall moonfaced woman in capacious green pajamas. He has never really cared for talking to women. Ironic.

"I suppose," he says aloud, "it's possible that in some sense we are not here."

That doesn't sound too clear, but she nods interestedly. She's watching my reactions, Lorimer tells himself. Women are natural poisoners. Has he said that aloud too? Her expression doesn't change. His vision is taking on a pleasing local clarity. Connie's skin strikes him as quite fine, healthy-looking. Olive tan even after two years in space. She was a farmer, he recalls. Big pores, but without the caked look he associates with women her age.

"You probably never wore make-up," he says. She looks puzzled. "Face paint, powder. None of you have."

"Oh!" Her smile shows a chipped front tooth. "Oh yes, I think Andy has."

"Andy?"

"For plays. Historical plays, Andy's good at that."

"Of course. Historical plays."

Lorimer's brain seems to be expanding, letting in light. He is understanding actively now, the myriad bits and pieces linking into patterns. Deadly patterns, he perceives; but the drug is shielding him in some way. Like an amphetamine high without the pressure. Maybe it's something they use socially? No, they're watching, too.

"Space bunnies, I still don't dig it," Bud Geirr laughs infectiously. He has a friendly buoyant voice people like; Lorimer still likes it after two years.

"You chicks have kids back home, what do your folks think about you flying around out here with old Andy, h'mm?" Bud floats into view, his arm draped around a twin's shoulders. The one called Judy Paris, Lorimer decides; the twins are hard to tell. She drifts passively at an angle to Bud's big body: jut-breasted plain girl in flowing yellow pajamas, her black hair raying out. Andy's red head swims up to them. He is holding a big green spaceball, looking about sixteen.

"Old Andy." Bud shakes his head, his grin flashing under his thick dark mustache. "When I was your age folks didn't let their women fly around with me."

Connie's lips quirk faintly. In Lorimer's head the pieces slide toward pattern. I know, he thinks. Do you know I know? His head is vast and crystalline, very nice really. Easier to think. Women. . . . No compact generalisation forms in his mind, only a few speaking faces on a matrix of pervasive irrelevance. Human, of course. Biological necessity. Only so, so . . . diffuse? Pointless? . . . His sister Amy, *soprano con tremulo: Of course women could contribute as much as men if you'd treat us as equals. You'll see!* and then marrying that idiot the second time. Well, now he can see.

"Kudzu vines," he says aloud. Connie smiles. How they all smile.

"How 'boot that?" Bud says happily, "Ever think we'd see chicks in zero gee, hey, Dave? Artits-stico. Woo-ee!" Across the cabin Dave's bearded head turns to him, not smiling.

"And ol' Andy's had it all to his self. Stunt your growth, lad." He punches Andy genially on the arm, Andy catches himself on the bulkhead. Bud can't be drunk, Lorimer thinks; not on that fruit cider. But he doesn't usually sound so much like a stage Texan either. A drug.

"Hey, no offense," Bud is saying earnestly to the boy, "I mean that. You have to forgive one underprilly, underprivileged brother. These chicks are good people. Know what?" he tells the girl, "You could look stu-pendous if you fix yourself up a speck. Hey, I can show you, old Buddy's a expert. I hope you don't mind my saying that. As a matter of fact you look real stupendous to me right now."

He hugs her shoulders, flings out his arm and hugs Andy too. They float upwards in his grasp, Judy grinning excitedly, almost pretty.

"Let's get some more of that good stuff." Bud propels them both toward the serving rack which is decorated for the occasion with sprays of greens and small real daisies.

"Happy New Year! Hey, Happy New Year, y'all!"

Faces turn, more smiles. Genuine smiles, Lorimer thinks,

maybe they really like their new years. He feels he has infinite time to examine every event, the implications evolving in crystal facts. I'm an echo chamber. Enjoyable, to be the observer. But others are observing too. They've started something here. Do they realise? So vulnerable, three of us, five of them in this fragile ship. They don't know. A dread unconnected to action lurks behind his mind.

"By god we made it," Bud laughs. "You space chickies, I have to give it to you. I commend you, by god I say it. We wouldn't be here, wherever we are. Know what, I jus' might decide to stay in the service after all. Think they have room for old Bud in your space program, sweetie?"

"Knock that off, Bud," Dave says quietly from the far wall. "I don't want to hear us use the name of the Creator like that." The full chestnut beard gives him a patriarchal gravity. Dave is forty-six, a decade older than Bud and Lorimer. Veteran of six successful missions.

"Oh my apologies, Major Dave old buddy." Bud chuckles intimately to the girl. "Our commanding ossifer. Stupendous guy. Hey, Doc!" he calls, "How's your attitude? You making out dinko?"

"Cheers," Lorimer hears his voice reply, the complex stratum of his feelings about Bud rising like a kraken in the moonlight of his mind. The submerged silent thing he has about them all, all the Buds and Daves and big, indomitable, cheerful, able, disciplined, slow-minded mesomorphs he has cast his life with. Meso-ectos, he corrected himself; astronauts aren't muscleheads. They like him, he has been careful about that. Liked him well enough to get him on *Sunbird*, to make him the official scientist on the first circumsolar mission. That little Doc Lorimer, he's cool, he's on the team. No shit from Lorimer, not like those other scientific assholes. He does the bit well with his small neat build and his dead-pan remarks. And the years of turning out for the bowling, the volleyball, the tennis, the skeet, the skiing that broke his ankle, the touch football that broke his collarbone. Watch that Doc, he's a sneaky one. And the big men banging him on the back, accepting him. Their token scientist . . . The trouble is, he isn't any kind of scientist any more. Living off his postdoctoral plasma work, a lucky hit. He hasn't really been into the math for years, he isn't up to it now. Too many other interests, too much time spent explaining elementary stuff. I'm a half-jock, he thinks. A foot taller and a hundred pounds heavier and I'd be just like them. One of them. An alpha. They probably sense it underneath, the beta bile. Had the jokes worn a shade thin in *Sunbird*, all that year going out? A year of Bud and Dave playing gin. That damn exercycle, gearing it up too tough for me. They didn't mean it, though. We were a team.

The memory of gaping jeans flicks at him, the painful end part—the grinning faces waiting for him when he stumbled out. The howls, the dribble down his leg. Being cool, pretending to laugh too. You shit-heads, I'll show you. I am not a girl.

Bud's voice rings out, chanting "And a Hap-pee New Year to you-all down there!" Parody of the oily NASA tone. "Hey, why don't we shoot 'em a signal? Greetings to all you Earthlings, I mean, all you little Lunies. Hap-py New Year in the good year whatsis." He snuffles comically. "There is a Santy Claus, Houston, ye-ew nevah saw nothin' like this! Houston, wherever you are," he sings out. "Hey, Houston! Do you read?"

In the silence Lorimer sees Dave's face set into Major Norman Davis, commanding.

And without warning he is suddenly back there, back a year ago in the cramped, shook-up command module of *Sunbird*, coming out from behind the sun. It's the drug doing this, he thinks as memory closes around him, it's so real. Stop. He tries to hang onto reality, to the sense of trouble building underneath.

—But he can't, he is *there*, hovering behind Dave and Bud in the triple couches, as usual avoiding his official station in the middle, seeing beside them their reflections against blackness in the useless port window. The outer layer has been annealed, he can just make out a bright smear that has to be Spica floating through the image of Dave's head, making the bandage look like a kid's crown.

"Houston, Houston, *Sunbird*," Dave repeats; "*Sunbird* calling Houston. Houston, do you read? Come in, Houston."

The minutes start by. They are giving it seven out, seven back; seventy-eight million miles, ample margin.

"The high gain's shot, that's what it is," Bud says cheerfully. He says it almost every day.

"No way." Dave's voice is patient, also as usual. "It checks out. Still too much crap from the sun, isn't that right, Doc?"

"The residual radiation from the flare is just about in line with us," Lorimer says. "They could have a hard time sorting us out." For the thousandth time he registers his own faint, ridiculous gratification at being consulted.

"Shit, we're outside Mercury." Bud shakes his head. "How we gonna find out who won the Series?"

He often says that too. A ritual, out here in eternal night. Lorimer watches the sparkle of Spica drift by the reflection of Bud's curly face-bush. His own whiskers are scant and scraggly, like a blond Fu Manchu. In the aft corner of the window is a striped glare that must be the remains of their port energy accumulators, fried off in the solar explosion that hit them a month ago and fused the outer layers of their windows. That was when Dave cut his head open on the sexlogic panel. Lorimer had been banged in among the gravity wave experiment, he still doesn't trust the readings. Luckily the particle stream has missed one piece of the front window; they still have about twenty degrees of clear vision straight ahead. The brilliant web of the Pleiades shows there, running off into a blur of light.

Twelve minutes ... thirteen. The speaker sighs and clicks emptily. Fourteen. Nothing.

"*Sunbird* to Houston, *Sunbird* to Houston. Come in, Houston. *Sunbird* out." Dave puts the mike back in its holder. "Give it another twenty-four."

They wait ritually. Tomorrow Packard will reply. Maybe.

"Be good to see old Earth again," Bud remarks.

"We're not using any more fuel on attitude," Dave reminds him. "I trust Doc's figures."

It's not my figures, it's the elementary facts of celestial mechanics. Lorimer thinks; in October there's only one place for Earth to be. He never says it. Not to a man who can fly two-body solutions by intuition once he knows where the bodies are. Bud is a good pilot and a better engineer; Dave is the best there is. He takes no pride in it. "The Lord helps us, Doc, if we let Him."

"Going to be a bitch docking if the radar's screwed up," Bud says idly. They all think about that for the hundredth time. It will be a bitch. Dave will do it. That was why he is hoarding fuel.

The minutes tick off.

"That's it," Dave says—and a voice fills the cabin, shockingly.

"Judy?" It is high and clear. A girl's voice.

"Judy, I'm so glad we got you. What are you doing on this band?"

Bud blows out his breath; there is a frozen instant before Dave snatches up the mike.

"*Sunbird*, we read you. This is Mission *Sunbird* calling Houston, ah, *Sunbird One* calling Houston Ground Control. Identify, who are you? Can you relay our signal? Over."

"Some skip," Bud says. "Some incredible ham."

"Are you in trouble, Judy?" the girl's voice asks. "I can't hear, you sound terrible. Wait a minute."

"This is United States Space Mission *Sunbird One*," Dave repeats. "Mission *Sunbird* calling Houston Space Center. You are dee-exxing our channel. Identify, repeat identify yourself and say if you can relay to Houston. Over."

"Dinko, Judy, try it again," the girl says.

Lorimer abruptly pushes himself up to the Lurp, the Long-Range Particle Density Cumulator experiment, and activates its shaft motor. The shaft whines, jars; lucky it was retracted during the flare, lucky it hasn't fused shut. He sets the probe pulse on max and begins a rough manual scan.

"You are intercepting official traffic from the United States space mission to Houston Control," Dave is saying forcefully. "If you cannot relay to Houston get off the air, you are committing a federal offence. Say again, can you relay our signal to Houston Space Center? Over."

"You still sound terrible," the girl says. "What's Houston? Who's talking, anyway? You know we don't have much time." Her voice is sweet but very nasal.

"Jesus, that's close," Bud says. "That is close."

"Hold it." Dave twists around to Lorimer's improvised radarscope.

"There." Lorimer points out a tiny stable peak at the extreme edge of the read-out slot, in the transcoronal scatter. Bud cranes too.

"A bogey!"

"Somebody else out here."

"Hello, hello? We have you now," the girl says. "Why are you so far out? Are you dinko, did you catch the flare?"

"Hold it," warns Dave. "What's the status, Doc?"

"Over three hundred thousand kilometers, guesstimated. Possibly headed away from us, going around the sun. Could be cosmonauts, a Soviet mission?"

"Out to beat us. They missed."

"With a *girl*?" Bud objects.

"They've done that. You taping this, Bud?"

"Roger-r-r." He grins. "That sure didn't sound like a Russky chick. Who the hell's Judy?"

Dave thinks for a second, clicks on the mike. "This is

Major Norman Davis commanding United States spacecraft *Sunbird One*. We have you on scope. Request you identify yourself. Repeat, who are you? Over."

"Judy, stop joking," the voice complains. "We'll lose you in a minute, don't you realise we worried about you?"

"*Sunbird* to unidentified craft. This is not Judy. I say again, this is not Judy. Who are you? Over."

"What—" the girl says, and is cut off by someone saying, "Wait a minute, Ann." The speaker squeals. Then a different woman says, "This is Lorna Bethune in *Escondita*. What is going on here?"

"This is Major Davis commanding United States Mission *Sunbird* on course for Earth. We do not recognise any spacecraft *Escondita*. Will you identify yourself? Over."

"I just did." She sounds older with the same nasal drawl. "There is no spaceship *Sunbird* and you're not on course for Earth. If this is an andy joke it isn't any good."

"This is no joke, madam!" Dave explodes. "This is the American circumsolar mission and we are American astronauts. We do not appreciate your interference. Out."

The woman starts to speak and is drowned in a jibber of static. Two voices come through briefly. Lorimer thinks he hears the words "*Sunbird* program" and something else. Bud works the squelcher; the interference subsides to a drone.

"Ah, Major Davis?" The voice is fainter. "Did I hear you say you are on course for Earth?"

Dave frowns at the speaker and then says curtly, "Affirmative."

"Well, we don't understand your orbit. You must have very unusual flight characteristics, our readings show you won't node with anything on your present course. We'll lose the signal in a minute or two. Ah, would you tell us where you see Earth now? Never mind the coordinates, just tell us the constellation."

Dave hesitates and then holds up the mike. "Doc."

"Earth's apparent position is in Pisces," Lorimer says to the voice. "Approximately three degrees from P. Gamma."

"It is not," the woman says. "Can't you see it's in Virgo? Can't you see out at all?"

Lorimer's eyes go to the bright smear in the port window. "We sustained some damage—"

"Hold it," snaps Dave.

"—to one window during a disturbance we ran into a perihelion. Naturally we know the relative direction of Earth on this date, October nineteen."

"October? It's March, March fifteen. You must—" Her voice is lost in a shriek.

"E-M front," Bud says, tuning. They are all leaning at the speaker from different angles, Lorimer is head-down. Space-noise wails and crashes like surf, the strange ship is too close to the coronal horizon. "—Behind you," they hear. More howls. "Band, try . . . ship . . . if you can, your signal—" Nothing more comes through.

Lorimer pushes back, staring at the spark in the window. It has to be Spica. But it is elongated, as if a second point-source is beside it? Impossible. An excitement is trying to flare out inside him, the women's voices resonate in his head.

"Playback," Dave says. "Houston will really like to hear this."

They listen again to the girl calling Judy, the woman saying she is Lorna Bethune. Bud holds up a finger. "Man's voice in there." Lorimer listens hard for the words he thought he heard. The tape ends.

"Wait till Packard gets this one." Dave rubs his arms. "Remember what they pulled on Howie? Claiming they rescued him."

"Seems like they want us on their frequency." Bud grins. "They must think we're fa-a-ar gone. Hey, looks like this other capsule's going to show up, getting crowded out here."

"If it shows up," Dave says. "Leave it on voice alert, Bud. The batteries will do that."

Lorimer watches the spark of Spica, or Spica-plus-something, wondering if he will ever understand. The casual acceptance of some trick or ploy out here in this incredible loneliness. Well, if these strangers are from the same mold, maybe that is it. Aloud, he says, "*Escondita* is an odd name for a Soviet mission. I believe it means 'hidden' in Spanish."

"Yeah," says Bud. "Hey, I know what that accent is, it's Australian. We had some Aussie bunnies at Hickam. Or-stryle-ya, woo-ee! You s'pose Woomara is sending up some kind of com-bined do?"

Dave shakes his head. "They have no capability whatsoever."

"We ran into some fairly strange phenomena back there, Dave," Lorimer says thoughtfully. "I'm beginning to wish we could take a visual check."

"Did you goof, Doc?"

"No. Earth is where I said, if it's October. Virgo is where it would appear in March."

"Then that's it," Dave grins, pushing out of the couch. "You been asleep five months, Rip van Winkle? Time for a hand before we do the roadwork."

"What I'd like to know is what that chick looks like," says Bud, closing down the transceiver. "Can I help you into your space-suit, Miss? Hey, Miss, pull that in, psst-psst-psst! You going to listen, Doc?"

"Right." Lorimer is getting out his charts. The others go aft through the tunnel to the small day-room, making no further comment on the presence of the strange ship or ships out here. Lorimer himself is more shaken than he likes; it was that damn phrase.

The tedious exercise period comes and goes. Lunchtime: they give the containers a minimum warm to conserve the batteries. Chicken à *la* king again; Bud puts ketchup on his and breaks their usual silence with a funny anecdote about an Australian girl, laboriously censoring himself to conform to *Sunbird's* unwritten code on talk. After lunch Dave goes forward to the command module. Bud and Lorimer continue their current task of checking out the suits and packs for a damage-assessment EVA to take place as soon as the radiation count drops.

They are just clearing away when Dave calls them. Lorimer comes through the tunnel to hear a girl's voice blare, "—dinko trip. What did Lorna say? *Gloria* over!"

He starts up the Lurp and begins scanning. No results this time. "They're either in line behind us or in the sunward quadrant," he reports finally. "I can't isolate them."

Presently the speaker holds another thin thread of sound.

"That could be their ground control," says Dave. "How's the horizon, Doc?"

"Five hours; Northwest Siberia, Japan, Australia."

"I told you the high gain is fucked up." Bud gingerly feeds power to his antenna motor. "Easy, eas-ee. The frame is twisted, that's what it is."

"Don't snap it," Dave says, knowing Bud will not.

The squeaking fades, pulses back. "Hey, we can really use this," Bud says. "We can calibrate on them."

A hard soprano says suddenly "—should be outside your orbit. Try around Beta Aries."

"Another chick. We have a fix," Bud says happily. "We

have a fix now. I do believe our troubles are over. That monkey was torqued one hundred forty-nine degrees. Woo-ee!"

The first girl comes back. "We see them, Margo! But they're so small, how can they live in there? Maybe they're tiny aliens! Over."

"That's Judy," Bud chuckles. "Dave, this is screwy, it's all in English. It has to be some U.N. thingie."

Dave massages his elbows, flexes his fists; thinking. They wait. Lorimer considers a hundred and forty-nine degrees from Gamma Piscium.

In thirteen minutes the voice from Earth says, "Judy, call the others, will you? We're going to play you the conversation, we think you should all hear. Two minutes. Oh, while we're waiting, Zebra wants to tell Connie the baby is fine. And we have a new cow."

"Code," says Dave.

The recording comes on. The three men listen once more to Dave calling Houston in a rattle of solar noise. The transmission clears up rapidly and cuts off with the woman saying that another ship, the *Gloria*, is behind them, closer to the sun.

"We looked up history," the Earth voice resumes. "There was a Major Norman Davis on the first *Sunbird* flight. Major was a military title. Did you hear them say 'Doc'? There was a scientific doctor on board, Doctor Orren Lorimer. The third member was Captain—that's another title—Bernhard Geirr. Just the three of them, all males of course. We think they had an early reaction engine and not too much fuel. The point is, the first *Sunbird* mission was lost in space. They never came out from behind the sun. That was about when the big flares started. Jan thinks they must have been close to one, you heard them say they were damaged."

Dave grunts. Lorimer is fighting excitement like a brush discharge sparkling in his gut.

"Either they are who they say they are or they're ghosts; or they're aliens pretending to be people. Jan says maybe the disruption in those super-flares could collapse the local time dimension. Pluggo. What did you observe there, I mean the highlights?"

Time dimension ... never came back ... Lorimer's mind narrows onto the reality of the two unmoving bearded heads before him, refuses to admit the words he thought he heard: *Before the year two thousand.* The language, he thinks. The language would have to have changed. He feels better.

A deep baritone voice says, "Margo?" In *Sunbird* eyes come alert.

"—like the big one fifty years ago." The man has the accent too. "We were really lucky being right there when it popped. The most interesting part is that we confirmed the gravity turbulence. Periodic but not waves. It's violent, we got pushed around some. Space is under monster stess in those things. We think France's theory that our system is passing through a micro-black-hole cluster looks right so long as one doesn't plonk us."

"France?" Bud mutters. Dave looks at him speculatively.

"It's hard to imagine anything being kicked out in time. But they're here, whatever they are, they're over eight hundred kays outside us scooting out toward Aldebaran. As Lorna said, if they're trying to reach Earth they're in trouble unless they have a lot of spare gees. Should we try to talk to them? Over. Oh, great about the cow. Over again."

"Black holes," Bud whistles softly. "That's one for you, Doc. Was we in a black hole?"

"Not in one or we wouldn't be here." If we are here, Lorimer adds to himself. A micro-black-hole cluster ... what happens when fragments of totally collapsed matter approach each other, or collide, say in the photosphere of a star? Time disruption? Stop it. Aloud he says, "They could be telling us something, Dave."

Dave says nothing. The minutes pass.

Finally the Earth voice comes back, saying that it will try to contact the strangers on their original frequency. Bud glances at Dave, tunes the selector.

"Calling *Sunbird One*?" the girl says slowly through her nose. "This is Luna Central calling Major Norman Davis of *Sunbird One*. We have picked up your conversation with our ship *Escondita*. We are very puzzled as to who you are and how you got here. If you really are *Sunbird One* we think you must have been jumped forward in time when you passed the solar flare." She pronounces it Cockney-style, "toime."

"Our ship *Gloria* is near you, they see you on their radar. We think you may have a serious course problem because you told Lorna you were headed for Earth and you think it is now October with Earth in Pisces. It is not October, it is March fifteen. I repeat, the Earth date—" she says "dyte" "—is March fifteen, time twenty hundred hours. You should be able to see Earth very close to Spica in Virgo. You said your window is damaged. Can't you go out and look? We think you have to make a big course correction. Do you have enough fuel? Do you have a computer? Do you have enough air and water and food? Can we help you? We're listening on this frequency. Luna to *Sunbird One*, come in."

On *Sunbird* nobody stirs. Lorimer struggles against internal eruptions. *Never came back. Jumped forward in time.* The cyst of memories he has schooled himself to suppress bulges up in the lengthening silence. "Aren't you going to answer?"

"Don't be stupid," Dave says.

"Dave. A hundred and forty-nine degrees is the difference between Gamma Piscium and Spica. That transmission is coming from where they say Earth is."

"You goofed."

"I did not goof. It has to be March."

Dave blinks as if a fly is bothering him.

In fifteen minutes the Luna voice runs through the whole thing again, ending "Please, come in."

"Not a tape." Bud unwraps a stick of gum, adding the plastic to the neat wad back of the gyro leads. Lorimer's skin crawls, watching the ambiguous dazzle of Spica. Spica-plus-Earth? Unbelief grips him, rocks him with a complex pang compounded of faces, voices, the sizzle of bacon frying, the creak of his father's wheelchair, chalk on a sunlit blackboard, Ginny's bare legs on the flowered couch, Jenny and Penny running dangerously close to the lawnmower. The girls will be taller now, Jenny is already as tall as her mother. His father is living with Amy in Denver, determined to last till his son gets home. *When I get home.* This has to be insanity. Dave's right; it's a trick, some crazy trick. The language.

Fifteen minutes more; the flat, earnest female voice comes back and repeats it all, putting in more stresses. Dave wears a remote frown, like a man listening to a lousy sports program. Lorimer has the notion he might switch off and propose a hand of gin; wills him to do so. The voice says it will now change frequencies.

Bud tunes back, chewing calmly. This time the voice stumbles on a couple of phrases. It sounds tired.

Another wait; an hour, now. Lorimer's mind holds only the bright point of Spica digging at him. Bud hums a bar of *Yellow Ribbons,* falls silent again.

"Dave," Lorimer says finally, "our antenna is pointed straight at Spica. I don't care if you think I goofed, if Earth is over there we have to change course soon. Look, you can see it could be a double light source. We have to check this out."

Dave says nothing. Bud says nothing but his eyes rove to the port window, back to his instrument panel, to the window again. In the corner of the panel is a polaroid snap of his wife. Patty: a tall, giggling, rump-switching red-head; Lorimer has occasional fantasies about her. Little-girl voice, though. And so tall. . . . Some short men chase tall women; it strikes Lorimer as undignified. Ginny is an inch shorter than he. Their girls will be taller. And Ginny insisted on starting a pregnancy before he left, even though he'll be out of commo. Maybe, maybe a boy, a son—*stop it*. Think about anything. Bud. . . . Does Bud love Patty? Who knows? He loves Ginny. At seventy million miles. . . .

"Judy?" Luna Central or whoever it is says. "They don't answer. You want to try? But listen, we've been thinking. If these people really are from the past this must be very traumatic for them. They could be just realising they'll never see their world again. Myda says these males had children and women they stayed with, they'll miss them terribly. This is exciting for us but it may seem awful to them. They could be too shocked to answer. They could be frightened, maybe they think we're aliens or hallucinations even. See?"

Five seconds later the nearby girl says, "Da, Margo, we were into that too. Dinko. Ah, *Sunbird?* Major Davis of *Sunbird*, are you there? This is Judy Paris in the ship *Gloria*, we're only about a million kay from you, we see you on our screen." She sounds young and excited. "Luna Central has been trying to reach you, we think you're in trouble and we want to help. Please don't be frightened, we're people just like you. We think you're way off course if you want to reach Earth. Are you in trouble? Can we help? If your radio is out can you make any sort of signal? Do you know Old Morse? You'll be off our screen soon, we're truly worried about you. Please reply somehow if you possibly can, *Sunbird,* come in!"

Dave sits impassive. Bud glances at him, at the port window, gazes stolidly at the speaker, his face blank. Lorimer has exhausted surprise, he wants only to reply to the voices. He can manage a rough signal by heterodyning the probe beam. But what then, with them both against him?

The girl's voice tries again determinedly. Finally she says, "Margo, they won't peep. Maybe they're dead? I think they're aliens."

Are we not?, Lorimer thinks. The Luna station comes back with a different, older voice.

"Judy, Myda here, I've had another thought. These people had a very rigid authority code. You remember your history, they peck-ordered everything. You notice Major Davis repeated about being commanding. That's called dominance-submission structure, one of them gave orders and the others did whatever they were told, we don't know quite why. Perhaps they were frightened. The point is that if the dominant one is in shock or panicked maybe the others can't reply unless this Davis lets them."

Jesus Christ, Lorimer thinks. Jesus H. Christ in colors. It is his father's expression for the inexpressible. Dave and Bud sit unstirring.

"How weird," the Judy voice says. "But don't they know they're on a bad course? I mean, could the dominant one make the others fly right out of the system? Truly?"

It's happened, Lorimer thinks; it has happened. I have to stop this. I have to act now, before they lose us. Desperate visions of himself defying Dave and Bud loom before him. Try persuasion first.

Just as he opens his mouth he sees Bud stir slightly, and with immeasurable gratitude hears him say, "Dave-o, what say we take an eyeball look? One little old burp won't hurt us."

Dave's head turns a degree or two.

"Or should I go out and see, like the chick said?" Bud's voice is mild.

After a long minute Dave says neutrally, "All right. . . . Attitude change." His arm moves up as though heavy; he starts methodically setting in the values for the vector that will bring Spica in line with their functional window.

Now why couldn't I have done that, Lorimer asks himself for the thousandth time, following the familiar check sequence. Don't answer. . . . And for the thousandth time he is obscurely moved by the rightness of them. The authentic ones, the alphas. Their bond. The awe he had felt first for the absurd jocks of his school ball team.

"That's go, Dave, assuming nothing got creamed."

Dave throws the ignition safety, puts the computer on real time. The hull shudders. Everything in the cabin drifts sidewise while the bright point of Spica swims the other way, appears on the front window as the retros cut in. When the star creeps out onto clear glass Lorimer can clearly see its companion. The double light steadies there; a beautiful job. He hands Bud the telescope.

"The one on the left."

Bud looks. "There she is, all right. Hey, Dave, look at that!"

He puts the scope in Dave's hand. Slowly, Dave raises it and looks. Lorimer can hear him breathe. Suddenly Dave pulls up the mike.

"Houston!" he says harshly. "*Sunbird* to Houston, *Sunbird* calling Houston. Houston, come in!"

Into the silence the speaker squeals, "They fired their engines—wait, she's calling!" And shuts up.

In *Sunbird*'s cabin nobody speaks. Lorimer stares at the twin stars ahead, impossible realities shifting around him as the minutes congeal. Bud's reflected face looks downwards, grin gone. Dave's beard moves silently; praying, Lorimer realises. Alone of the crew Dave is deeply religious; at Sunday meals he gives a short, dignified grace. A shocking pity for Dave rises in Lorimer; Dave is so deeply involved with his family, his four sons, always thinking about their training, taking them hunting, fishing, camping. And Doris his wife so incredibly active and sweet, going on their trips, cooking and doing things for the community. Driving Penny and Jenny to classes while Ginny was sick that time. Good people, the backbone. . . . This can't be, he thinks; Packard's voice is going to come through in a minute, the antenna's beamed right now. Six minutes now. This will all go away. *Before the year two thousand*—stop it, the language would have changed. Think of Doris. . . . She has that glow, feeding her five men; women with sons are different. But Ginny, but his dear woman, his *wife*, his *daughters*—grandmothers now? All dead and dust? *Quit that.* Dave is still praying. . . . Who knows what goes on inside those heads? Dave's cry. . . . Twelve minutes, it has to be all right. The second sweep is stuck, no, it's moving. Thirteen. It's all insane, a dream. Thirteen plus. . . . fourteen. The speaker hissing and clicking vacantly. Fifteen now. A dream. . . . Or are those women staying off, letting us see? Sixteen. . . .

At twenty Dave's hand moves, stops again. The seconds jitter by, space crackles. Thirty minutes coming up.

"Calling Major Davis in *Sunbird?*" It is the older woman, a gentle voice. "This is Luna Central. We are the service and communication facility for space flight now. We're sorry to have to tell you that there is no space center at Houston any more. Houston itself was abandoned when the shuttle base moved to White Sands, over two centuries ago."

A cool dust-colored light enfolds Lorimer's brain, isolating it. He will remain so a long time.

The woman is explaining it all again, offering help, asking if they were hurt. A nice dignified speech. Dave still sits immobile, gazing at Earth. Bud puts the mike in his hand.

"Tell them, Dave-o."

Dave looks at it, takes a deep breath, presses the send button.

"*Sunbird* to Luna Control," he says quite normally. (It's "Central," Lorimer thinks.) "We copy. Ah, negative on life support, we have no problems. We copy the course change suggestion and are proceeding to recompute. Your offer of computer assistance is appreciated. We suggest you transmit position data so we can get squared away. Ah, we are economising on transmission until we see how our accumulators have held up. *Sunbird* out."

And so it had begun.

Lorimer's mind floats back to himself now floating in *Gloria*, nearly a year, or three hundred years, later; watching and being watched by them. He still feels light, contented; the dread underneath has come no nearer. But it is so silent. He seems to have heard no voices for a long time. Or was it a long time? Maybe the drug is working on his time sense, maybe it was only a minute or two.

"I've been remembering," he says to the woman Connie, wanting her to speak.

She nods. "You have so much to remember. Oh, I'm sorry—that wasn't good to say." Her eyes speak sympathy.

"Never mind." It is all dreamlike now, his lost world and this other which he is just now seeing plain. "We must seem like very strange beasts to you."

"We're trying to understand," she says. "It's history, you learn the events but you don't really feel what the people were like, how it was for them. We hope you'll tell us."

The drug, Lorimer thinks, that's what they're trying. Tell them . . . how can he? Could a dinosaur tell how it was? A montage flows through his mind, dominated by random shots of Operations' north parking lot and Ginny's yellow kitchen telephone with the sickly ivy vines. . . . Women and vines. . . .

A burst of laughter distracts him. It's coming from the chamber they call the gym, Bud and the others must be playing ball in there. Bright idea, really, he muses: Using muscle power, sustained mild exercise. That's why they are all so fit. The gym is a glorified squirrel-wheel, when you climb or pedal up the walls it revolves and winds a gear train, which among other things rotates the sleeping drum. A real Woolagong. . . . Bud and Dave usually take their shifts together, scrambling the spinning gym like big pale apes. Lorimer prefers the easy rhythm of the woman, and the cycle here fits him nicely. He usually puts in his shift with Connie, who doesn't talk much, and one of the Judys, who do.

No one is talking now, though. Remotely uneasy he looks around the big cylinder of the cabin, sees Dave and Lady Blue by the forward window. Judy Dakar is behind them, silent for once. They must be looking at Earth; it has been a beautiful expanding disk for some weeks now. Dave's beard is moving, he is praying again. He has taken to doing that, not ostentatiously, but so obviously sincere that Lorimer, a life atheist, can only sympathise.

The Judys have asked Dave what he whispers, of course. When Dave understood that they had no concept of prayer and had never seen a Christian Bible there had been a heavy silence.

"So you have lost all faith," he said finally.

"We have faith," Judy Paris protested.

"May I ask in what?"

"We have faith in ourselves, of course," she told him.

"Young lady, if you were my daughter I'd tan your britches," Dave said, not joking. The subject was not raised again.

But he came back so well after that first dreadful shock, Lorimer thinks. A personal god, a father-model, man needs that. Dave draws strength from it and we lean on him. Maybe leaders have to believe. Dave was so great; cheerful, unflappable, patiently working out alternatives, making his decisions on the inevitable discrepancies in the position readings in a way Lorimer couldn't do. A bitch. . . .

Memory takes him again; he is once again back in *Sunbird*, gritty-eyed, listening to the women's chatter, Dave's terse replies. God, how they chattered. But their computer work checks out. Lorimer is suffering also from a quirk of Dave's, his reluctance to transmit their exact thrust and fuel reserve. He keeps holding out a margin and making Lorimer compute it back in.

But the margins don't help; it is soon clear that they are in big trouble. Earth will pass too far ahead of them on their orbit, they don't have the acceleration to catch up with her before they cross her path. They can carry out an ullage manoeuver, they can kill enough velocity to let Earth catch them on the second go-by; but that would take an extra year and their life-support would be long gone. The grim question of whether they have enough to enable a single man to wait it out pushes into Lorimer's mind. He pushes it back; that one is for Dave.

There is a final possibility: Venus will approach their trajectory three months hence and they may be able to gain velocity by swinging by it. They go to work on that.

Meanwhile Earth is steadily drawing away from them and so is *Gloria*, closer toward the sun. They pick her out of the solar interference and then lose her again. They know her crew now: the man is Andy Kay, the senior woman is Lady Blue Parks; they appear to do the navigating. Then there is a Connie Morelos and the two twins, Judy Paris and Judy Dakar, who run the communications. The chief Luna voices are women too, Margo and Azella. The men can hear them talking to the *Escondita* which is now swinging in toward the far side of the sun. Dave insists on monitoring and taping everything that comes through. It proves to be largely replays of their exchanges with Luna and *Gloria*, mixed with a variety of highly personal messages. As references to cows, chickens and other livestock multiply Dave reluctantly gives up his idea that they are code. Bud counts a total of five male voices.

"Big deal," he says. "There were more chick drivers on the road when we left. Means space is safe now, the girlies have taken over. Let them sweat their little asses off." He chuckles. "When we get this bird down, the stars ain't gonna study old Buddy no more, no ma'am. A nice beach and about a zillion steaks and ale and all those sweet things. Hey, we'll be living history, we can charge admission."

Dave's face takes on the expression that means an inappropriate topic has been breached. Much to Lorimer's impatience, Dave discourages all speculation as to what may await them on this future Earth. He confines their transmissions strictly to the problem in hand; when Lorimer tries to get him at least to mention the unchanged-language puzzle Dave only says firmly, "Later." Lorimer fumes; inconceivable that he is three centuries in the future, unable to learn a thing.

They do glean a few facts from the women's talk. There have been nine successful *Sunbird* missions after theirs and one other casualty. And the *Gloria* and her sister ship are on a long-planned fly-by of the two inner planets.

"We always go along in pairs" Judy says. "But those planets are no good. Still, it was worth seeing."

"For Pete's sake Dave, ask them how many planets have been visited," Lorimer pleads.

"Later."

But about the fifth meal-break Luna suddenly volunteers.

"Earth is making up a history for you, *Sunbird*," the Margo voice says. "We know you don't want to waste power asking so we thought we'd send you a few main points right now." She laughs. "It's much harder than we thought, nobody here does history."

Lorimer nods to himself; he has been wondering what he could tell a man from 1690 who would want to know what happened to Cromwell—was Cromwell then?—and who had never heard of electricity, atoms or the U.S.A.

"Let's see, probably the most important is that there aren't as many people as you had, we're just over two million. There was a world epidemic not long after your time. It didn't kill people but it reduced the population. I mean there weren't any babies in most of the world. Ah, sterility. The country called Australia was affected least." Bud holds up a finger.

"And North Canada wasn't too bad. So the survivors all got together in the south part of the American states where they could grow food and the best communications and factories were. Nobody lives in the rest of the world but we travel there sometimes. Ah, we have five main activities, was industries the word? Food, that's farming and fishing. Communications, transport, and space—that's us. And the factories they need. We live a lot simpler than you did, I think. We see your things all over, we're very grateful to you. Oh, you'll be interested to know we use zeppelins just like you did, we have six big ones. And our fifth thing is the children. Babies. Does that help? I'm using a children's book we have here."

The men have frozen during this recital; Lorimer is holding a cooling bag of hash. Bud starts chewing again and chokes.

"Two million people and a space capability?" He coughs. "That's incredible."

Dave gazes reflectively at the speaker. "There's a lot they're not telling us."

"I gotta ask them," Bud says. "Okay?"

Dave nods. "Watch it."

"Thanks for the history, Luna," Bud says. "We really appreciate it. But we can't figure out how you maintain a space program with only a couple of million people. Can you tell us a little more on that?"

In the pause Lorimer tries to grasp the staggering figures. From eight billion to two million ... Europe, Asia, Africa, South America, America itself—wiped out. *There weren't any more babies.* World sterility, from what? The Black Death, the famines of Asia—those had been decimations. This is magnitudes worse. No, it is all the same: beyond comprehension. An empty world, littered with junk.

"Sunbird?" says Margo, "Da, I should have thought you'd want to know about space. Well, we have only the four real spaceships and one building. You know the two here. Then there's *Indira* and *Pech*, they're on the Mars run now. Maybe the Mars dome was since your day. You had the satellite stations though, didn't you? And the old Luna dome, of course—I remember now, it was during the epidemic. They tried to set up colonies to, ah, breed children, but the epidemic got there too. They struggled terribly hard. We owe a lot to you really, you men I mean. The history has it all, how you worked out a minimal viable program and trained everybody and saved it from the crazies. It was a glorious achievement. Oh, the Marker here has one of your names on it. Lorimer. We love to keep it all going and growing, we all love travelling. Man is a rover, that's one of our mottoes."

"Are you hearing what I'm hearing?" Bud asks, blinking comically.

Dave is still staring at the speaker. "Not one word about their government," he says slowly. "Not a word about economic conditions. We're talking to a bunch of monkeys."

"Should I ask them?"

"Wait a minute ... Roger, ask the name of their chief of state and the head of the space program. And—no, that's all."

"President?" Margo echoes Bud's query. "You mean like queens and kings? Wait, here's Myda. She's been talking about you with Earth."

The older woman they hear occasionally says *"Sunbird?* Da, we realise you had a very complex activity, your governments. With so few people we don't have that type of formal structure at all. People from the different activities meet periodically and our communications are good, everyone is kept informed. The people in each activity are in charge of doing it while they're there. We rotate, you see. Mostly in five-year hitches, for example Margo here was on the zeppelins and I've been on several factories and farms and of course the, well, the education, we all do that. I believe that's one big difference from you. And of course we all work. And things are basically far more stable now, I gather. We change slowly. Does that answer you? Of course you can always ask Registry, they keep track of us all. But we can't, ah, take you to our leader, if that's what you mean." She laughs, a genuine, jolly sound. "That's one of our old jokes. I must say," she goes on seriously, "it's been a joy to us that we can understand you so well. We make a big effort not to let the language drift, it would be tragic to lose touch with the past."

Dave takes the mike. "Thank you, Luna. You've given us something to think about. *Sunbird* out."

"How much of that is for real, Doc?" Bud rubs his curly head. "They're giving us one of your science fiction stories."

"The real story will come later," says Dave. "Our job is to get there."

"That's a point that doesn't look too good."

By the end of the session it looks worse. No Venus trajectory is any good. Lorimer reruns all the computations; same result.

"There doesn't seem to be any solution to this one, Dave," he says at last. "The parameters are just too tough. I think we've had it."

Dave massages his knuckles thoughtfully. Then he nods. "Roger. We'll fire the optimum sequence on the Earth heading."

"Tell them to wave if they see us go by," says Bud.

They are silent, contemplating the prospect of a slow death in space eighteen months hence. Lorimer wonders if he can raise the other question, the bad one. He is pretty sure what Dave will say. What will he himself decide, what will he have the guts to do?

"Hello, *Sunbird*?" the voice of *Gloria* breaks in. "Listen, we've been figuring. We think if you use all your fuel you could come back in close enough to our orbit so we could swing out and pick you up. You'd be using solar gravity that way. We have plenty of manoeuver but much less acceleration than you do. You have suits and some kind of propellants, don't you? I mean, you could fly across a few kays?"

The three men look at each other; Lorimer guesses he had not been the only one to speculate on that.

"That's a good thought, *Gloria*," Dave says. "Let's hear what Luna says."

"Why?" asks Judy. "It's our business, we wouldn't endanger the ship. We'd only miss another look at Venus, who cares. We have plenty of water and food and if the air gets a little smelly we can stand it."

"Hey, the chicks are all right," Bud says. They wait.

The voice of Luna comes on. "We've been looking at that too, Judy. We're not sure you understand the risk. Ah, *Sunbird*, excuse me. Judy, if you manage to pick them up you'll have to spend nearly a year in the ship with these three male persons from a *very different culture*. Myda says you should remember history and it's a risk no matter what Connie says. *Sunbird*, I hate to be so rude. Over."

Bud is grinning broadly, they all are. "Cave men," he chuckles. "All the chicks land preggers."

"Margo, they're human beings," the Judy voice protests. "This isn't just Connie, we're all agreed. Andy and Lady Blue say it would be very interesting. If it works, that is. We can't let them go without trying."

"We feel that way too, of course," Luna replies. "But there's another problem. They could be carrying diseases. *Sunbird*, I know you've been isolated for fourteen months, but Murti says people in your day were immune to organisms that aren't around now. Maybe some of ours could harm you, too. You could all get mortally sick and lose the ship."

"We thought of that, Margo," Judy says impatiently. "Look, if you have contact with them at all somebody has to test, true? So we're ideal. By the time we get home you'll know. And how could we get sick so fast we couldn't put *Gloria* in a stable orbit where you could get her later on?"

They wait. "Hey, what about that epidemic?" Bud pats his hair elaborately. "I don't know if I want a career in gay lib."

"You rather stay out here?" Dave asks.

"Crazies," says a different voice from Luna. "*Sunbird*, I'm Murti, the health person here. I think what we have to fear most is the meningitis-influenza complex, they mutate so readily. Does your Doctor Lorimer have any suggestions?"

"Roger, I'll put him on," says Dave. "But as to your first point, madam, I want to inform you that at time of takeoff the incidence of rape in the United States space cadre was zero point zero. I guarantee the conduct of my crew provided you can control yours. Here is Doctor Lorimer."

But Lorimer can not of course tell them anything useful. They discuss the men's polio shots, which luckily have used killed virus, and various childhood diseases which still seem to be around. He does not mention their epidemic.

"Luna, we're going to try it," Judy declares. "We couldn't live with ourselves. Now let's get the course figured before they get any farther away."

From there on there is no rest on *Sunbird* while they set up and refigure and rerun the computations for the envelope of possible intersecting trajectories. The *Gloria*'s drive, they learn, is indeed low-thrust, although capable of sustained operation. *Sunbird* will have to get most of the way to the rendez-vous on her own if they can cancel their outward velocity.

The tension breaks once during the long session, when Luna calls *Gloria* to warn Connie to be sure the female crew members wear concealing garments at all times if the men came aboard.

"Not suit-liners, Connie, they're much too tight." It is the older woman, Myda. Bud chuckles.

"Your light sleepers, I think. And when the men unsuit, your Andy is the only one who should help them. You others stay away. The same for all body functions and sleeping. This is very important, Connie, you'll have to watch it the whole way home. There are a great many complicated taboos. I'm putting an instruction list on the bleeper, is your receiver working?"

"Da, we used it for France's black hole paper."

"Good. Tell Judy to stand by. Now listen, Connie, listen carefully. Tell Andy he has to read it all. I repeat, *he* has to read every word. Did you hear that?"

"Ah, dinko," Connie answers. "I understand, Myda. He will."

"I think we just lost the ball game, fellas," Bud laments. "Old mother Myda took it all away."

Even Dave laughs. But later when the modulated squeal that is a whole text comes through the speaker, he frowns again. "There goes the good stuff."

The last factors are cranked in; the revised program spins, and Luna confirms them. "We have a pay-out, Dave," Lorimer reports. "It's tight but there are at least two viable options. Provided the main jets are fully functional."

"We're going EVA to check."

That is exhausting; they find a warp in the deflector housing of the port engines and spend four sweating hours trying to wrestle it back. It is only Lorimer's third sight of open space but he is soon too tired to care.

"Best we can do," Dave pants finally. "We'll have to compensate in the psychic mode."

"You can do it, Dave-o," says Bud. "Hey, I gotta change those suit radios, don't let me forget."

In the psychic mode . . . Lorimer surfaces back to his real self, cocooned in *Gloria*'s big cluttered cabin, seeing Connie's living face. It must be hours, how long has he been dreaming?

"About two minutes," Connie smiles.

"I was thinking of the first time I saw you."

"Oh yes. We'll never forget that, ever."

Nor will he . . . He lets it unroll again in his head. The interminable hours after the first long burn, which has sent *Sunbird* yawing so they all have to gulp nausea pills. Judy's breathless voice reading down their approach: "Oh, very good, four hundred thousand . . . Oh, great, *Sunbird*, you're almost three, you're going to break a hundred for sure—" Dave has done it, the big one.

Lorimer's probe is useless in the yaw, it isn't until they stabilise enough for the final burst that they can see the strange blip bloom and vanish in the slot. Converging, hopefully, on a theoretical near-intersection point.

"Here goes everything."

The final burn changes the yaw into a sickening tumble with the starfield looping past the glass. The pills are no more use and the fuel feed to the attitude jets goes sour. They are all vomiting before they manage to hand-pump the last of the fuel and slow the tumble.

"That's it, *Gloria*. Come and get us. Lights on, Bud. Let's get those suits up."

Fighting nausea they go through the laborious routine in the fouled cabin. Suddenly Judy's voice sings out, "We see you, *Sunbird*! We see your light! Can't you see us?"

"No time," Dave says. But Bud, half-suited, points at the window. "Fellas, oh, hey, look at that."

Lorimer stares, thinks he sees a faint spark between the whirling stars before he has to retch.

"Father, we thank you," says Dave quietly. "All right, move it on, Doc. Packs."

The effort of getting themselves plus the propulsion units and a couple of cargo nets out of the rolling ship drives everything else out of mind. It isn't until they are floating linked together and stabilised by Dave's hand jet that Lorimer has time to look.

The sun blanks out their left. A few meters below them *Sunbird* tumbles empty, looking absurdly small. Ahead of them, infinitely far away, is a point too blurred and yellow to be a star. It creeps: *Gloria,* on her approach tangent.

"Can you start, *Sunbird?*" says Judy in their helmets. "We don't want to brake any more on account of our exhaust. We estimage fifty kay in an hour, we're coming out on a line."

"Roger. Give me your jet, Doc."

"Goodbye, *Sunbird,*" says Bud. "Plenty of lead, Dave-o."

Lorimer finds it restful in a childish way, being towed across the abyss tied to the two big men. He has total confidence in Dave, he never considers the possibility that they will miss, sail by and be lost. Does Dave feel contempt? Lorimer wonders; that banked-up silence, is it partly contempt for those who can manipulate only symbols, who have no mastery of matter?... He concentrates on mastering his stomach.

It is a long, dark trip. *Sunbird* shrinks to a twinkling light, slowly accelerating on the spiral course that will end her ultimately in the sun with her precious records that are three hundred years obsolete. With, also, the packet of photos and letters that Lorimer has twice put in his suit-pouch and twice taken out. Now and then he catches sight of *Gloria,* growing from a blur to an incomprehensible tangle of lighted crescents.

"Woo-ee, it's big," Bud says. "No wonder they can't accelerate, that thing is a flying trailer park. I'd break up."

"It's a space ship. Got those nets tight, Doc?"

Judy's voice suddenly fills their helmets. "I see your lights! Can you see me? Will you have enough left to brake at all?"

"Affirmative to both, *Gloria,*" says Dave.

At that moment Lorimer is turned slowly forward again and he sees—will see it forever: the alien ship in the starfield and on its dark side the tiny lights that are women in the stars, waiting for them. Three—no, four; one suit-light is way out, moving. If that is a tether it must be over a kilometer.

"Hello, I'm Judy Dakar!" The voice is close. "Oh, mother, you're big! Are you all right? How's your air?"

"No problem."

They are in fact stale and steaming wet; too much adrenalin. Dave uses the jets again and suddenly she is growing, is coming right at them, a silvery spider on a training thread. Her suit looks trim and flexible; it is mirror-bright, and the pack is quite small. Marvels of the future, Lorimer thinks; Paragraph One.

"You made it, you made it! Here, tie in. Brake!"

"There ought to be some historic words," Bud murmurs. "If she gives us a chance."

"Hello, Judy," says Dave calmly. "Thanks for coming."

"Contact!" She blasts their ears. "Haul us in, Andy! Brake, brake—the exhaust is back there!"

And they are grabbed hard, deflected into a great arc toward the ship. Dave uses up the last jet. The line loops.

"Don't jerk it," Judy cries. "Oh, I'm *sorry*." She is clinging on them like a gibbon, Lorimer can see her eyes, her excited mouth. Incredible. "Watch out, it's slack."

"Teach me, honey," says Andy's baritone. Lorimer twists and sees him far back at the end of a heavy tether, hauling them smoothly in. Bud offers to help, is refused. "Just hang loose, please," a matronly voice tells them. It is obvious Andy has done this before. They come in spinning slowly, like space fish. Lorimer finds he can no longer pick out the twinkle that is *Sunbird*. When he is swung back, *Gloria* has changed to a disorderly cluster of bulbs and spokes around a big central cylinder. He can see pods and miscellaneous equipment stowed all over her. Not like science fiction.

Andy is paying the line into a floating coil. Another figure floats beside him. They are both quite short, Lorimer realises as they near.

"Catch the cable," Andy tells them. There is a busy moment of shifting inertial drag.

"Welcome to *Gloria*, Major Davis, Captain Geirr, Doctor Lorimer. I'm Lady Blue Parks. I think you'll like to get inside as soon as possible. If you feel like climbing go right ahead, we'll pull all this in later."

"We appreciate it, Ma'm."

They start hand-over-hand along the catenary of the main tether. It has a good rough grip. Judy coasts up to peer at them, smiling broadly, towing the coil. A taller figure waits by the ship's open airlock.

"Hello, I'm Connie. I think we can cycle in two at a time. Will you come with me, Major Davis?"

It is like an emergency on a plane, Lorimer thinks as Dave

follows her in. Being ordered about by supernaturally polite little girls.

"Space-going stews," Bud nudges him. "How 'bout that?" His face is sprouting sweat. Lorimer tells him to go next, his own LSP has less load.

Bud goes in with Andy. The woman named Lady Blue waits beside Lorimer while Judy scrambles on the hull securing their cargo nets. She doesn't seem to have magnetic soles; perhaps ferrous metals aren't used in space now. When she begins hauling in the main tether on a simple hand winch Lady Blue looks at it critically.

"I used to make those," she says to Lorimer. What he can see of her features looks compressed, her dark eyes twinkle. He has the impression she is part Black.

"I ought to get over and clean that aft antenna." Judy floats up. "Later," says Lady Blue. They both smile at Lorimer. Then the hatch opens and he and Lady Blue go in. When the toggles seat there comes a rising scream of air and Lorimer's suit collapses.

"Can I help you?" She has opened her faceplate, the voice is rich and live. Eagerly Lorimer catches the latches in his clumsy gloves and lets her lift the helmet off. His first breath surprises him, it takes an instant to identify the gas as fresh air. Then the inner hatch opens, letting in greenish light. She waves him through. He swims into a short tunnel. Voices are coming from around the corner ahead. His hand finds a grip and he stops, feeling his heart shudder in his chest.

When he turns that corner the world he knows will be dead. Gone, rolled up, blown away forever with *Sunbird*. He will be irrevocably in the future. A man from the past, a time traveller. In the future. . . .

He pulls himself around the bend.

The future is a vast bright cylinder, its whole inner surface festooned with unidentifiable objects, fronds of green. In front of him floats an odd tableau: Bud and Dave, helmets off, looking enormous in their bulky white suits and packs. A few meters away hang two bare-headed figures in shiny suits and a dark-haired girl in flowing pink pajamas.

They are all simply staring at the two men, their eyes and mouths open in identical expressions of pleased wonder. The face that has to be Andy's is grinning open-mouthed like a kid at the zoo. He is a surprisingly young boy, Lorimer sees, in spite of his deep voice; blond, downy-cheeked, compactly muscular. Lorimer finds he can scarcely bear to look at the pink woman, can't tell if she really is surpassingly beautiful or plain. The taller suited woman has a shiny, ordinary face.

From overhead bursts an extraordinary sound which he finally recognises as a chicken cackling. Lady Blue pushes past him.

"All right, Andy, Connie, stop staring and help them get their suits off. Judy, Luna is just as eager to hear about this as we are."

The tableau jumps to life. Afterwards Lorimer can recall mostly eyes, bright curious eyes tugging his boots, smiling eyes up-side-down over his pack—and always that light, ready laughter. Andy is left alone to help them peel down, blinking at the fittings which Lorimer still finds embarrassing. He seems easy and nimble in his own half-open suit. Lorimer struggles out of the last lacings, thinking, a boy! A boy and four women orbiting the sun, flying their big junky ships to Mars. Should he feel humiliated? He only feels grateful, accepting a short robe and a bulb of tea somebody—Connie?—gives him.

The suited Judy comes in with their nets. The men follow Andy along another passage, Bud and Dave clutching at the small robes. Andy stops by a hatch.

"This greenhouse is for you, it's your toilet. Three's a lot but you have full sun."

Inside is a brilliant jungle, foliage everywhere, glittering water droplets, rustling leaves. Something whirs away—a grasshopper.

"You crank that handle." Andy points to a seat on a large cross-duct. "The piston rams the gravel and waste into a compost process and it ends up in the soil core. That vetch is a heavy nitrogen user and a great oxidator. We pump CO_2 in and oxy out. It's a real Woolagong."

He watches critically while Bud tries out the facility.

"What's a Woolagong?" asks Lorimer dazedly.

"Oh, she's one of our inventors. Some of her stuff is weird. When we have a pluggy-looking thing that works we call it a Woolagong." He grins. "The chickens eat the seeds and the hoppers, see, and the hoppers and iguanas eat the leaves. When a greenhouse is going darkside we turn them in to harvest. With this much light I think we could keep a goat, don't you? You don't have any life at all on your ship, true?"

"No," Lorimer says, "not a single iguana."

"They promised us a Shetland pony for Christmas," says Bud, rattling gravel. Andy joins perplexedly in the laugh.

Lorimer's head is foggy; it isn't only fatigue, the year in *Sunbird* has atrophied his ability to take in novelty. Numbly he uses the Woolagong and they go back out and forward to *Gloria*'s big control room, where Dave makes a neat short speech to Luna and is answered graciously.

"We have to finish changing course now," Lady Blue says. Lorimer's impression has been right, she is a small light part-Negro in late middle age. Connie is part something exotic too, he sees; the others are European types.

"I'll get you something to eat," Connie smiles warmly. "Then you probably want to rest. We saved all the cubbies for you." She says "syved"; their accents are all identical.

As they leave the control room Lorimer sees the withdrawn look in Dave's eyes and knows he must be feeling the reality of being a passenger in an alien ship; not in command, not deciding the course, the communications going on unheard.

That is Lorimer's last coherent observation, that and the taste of the strange, good food. And then being led aft through what he now knows is the gym, to the shaft of the sleeping drum. There are six irised ports like dog-doors; he pushes through his assigned port and finds himself facing a roomy mattress. Shelves and a desk are in the wall.

"For your excretions." Connie's arm comes through the iris, pointing at bags. "If you have a problem stick your head out and call. There's water."

Lorimer simply drifts toward the mattress, too sweated out to reply. His drifting ends in a curious heavy settling and his final astonishment: the drum is smoothly, silently starting to revolve. He sinks gratefully onto the pad, growing "heavier" as the minutes pass. About a tenth gee, maybe more, he thinks, it's still accelerating. And falls into the most restful sleep he has known in the long weary year.

It isn't till next day that he understands that Connie and two others have been on the rungs of the gym chamber, sending it around hour after hour without pause or effort and chatting as they went.

How they talk, he thinks again floating back to real present time. The bubbling irritant pours through his memory, the voices of Ginny and Jenny and Penny on the kitchen telephone, before that his mother's voice, his sister Amy's interminable. What do they always have to talk, talk, talk of?

"Why, everything," says the real voice of Connie beside him now, "it's natural to share."

"Natural. . . ." Like ants, he thinks. They twiddle their antennae together every time they meet. Where did you go, what did you do? Twiddle-twiddle. How do you *feel*? Oh, I feel this, I feel that, blah blah twiddle-twiddle. Total coordination of the hive. Women have no self-respect. Say anything, no sense of the strategy of words, the dark danger of naming. Can't hold in.

"Ants, bee-hives," Connie laughs, showing the bad tooth. "You truly see us as insects, don't you? Because they're females?"

"Was I talking aloud? I'm sorry." He blinks away dreams.

"Oh, please don't be. It's so sad to hear about your sister and your children and you, your wife. They must have been wonderful people. We think you're very brave."

But he has only thought of Ginny and them all for an instant—what has he been babbling? What is the drug doing to him?

"What are you doing to us?" he demands, lanced by real alarm now, almost angry.

"It's all right, truly." Her hand touches his, warm and somehow shy. "We all use it when we need to explore something. Usually it's pleasant. It's a laevonoramine compound, a disinhibitor, it doesn't dull you like alcohol. We'll be home so soon, you see. We have the responsibility to understand and you're so locked in." Her eyes melt at him. "You don't feel sick, do you? We have the antidote."

"No . . ." His alarm has already flowed away somewhere. Her explanation strikes him as reasonable enough. "We're not locked in," he says or tries to say. "We talk . . ." He gropes for a word to convey the judiciousness, the adult restraint. Objectivity, maybe? "We talk when we have something to say." Irrelevantly he thinks of a mission coordinator named Forrest, famous for his blue jokes. "Otherwise it would all break down," he tells her. "You'd fly right out of the system." That isn't quite what he means; let it pass.

The voices of Dave and Bud ring out suddenly from opposite ends of the cabin, awakening the foreboding of evil in his mind. They don't know us, he thinks. They should look out, stop this. But he is feeling too serene, he wants to think about his own new understanding, the pattern of them all he is seeing at last.

"I feel lucid," he manages to say, "I want to think."

She looks pleased. "We call that the ataraxia effect. It's so nice when it goes that way."

Ataraxia, philosophical calm. Yes. But there are monsters

in the deep, he thinks or says. The night side. The night side of Orren Lorimer, a self hotly dark and complex, waiting in leash. They're so vulnerable. They don't know we can take them. Images rush up: a Judy spread-eagled on the gym rungs, pink pajamas gone, open to him. Flash sequence of the three of them taking over the ship, the women tied up, helpless, shrieking, raped and used. The team—get the satellite station, get a shuttle down to Earth. Hostages. Make them do anything, no defense whatever . . . Has Bud actually said that? But Bud doesn't know, he remembers. Dave knows they're hiding something, but he thinks it's socialism or sin. When they find out. . . .

How has he himself found out? Simply listening, really, all these months. He listens to their talk much more than the others; "fraternising," Dave calls it. . . . They all listened at first, of course. Listened and looked and reacted helplessly to the female bodies, the tender bulges so close under the thin, tantalising clothes, the magnetic mouths and eyes, the smell of them, their electric touch. Watching them touch each other, touch Andy, laughing, vanishing quietly into shared bunks. *What goes on? Can I? My need, my need—*

The power of them, the fierce resentment. . . . Bud muttered and groaned meaningfully despite Dave's warnings. He kept needling Andy until Dave banned all questions. Dave himself was noticeably tense and read his Bible a great deal. Lorimer found his own body pointing after them like a famished hound, hoping to Christ the cubicles are as they appeared to be, unwired.

All they learn is that Myda's instructions must have been ferocious. The atmosphere has been implacably antiseptic, the discretion impenetrable. Andy politely ignored every probe. No word or act has told them what, if anything, goes on; Lorimer was irresistibly reminded of the weekend he spent at Jenny's scout camp. The men's training came presently to their rescue, and they resigned themselves to finishing their mission on a super-*Sunbird*, weirdly attended by a troop of Boy and Girl Scouts.

In every other way their reception couldn't be more courteous. They have been given the run of the ship and their own dayroom in a cleaned-out gravel storage pod. They visit the control room as they wish. Lady Blue and Andy give them specs and manuals and show them every circuit and device of *Gloria*, inside and out. Luna has bleeped up a stream of science texts and the data on all their satellites and shuttles and the Mars and Luna dome colonies.

Dave and Bud plunged into an orgy of engineering. *Gloria* is, as they suspected, powered by a fission plant that uses a range of Lunar minerals. Her ion drive is only slightly advanced over the experimental models of their own day. The marvels of the future seem so far to consist mainly of ingenious modifications.

"It's primitive," Bud tells him. "What they've done is sacrifice everything to keep it simple and easy to maintain. Believe it, they can hand-feed fuel. And the backups, brother! They have redundant redundancy."

But Lorimer's technical interest soon flags. What he really wants is to be alone a while. He makes a desultory attempt to survey the apparently few new developments in his field, and finds he can't concentrate. What the hell, he tells himself, I stopped being a physicist three hundred years ago. Such a relief to be out of the cell of *Sunbird*; he has given himself up to drifting solitary through the warren of the ship, using their excellent 400 mm telescope, noting the odd life of the crew.

When he finds that Lady Blue likes chess they form a routine of bi-weekly games. Her personality intrigues him; she has reserve and an aura of authority. But she quickly stops Bud when he calls her "Captain."

"No one here commands in your sense. I'm just the oldest." Bud goes back to "Ma'm."

She plays a solid positional game, somewhat more erratic than a man but with occasional elegant traps. Lorimer is astonished to find that there is only one new chess opening, an interesting queen-side gambit called the Dagmar. One new opening in three centuries? He mentions it to the others when they come back from helping Andy and Judy Paris overhaul a standby converter.

"They haven't done much anywhere," Dave says. "Most of your new stuff dates from the epidemic, Andy, if you'll pardon me. The program seems to be stagnating. You've been gearing up this Titan project for eighty years."

"We'll get there." Andy grins.

"C'mon Dave," says Bud. "Judy and me are taking on you two for the next chicken dinner, we'll get a bridge team here yet. Woo-ee, I can taste that chicken! Losers get the iguana."

The food is so good. Lorimer finds himself lingering around the kitchen end, helping whoever is cooking, munching on their various seeds and chewy roots as he listens to them talk. He even likes the iguana. He begins to put on weight, in fact they all do. Dave decrees double exercise shifts.

"You going to make us *climb* home, Dave-o?" Bud groans. But Lorimer enjoys it, pedalling or swinging easily along the rungs while the women chat and listen to tapes. Familiar music: he identifies a strange spectrum from Handel, Brahms, Sibelius, through Strauss to ballad tunes and intricate light jazz-rock. No lyrics. But plenty of informative texts doubtless selected for his benefit.

From the promised short history he finds out more about the epidemic. It seems to have been an air-borne quasi-virus escaped from Franco-Arab military labs, possibly potentiated by pollutants.

"It apparently damaged only the reproductive cells," he tells Dave and Bud. "There was little actual mortality, but almost universal sterility. Probably a molecular substitution in the gene code in the gametes. And the main effect seems to have been on the men. They mention a shortage of male births afterwards, which suggests that the damage was on the Y-chromosome where it would be selectively lethal to the male fetus."

"Is it still dangerous, Doc?" Dave asks. "What happens to us when we get back home?"

"They can't say. The birth-rate is normal now, about two percent and rising. But the present population may be resistant. They never achieved a vaccine."

"Only one way to tell," Bud says gravely. "I volunteer."

Dave merely glances at him. Extraordinary how he still commands, Lorimer thinks. Not submission, for Pete's sake. A team.

The history also mentions the riots and fighting which swept the world when humanity found itself sterile. Cities bombed, and burned, massacres, panics, mass rapes and kidnapping of women, marauding armies of biologically desperate men, bloody cults. The crazies. But it is all so briefly told, so long ago. Lists of honoured names. "We must always be grateful to the brave people who held the Denver Medical Laboratories—" And then on to the drama of building up the helium supply for the dirigibles.

In three centuries it's all dust, he thinks. What do I know of the hideous Thirty Years War that was three centuries back for me? *Fighting devastated Europe for two generations.* Not even names.

JAMES TIPTREE, JR.   249

The description of their political and economic structure is
even briefer. They seem to be, as Myda had said, almost un-
governed.

"It's a form of loose social credit system run by
consensus," he says to Dave. "Somewhat like a permanent
frontier period. They're building up slowly. Of course they
don't need an army or airforce. I'm not sure if they even use
cash money or recognise private ownership of land. I did notice one favorable reference to early Chinese communalism,"
he adds to see Dave's mouth set. "But they aren't tied to a
community. They travel about. When I asked Lady Blue
about their police and legal system she told me to wait and
talk with real historians. This Registry seems to be just that,
it's not a policy organ."

"We've run into a situation here, Lorimer," Dave says so-
berly. "Stay away from it. They're not telling the story."

"You notice they never talk about their husbands?" Bud
laughs. "I asked a couple of them what their husbands did
and I swear they had to think. And they all have kids. Believe me, it's a swinging scene down there, even if old Andy
acts like he hasn't found out what it's for."

"I don't want any prying into their personal family lives
while we're on this ship, Geirr. None whatsoever. That's an
order."

"Maybe they don't have families. You ever hear 'em mention anybody getting married? That has to be the one thing
on a chick's mind. Mark my words, there's been some
changes made."

"The social mores are bound to have changed to some extent," Lorimer says. "Obviously you have women doing more
work outside the home, for one thing. But they have family
bonds; for instance Lady Blue has a sister in an aluminum
mill and another in health. Andy's mother is on Mars and his
sister works in Registry. Connie has a brother or brothers on
the fishing fleet near Biloxi, and her sister is coming out to
replace her here next trip, she's making yeast now."

"That's the top of the iceberg."

"I doubt the rest of the iceberg is very sinister, Dave."

But somewhere along the line the blandness begins to
bother Lorimer too. So much is missing. Marriage, love-af-
fairs, children's troubles, jealousy squabbles, status, possessions, money problems, sicknesses, funerals even—all the
daily minutiae that occupied Ginny and her friends seems to
have been edited out of these women's talk. *Edited.* . . . Can

Dave be right, is some big, significant aspect being deliberately kept from them?

"I'm still surprised your language hasn't changed more," he says one day to Connie during their exertions in the gym.

"Oh, we're very careful about that." She climbs at an angle beside him, not using her hands. "It would be a dreadful loss if we couldn't understand the books. All the children are taught from the same original tapes, you see. Oh, there's faddy words we use for a while, but our communicators have to learn the old texts by heart, that keeps us together."

Judy Paris grunts from the pedicycle. "You, my dear children, will never know the oppression we suffered," she declaims mockingly.

"Judys talk too much," says Connie.

"We do, for a fact." They both laugh.

"So you still read our so-called great books, our fiction and poetry?" asks Lorimer. "Who do you read, H.G. Wells? Shakespeare? Dickens, ah, Balzac, Kipling, Brian?" He gropes; Brian had been a bestseller Ginny liked. When had he last looked at Shakespeare or the others?

"Oh, the historicals," Judy says. "It's interesting, I guess. Grim. They're not very realistic. I'm sure it was to you," she adds generously.

And they turn to discussing whether the laying hens are getting too much light, leaving Lorimer to wonder how what he supposes are the eternal verities of human nature can have faded from a world's reality. Love, conflict, heroism, tragedy—all "unrealistic"? Well, flight crews are never great readers; still, women read more. . . . Something *has* changed, he can sense it. Something basic enough to affect human nature. A physical development perhaps; a mutation? What is really under those floating clothes?

It is the Judys who give him part of it.

He is exercising alone with both of them, listening to them gossip about some legendary figure named Dagmar.

"The Dagmar who invented the chess opening?" he asks.

"Yes. She does anything, when she's good she's great."

"Was she bad sometimes?"

A Judy laughs. "The Dagmar problem, you can say. She has this tendency to organise everything. It's fine when it works but every so often it runs wild, she thinks she's queen or what. Then they have to get out the butterfly nets."

All in present tense—but Lady Blue has told him the Dagmar gambit is over a century old.

Longevity, he thinks; by god, that's what they're hiding. Say they've achieved a doubled or tripled life span, that would certainly change human psychology, affect their outlook, on everything. Delayed maturity, perhaps? We were working on endocrine cell juvenescence when I left. How old are these girls, for instance?

He is framing a question when Judy Dakar says, "I was in the creche when she went pluggo. But she's good, I loved her later on."

Lorimer thinks she has said "crash" and then realises she means a communal nursery. "Is that the same Dagmar?" he asks. "She must be very old."

"Oh no, her sister."

"A sister a hundred years apart?"

"I mean, her daughter. Her, her *grand*-daughter." She starts pedalling fast.

"Judys," says her twin, behind them.

Sister again. Everybody he learns of seems to have an extraordinary number of sisters, Lorimer reflects. He hears Judy Paris saying to her twin, "I think I remember Dagmar at the creche. She started uniforms for everybody. Colors and numbers."

"You couldn't have, you weren't born," Judy Dakar retorts.

There is a silence in the drum.

Lorimer turns on the rungs to look at them. Two flushed cheerful faces stare back warily, make identical head-dipping gestures to swing the black hair out of their eyes. Identical. . . . But isn't the Dakar girl on the cycle a shade more mature, her face more weathered?

"I thought you were supposed to be twins."

"Ah, Judys talk a lot," they say together—and grin guiltily.

"You aren't sisters," he tells them. "You're what we called clones."

Another silence.

"Well, yes," says Judy Dakar. "We call it sisters. Oh, mother! We weren't supposed to tell you, Myda said you would be frightfully upset. It was illegal in your day, true?"

"Yes. We considered it immoral and unethical, experimenting with human life. But it doesn't upset me personally."

"Oh, that's beautiful, that's great," they say together. "We think of you as different," Judy Paris blurts, "you're more hu—more like us. Please, you don't have to tell the others, do you? Oh, *please* don't."

"It was an accident there were two of us here," says Judy Dakar. "Myda *warned* us. Can't you wait a little while?" Two identical pairs of dark eyes beg him.

"Very well," he says slowly. "I won't tell my friends for the time being. But if I keep your secret you have to answer some questions. For instance, how many of your people are created artificially this way?"

He begins to realise he *is* somewhat upset. Dave is right, damn it, they are hiding things. Is this brave new world populated by subhuman slaves, run by master brains? Decorticate zombies, workers without stomachs or sex, human cortexes wired into machines, monstrous experiments rush through his mind. He had been naive again. These normal-looking women can be fronting for a hideous world.

"How many?"

"There's only about eleven thousand of us," Judy Dakar says. The two Judys look at each other, transparently confirming something. They're unschooled in deception, Lorimer thinks; is that good? And is diverted by Judy Paris exclaiming, "What we can't figure out is why did you think it was wrong?"

Lorimer tries to tell them, to convey the horror of manipulating human identity, creating abnormal life. The threat to individuality, the fearful power it would put in a dictator's hand.

"Dictator?" one of them echoes blankly. He looks at their faces and can only say, "Doing things to people without their consent. I think it's sad."

"But that's just what we think about you," the younger Judy bursts out. "How do you know who you *are*? Or who anybody is? All alone, no sisters to share with! You don't know what you can do, or what would be interesting to try. All you poor singletons, you—why, you just have to blunder along and die, all for nothing!"

Her voice trembles. Amazed, Lorimer sees both of them are misty-eyed.

"We better get this m-moving," the other Judy says.

They swing back into the rhythm and in bits and pieces Lorimer finds out how it is. Not bottled embryos, they tell him indignantly. Human mothers like everybody else, young mothers, the best kind. A somatic cell nucleus is inserted in an enucleated ovum and re-implanted in the womb. They have each borne two "sister" babies in their late teens and nursed them a while before moving on. The creches always have plenty of mothers.

His longevity notion is laughed at; nothing but some rules of healthy living have as yet been achieved. "We should make ninety in good shape," they assure him. "A hundred and eight, that was Judy Eagle, she's our record. But she was pretty blah at the end."

The clone-strains themselves are old, they date from the epidemic. They were part of the first effort to save the race when the babies stopped and they've continued ever since.

"It's so perfect," they tell him. "We each have a book, it's really a library. All the recorded messages. The Book of Judy Shapiro, that's us. Dakar and Paris are our personal names, we're doing cities now." They laugh, trying not to talk at once about how each Judy adds her individual memoir, her adventures and problems and discoveries in the genotype they all share.

"If you make a mistake it's useful for the others. Of course you try not to—or at least make a *new* one."

"Some of the old ones aren't so realistic," her other self puts in. "Things were so different, I guess. We make excerpts of the parts we like best. And practical things, like Judys should watch out for skin cancer."

"But we have to read the whole thing every ten years," says the Judy called Dakar. "It's inspiring. As you get older you understand some of the ones you didn't before."

Bemused, Lorimer tries to think how it would be, hearing the voices of three hundred years of Orren Lorimers. Lorimers who were mathematicians or plumbers or artists or bums or criminals, maybe. The continuing exploration and completion of self. And a dozen living doubles; aged Lorimers, infant Lorimers. And other Lorimers' women and children ... would he enjoy it or resent it? He doesn't know.

"Have you made your records yet?"

"Oh, we're too young. Just notes in case of accident."

"Will we be in them?"

"You can say!" They laugh merrily, then sober. "Truly you won't tell?" Judy Paris asks. "Lady Blue, we have to let her know what we did. Oof. But truly you won't tell your friends?"

He hadn't told on them, he thinks now, emerging back into his living self. Connie beside him is drinking cider from a bulb. He has a drink in his hand too, he finds. But he hasn't told.

"Judys will talk." Connie shakes her head, smiling. Lorimer realises he must have gabbled out the whole thing.

"It doesn't matter," he tells her. "I would have guessed soon anyhow. There were too many clues ... Woolagongs invent, Mydas worry, Jans are brains, Billy Dees work so hard. I picked up six different stories of hydro-electric stations that were built or improved or are being run by one Lala Singh. Your whole way of life. I'm more interested in this sort of thing than a respectable physicist should be," he says wryly. "You're all clones, aren't you? Every one of you. What do Connies do?"

"You really do know." She gazes at him like a mother whose child has done something troublesome and bright. "Whew! Oh, well, Connies farm like mad, we grow things. Most of our names are plants. I'm Veronica, by the way. And of course the creches, that's our weakness. The runt mania. We tend to focus on anything smaller or weak."

Her warm eyes focus on Lorimer, who draws back involuntarily.

"We control it." She gives a hearty chuckle. "We aren't all that way. There's been engineering Connies, and we have two young sisters who love metallurgy. It's fascinating what the genotype can do if you try. The original Constantia Morelos was a chemist, she weighed ninety pounds and never saw a farm in her life." Connie looks down at her own muscular arms. "She was killed by the crazies, she fought with weapons. It's so hard to understand . . . And I had a sister Timothy who made dynamite and dug two canals and she wasn't even an andy."

"*An* andy," he says.

"Oh, dear."

"I guessed that too. Early androgen treatments."

She nods hesitantly. "Yes. We need the muscle-power for some jobs. A few. Kays are quite strong anyway. Whew!" She suddenly stretches her back, wriggles as if she'd been cramped. "Oh, I'm glad you know. It's been such a strain. We couldn't even sing."

"Why not?"

"Myda was sure we'd make mistakes, all the words we'd have had to change. We sing a lot." She softly hums a bar or two.

"What kinds of songs do you sing?"

"Oh, every kind. Adventure songs, work songs, mothering songs, roaming songs, mood songs, trouble songs, joke songs—everything."

"What about love songs?" he ventures. "Do you still have, well, love?"

"Of course, how could people not love?" But she looks at him doubtfully. "The love stories I've heard from your time are so, I don't know, so weird. Grim and pluggy. It doesn't seem like love. . . . Oh, yes, we have famous love songs. Some of them are partly sad too. Like Tamil and Alcmene O, they're fated together. Connies are fated too, a little," she grins bashfully. "We love to be with Ingrid Anders. It's more one-sided. I hope there'll be an Ingrid on my next hitch. She's so exciting, she's like a little diamond."

Implications are exploding all about him, sparkling with questions. But Lorimer wants to complete the darker pattern beyond.

"Eleven thousand genotypes, two million people: that averages two hundred of each of you alive now." She nods. "I suppose it varies? There's more of some?"

"Yes, some types aren't as viable. But we haven't lost any since early days. They tried to preserve all the genes they could, we have people from all the major races and a lot of small strains. Like me, I'm the Carib Blend. Of course we'll never know what was lost. But eleven thousand is a lot, really. We all try to know every one, it's a life hobby."

A chill penetrates his ataraxia. Eleven thousand, period. That is the true population of Earth now. He thinks of two hundred tall olive-skinned women named after plants, excited by two hundred little bright Ingrids; two hundred talkative Judys, two hundred self-possessed Lady Blues, two hundred Margos and Mydas and the rest. He shivers. The heirs, the happy pall-bearers of the human race.

"So evolution ends," he says somberly.

"No, why? It's just slowed down. We do everything much slower than you did, I think. We like to experience things *fully*. We have time." She stretches again, smiling. "There's all the time."

"But you have no new genotypes. It is the end."

"Oh, but there are, now. Last century they worked out the way to make haploid nuclei combine. We can make a stripped egg-cell function like pollen," she says proudly. "I mean sperm. It's tricky, some don't come out too well. But now we're finding both Xs viable we have over a hundred new types started. Of course it's hard for them, with no sisters. The donors try to help."

Over a hundred, he thinks. Well. Maybe. . . . But "both Xs viable," what does that means? She must be referring to the epidemic. But he had figured it primarily affected the men. His mind goes happily to work on the new puzzle, ignoring a sound from somewhere that is trying to pierce his calm.

"It was a gene or genes on the X-chromosome that was injured," he guesses aloud. "Not the Y. And the lethal trait had to be recessive, right? Thus there would have been no births at all for a time, until some men recovered or were isolated long enough to manufacture undamaged X-bearing gametes. But women carry their lifetime supply of ova, they could never regenerate productively. When they mated with the recovered males only female babies would be produced since the female carries two Xs and the mother's defective gene would be compensated by a normal X from the father. But the male is XY, he receives only the mother's defective X. Thus the lethal defect would be expressed, the male fetus would be finished. . . . A planet of girls and dying men. The few odd viables died off."

"You truly do understand," she says admiringly.

The sound is becoming urgent; he refuses to hear it, there is significance here.

"So we'll be perfectly all right on Earth. No problem. In theory we can marry again and have families, daughters anyway."

"Yes," she says. "In theory."

The sound suddenly broaches his defenses, becomes the loud voice of Bud Geirr raised in song. He sounds plain drunk now. It seems to be coming from the main garden pod, the one they use to grow vegetables, not sanitation. Lorimer feels the dread alive again, rising closer. Dave ought to keep an eye on him. But Dave seems to have vanished too, he recalls seeing him go toward Control with Lady Blue.

"OH, THE SUN SHINES BRIGHT ON PRET-TY RED WI-I-ING," carols Bud.

Something should be done, Lorimer decides painfully. He stirs; it is an effort.

"Don't worry," Connie says. "Andy's with them."

"You don't know, you don't know what you've started." He pushes off toward the garden hatchway.

"—AS SHE LAY SLE-EPING, A COWBOY CREE-E-EEPING—" General laughter from the hatchway. Lorimer coasts through into the green dazzle. Beyond the radial fence of snap-beans he sees Bud sailing in an exaggerated crouch after Judy Paris. Andy hangs by the iguana cages, laughing.

Bud catches one of Judy's ankles and stops them both with a flourish, making her yellow pajamas swirl. She giggles at him upside-down, making no effort to free herself.

"I don't like this," Lorimer whispers.

"Please don't interfere." Connie has hold of his arm, anchoring them both to the tool rack. Lorimer's alarm seems to have ebbed; he will watch, let serenity return. The others have not noticed them.

"Oh, there once was an Indian maid." Bud sings more restrainedly, "Who never was a-fraid, that some buckaroo would slip it up her, ahem, ahem," he coughs ostentatiously, laughing. "Hey, Andy, I hear them calling you."

"What?" says Judy, "I don't hear anything."

"They're calling you, lad. Out there."

"Who?" asks Andy, listening.

"*They* are, for Crissake." He lets go of Judy and kicks over to Andy. "Listen, you're a great kid. Can't you see me and Judy have some business to discuss in private?" He turns Andy gently around and pushes him at the bean-stakes. "It's New Year's Eve, dummy."

Andy floats passively away through the fence of vines, raising a hand at Lorimer and Connie. Bud is back with Judy.

"Happy New Year, kitten," he smiles.

"Happy New Year. Did you do special things on New Year?" she asks curiously.

"What we did on New Year's." He chuckles, taking her shoulders in his hands. "On New Year's Eve, yes we did. Why don't I show you some of our primitive Earth customs, h'mm?"

She nods, wide-eyed.

"Well, first we wish each other well, like this." He draws her to him and lightly kisses her cheek. "Kee-rist, what a dumb bitch," he says in a totally different voice. "You can tell you've been out too long when the geeks start looking good. Knockers, ahhh——" His hand plays with her blouse. The man is unaware, Lorimer realises. He doesn't know he's drugged, he's speaking his thoughts. I must have done that. Oh, god. . . . He takes shelter behind his crystal lens, an observer in the protective light of eternity.

"And then we smooch a little." The friendly voice is back, Bud holds the girl closer, caressing her back. "Fat ass." He puts his mouth on hers; she doesn't resist. Lorimer watches

Bud's arms tighten, his hands working on her buttocks, going under her clothes. Safe in the lens his own sex stirs. Judy's arms are waving aimlessly.

Bud breaks for breath, a hand at his zipper.

"Stop staring," he says hoarsely. "One fucking more word, you'll find out what that big mouth is for. Oh, man, a flagpole. Like steel. . . . Bitch, this is your lucky day." He is baring her breasts now, big breasts. Fondling them. "Two fucking years in the ass end of noplace," he mutters, "shit on me will you? Can't wait, watch it—titty-titty-titties—"

He kisses her again quickly and smiles down at her. "Good?" he asks in his tender voice, and sinks his mouth on her nipples, his hand seeking in her thighs. She jerks and says something muffled. Lorimer's arteries are pounding with delight, with dread.

"I, I think this should stop," he makes himself say falsely, hoping he isn't saying more. Through the pulsing tension he hears Connie whisper back, it sounds like "Don't worry, Judy's very athletic." Terror stabs him, they don't know. But he can't help.

"Cunt," Bud grunts, "you have to have a cunt in there, is it froze up? You dumb cunt—" Judy's face appears briefly in her floating hair, a remote part of Lorimer's mind notes that she looks amused and uncomfortable. His being is riveted to the sight of Bud expertly controlling her body in midair, peeling down the yellow slacks. Oh god—her dark pubic mat, the thick white thighs—a perfectly normal woman, no mutation. Ohhh, god. . . . But there is suddenly a drifting shadow in the way: Andy again floating over them with something in his hands.

"You dinko, Jude?" the boy asks.

Bud's face comes up red and glaring. "Bug out, you!"

"Oh, I won't bother."

"Jee-sus Christ." Bud lunges up and grabs Andy's arm, his legs still hooked around Judy. "This is man's business, boy, do I have to spell it out?" He shifts his grip. "Shoo!"

In one swift motion he has jerked Andy close and backhanded his face hard, sending him sailing into the vines.

Bud gives a bark of laughter, bends back to Judy. Lorimer can see his erection poking through his fly. He wants to utter some warning, tell them their peril, but he can only ride the hot pleasure surging through him, melting his crystal shell. Go on, more—avidly he sees Bud mouth her breasts again and then suddenly flip her whole body over, holding her wrists behind her in one fist, his legs pinning hers. Her bare buttocks bulge up helplessly, enormous moons. "Ass-s-s," Bud groans. "Up you bitch, ahhh-hh—" He pulls her butt onto him.

Judy gives a cry, begins to struggle futilely. Lorimer's shell boils and bursts. Amid the turmoil ghosts outside are trying to rush in. And something *is* moving, a real ghost—to his dismay he sees it is Andy again, floating toward the joined bodies, holding a whirring thing. Oh, no—a camera. The fools.

"Get away!" he tries to call to the boy.

But Bud's head turns, he has seen. "You little pissass." His long arm shoots out and captures Andy's shirt, his legs still locked around Judy.

"I've had it with you." His fist slams into Andy's mouth, the camera goes spinning away. But this time Bud doesn't let him go, he is battering the boy, all of them rolling in a tangle in the air.

"Stop!" Lorimer hears himself shout, plunging at them through the beans. "Bud, stop it! You're hitting a woman."

The angry face comes around, squinting at him.

"Get lost Doc, you little fart. Get your own ass."

"Andy is a *woman*, Bud. You're hitting a girl. She's not a man."

"Huh?" Bud glances at Andy's bloody face. He shakes the shirt-front. "Where's the boobs?"

"She doesn't have breasts, but she's a woman. Her real name is Kay. They're all women. Let her go, Bud."

Bud stares at the androgyne, his legs still pinioning Judy, his penis poking the air. Andy puts up his/her hands in a vaguely combative way.

"A dyke?" says Bud slowly. "A goddam little bull dyke? This I gotta see."

He feints casually, thrusts a hand into Andy's crotch.

"No balls!" he roars. "No balls at all!" Convulsing with laughter he lets himself tip over in the air, releasing Andy, his legs letting Judy slip free. "Na-ah," he interrupts himself to grab her hair and goes on guffawing. "A dyke! Hey, dykey!" He takes hold of his hard-on, waggles it at Andy. "Eat your heart out, little dyke." Then he pulls up Judy's head. She has been watching unresisting all along.

"Take a good look, girlie. See what old Buddy has for you? Tha-a-at's what you want, say it. How long since you saw a real man, hey, dog-face?"

Maniacal laughter bubbles up in Lorimer's gut, farce too strong for fear. "She never saw a man in her life before, none of them has. You imbecile, don't you get it? There aren't any other men, they've all been dead three hundred years."

Bud slowly stops chuckling, twists around to peer at Lorimer.

"What'd I hear you say, Doc?"

"The men are all gone. They died off in the epidemic. There's nothing but women left alive on Earth."

"You mean there's, there's two million women down there and no men?" His jaw gapes. "Only little bull dykes like Andy. . . . Wait a minute. Where do they get the kids?"

"They grow them artificially. They're all girls."

"Gawd. . . ." Bud's hand clasps his drooping penis, jiggles it absently. It stiffens. "Two million hot little cunts down there, waiting for old Buddy. Gawd. The last man on Earth. . . . You don't count, Doc. And old Dave, he's full of crap."

He begins to pump himself, still holding Judy by the hair. The motion sends them slowly backward. Lorimer sees that Andy—Kay—has the camera going again. There is a big star-shaped smear of blood on the boyish face; cut lip, probably. He himself feels globed in thick air, all action spent. Not lucid.

"Two million cunts," Bud repeats. "Nobody home, nothing but pussy everywhere. I can do anything I want, any time. No more shit." He pumps faster. "They'll be spread out for miles begging for it. Clawing each other for it. All for me, King Buddy. . . . I'll have strawberries and cunt for breakfast. Hot buttered boobies, man. 'N' head, there'll be a couple little twats licking whip cream off my cock all day long. . . . Hey, I'll have contests! Only the best for old Buddy now. Not you, cow." He jerks Judy's head. "Li'l teenies, tight li'l holes. I'll make the old broads hot 'em up while I watch." He frowns slightly, working on himself. In a clinical corner of his mind Lorimer guesses the drug is retarding ejaculation. He tells himself that he should be relieved by Bud's self-absorption, is instead obscurely terrified.

"King, I'll be their god," Bud is mumbling. "They'll make statues of me, my cock a mile high, all over. . . . His Majesty's sacred balls. They'll worship it. . . . Buddy Geirr, the last cock on Earth. Oh man, if old George could see that. When the boys hear that they'll really shit themselves, woo-ee!"

He frowns harder. "They can't all be gone." His eyes rove,

find Lorimer. "Hey, Doc, there's some men left someplace, aren't there? Two or three, anyway?"

"No." Effortfully Lorimer shakes his head. "They're all dead, all of them."

"Balls." Bud twists around, peering at them. "There has to be some left. Say it." He pulls Judy's head up. "*Say it*, cunt."

"No, it's true," she says.

"No men," Andy/Kay echoes.

"You're lying." Bud scowls, frigs himself faster, thrusting his pelvis. "There has to be some men, sure there are. . . . They're hiding out in the hills, that's what it is. Hunting, living wild. . . . Old wild men, I knew it."

"Why do there have to be men?" Judy asks him, being jerked to and fro.

"Why, you stupid bitch." He doesn't look at her, thrusts furiously. "Because, dummy, otherwise nothing counts, that's why. . . . There's some men, some good old buckaroos—Buddy's a good old buckaroo—"

"Is he going to emit sperm now?" Connie whispers.

"Very likely," Lorimer says, or intends to say. The spectacle is of merely clinical interest, he tells himself, nothing to dread. One of Judy's hands clutches something: a small plastic bag. Her other hand is on her hair that Bud is yanking. It must be painful.

"Uhhh, ahh," Bud pants distressfully, "fuck away, fuck—" Suddenly he pushes Judy's head into his groin, Lorimer glimpses her nonplussed expression.

"You have a mouth, bitch, get working! . . . Take it for shit's sake, *take* it! Uh, uh—" A small oyster jets limply from him. Judy's arm goes after it with the bag as they roll over in the air.

"Geirr!"

Bewildered by the roar, Lorimer turns and sees Dave—Major Norman Davis—looming in the hatchway. His arms are out, holding back Lady Blue and the other Judy.

"Geirr! I said there would be no misconduct on this ship and I mean it. Get away from that woman!"

Bud's legs only move vaguely, he does not seem to have heard. Judy swims through them bagging the last drops.

"You, what the hell are you doing?"

In the silence Lorimer hears his own voice say, "Taking a sperm sample, I should think."

"Lorimer? Are you out of your perverted mind? Get Geirr to his quarters."

Bud slowly rotates upright. "Ah, the reverend Leroy," he says tonelessly.

"You're drunk, Geirr. Go to your quarters."

"I have news for you, Dave-o," Bud tells him in the same flat voice. "I bet you don't know we're the last men on Earth. Two million twats down there."

"I'm aware of that," Dave says furiously. "You're a drunken disgrace. Lorimer, get that man out of here."

But Lorimer feels no nerve of action stir. Dave's angry voice has pushed back the terror, created a strange hopeful stasis encapsulating them all.

"I don't have to take that any more ..." Bud's head moves back and forth, silently saying no, no, as he drifts toward Lorimer. "Nothing counts any more. All gone. What for, friends?" His forehead puckers. "Old Dave, he's a man. I'll let him have some. The dummies. . . . Poor old Doc, you're a creep but you're better'n nothing, you can have some too. . . . We'll have places, see, big spreads. Hey, we can run drags, there has to be a million good old cars down there. We can go hunting. And then we find the wild men."

Andy, or Kay, is floating toward him, wiping off blood.

"Ah, no you don't!" Bud snarls and lunges for her. As his arm stretches out Judy claps him on the triceps.

Bud gives a yell that dopplers off, his limbs thrash—and then he is floating limply, his face suddenly serene. He is breathing, Lorimer sees, releasing his own breath, watching them carefully straighten out the big body. Judy plucks her pants out of the vines, and they start towing him out through the fence. She has the camera and the specimen bag.

"I put this in the freezer, dinko?" she says to Connie as they come by. Lorimer has to look away.

Connie nods. "Kay, how's your face?"

"I felt it!" Andy/Kay says excitedly through puffed lips, "I felt physical anger, I wanted to hit him. Woo-ee!"

"Put that man in my wardroom," Dave orders as they pass. He has moved into the sunlight over the lettuce rows. Lady Blue and Judy Dakar are back by the wall, watching. Lorimer remembers what he wanted to ask.

"Dave, do you really know? Did you find out they're all women?"

Dave eyes him broodingly, floating erect with the sun on his chestnut beard and hair. The authentic features of man. Lorimer thinks of his own father, a small pale figure like himself. He feels better.

"I always knew they were trying to deceive us, Lorimer. Now that this woman has admitted the fact I understand the full extent of the tragedy."

It is his deep, mild Sunday voice. The women look at him interestedly.

"They are lost children. They have forgotten. He who made them. For generations they have lived in darkness."

"They seem to be doing all right," Lorimer hears himself say. It sounds rather foolish.

"Women are not capable of running anything. You should know that, Lorimer. Look what they've done here, it's pathetic. Marking time, that's all. Poor souls." Dave sighs gravely. "It is not their fault. I recognise that. Nobody has given them any guidance for three hundred years. Like a chicken with its head off."

Lorimer recognises his own thought; the structureless, chattering, trivial, two-million-celled protoplasmic lump.

"The head of the woman is the man," Dave said crisply. "Corinthians one eleven three. No discipline whatsoever." He stretches out his arm, holding up his crucifix as he drifts toward the wall of vines. "Mockery. Abominations." He touches the stakes and turns, framed in the green arbor.

"We were sent here, Lorimer. This is God's plan. *I* was sent here. Not you, you're as bad as they are. My middle name is Paul," he adds in a conversational tone. The sun gleams on the cross, on his uplifted face, a strong, pure, apostolic visage. Despite some intellectual reservations Lorimer feels a forgotten nerve respond.

"Oh Father, send me strength," Dave prays quietly, his eyes closed. "You have spared us from the void to bring Your light to this suffering world. I shall lead Thy erring daughters out of the darkness. I shall be a stern but merciful father to them in Thy name. Help me to teach the children Thy holy law and train them in the fear of Thy righteous wrath. Let the women learn in silence and all subjection; Timothy two eleven. They shall have sons to rule over them and glorify Thy name."

He could do it, Lorimer thinks a man like that really could get life going again. Maybe there is some mystery, some plan. I was too ready to give up. No guts. . . . He becomes aware of women whispering.

"This tape is about through." It is Judy Dakar. "Isn't that enough? He's just repeating."

"Wait," murmurs Lady Blue.

"And she brought forth a man child to rule the nations with a rod of iron, Revelations twelve five," Dave says, louder. His eyes are open now, staring intently at the crucifix. *"For God so loved the world that he sent his only begotten son."*

Lady Blud nods; Judy pushes off toward Dave. Lorimer understands, protest rising in his throat. They mustn't do that to Dave, treating him like an animal for Christ's sake, a man—

"Dave! Look out, don't let her get near you!" he shouts.

"May I look, Major? It's beautiful, what is it?" Judy is coasting close, her hand out toward the crucifix.

"She's got a hypo, watch it!"

But Dave has already wheeled round. "Do not profane, woman!"

He thrusts the cross at her like a weapon, so menacing that she recoils in mid-air and shows the glinting needle in her hand.

"Serpent!" He kicks her shoulder away, sending himself upward. "Blasphemer. All right," he snaps in his ordinary voice, "there's going to be some order around here starting now. Get over by that wall, all of you."

Astounded, Lorimer sees that Dave actually has a weapon in his other hand, a small grey handgun. He must have had it since Houston. Hope and ataraxia shrivel away, he is shocked into desperate reality.

"Major Davis," Lady Blue is saying. She is floating right at him, they all are, right at the gun. Oh God, do they know what it is?

"Stop!" he shouts at them. "Do what he says, for god's sake. That's a ballistic weapon, it can kill you. It shoots metal slugs." He begins edging toward Dave along the vines.

"Stand back." Dave gestures with the gun. "I am taking command of this ship in the name of the United States of America under God."

"Dave, put that gun away. You don't want to shoot people."

Dave sees him, swings the gun around. "I warn you, Lorimer, get over there with them. Geirr's a man, when he sobers up." He looks at the women still drifting puzzledly toward him and understands. "All right, lesson one. Watch this."

He takes deliberate aim at the iguana cages and fires. There is a pinging crack. A lizard explodes bloodily, voices cry out. A loud mechanical warble starts up and overrides everything.

"A leak!" Two bodies go streaking toward the far end, everybody is moving. In the confusion Lorimer sees Dave calmly pulling himself back to the hatchway behind them, his gun ready. He pushes frantically across the tool rack to cut him off. A spray cannister comes loose in his grip, leaving him kicking in the air. The alarm warble dies.

"You will stay here until I decide to send for you," Dave announces. He has reached the hatch, is pulling the massive lock door around. It will seal off the pod, Lorimer realises.

"Don't do it, Dave! Listen to me, you're going to kill us all." Lorimer's own internal alarms are shaking him, he knows now what all that damned volleyball has been for and he is scared to death. "Dave, listen to me!"

"Shut up." The gun swings toward him. The door is moving. Lorimer gets a foot on solidity.

"Duck! It's a bomb!" With all his strength he hurls the massive cannister at Dave's head and launches himself after it.

"Look out!" And he is sailing helplessly in slow motion, hearing the gun go off again, voices yelling. Dave must have missed him, overhead shots are tough—and then he is doubling downwards, grabbing hair. A hard blow strikes his gut, it is Dave's leg kicking past him but he has his arm under the beard, the big man bucking like a bull, throwing him around.

"Get the gun, get it!" People are bumping him, getting hit. Just as his hold slips a hand snakes by him onto Dave's shoulder and they are colliding into the hatch door in a tangle. Dave's body is suddenly no longer at war.

Lorimer pushes free, sees Dave's contorted face tip slowly backward looking at him.

"Judas—"

The eyes close. It is over.

Lorimer looks around. Lady Blue is holding the gun, sighting down the barrel.

"Put that down," he gasps, winded. She goes on examining it.

"Hey, thanks!" Andy—Kay—grins lopsidedly at him, rubbing her jaw. They are all smiling, speaking warmly to him, feeling themselves, their torn clothes. Judy Dakar has a black eye starting, Connie holds a shattered iguana by the tail.

Beside him Dave drifts breathing stertorously, his blind

face pointing at the sun. *Judas* ... Lorimer feels the last shield break inside him, desolation flooding in. *On the deck my captain lies.*

Andy-who-is-not-a-man comes over and matter-of-factly zips up Dave's jacket, takes hold of it and begins to tow him out. Judy Dakar stops them long enough to wrap the crucifix chain around his hand. Somebody laughs, not unkindly, as they go by.

For an instant Lorimer is back in that Evanston toilet. But they are gone, all the little giggling girls. All gone forever, gone with the big boys waiting outside to jeer at him. Bud is right, he thinks. Nothing counts any more. Grief and anger hammer at him. He knows now what he has been dreading: not their vulnerability, his.

"They were good men," he says bitterly. "They aren't bad men. You don't know what bad means. You did it to them, you broke them down. You made them do crazy things. Was it interesting? Did you learn enough?" His voice is trying to shake. "Everybody has aggressive fantasies. They didn't act on them. Never. Until you poisoned them."

They gaze at him in silence. "But nobody does," Connie says finally. "I mean, the fantasies."

"They were good men," Lorimer repeats elegiacally. He knows he is speaking for it all, for Dave's Father, for Bud's manhood, for himself, for Cro-Magnon, for the dinosaurs too, maybe. "I'm a man. By god yes, I'm angry. I have a right. We gave you all this, we made it all. We built your precious civilisation and your knowledge and comfort and medicines and your dreams. All of it. We protected you, we worked our balls off keeping you and your kids. It was hard. It was a fight, a bloody fight all the way. We're tough. We had to be, can't you understand? Can't you for Christ's sake understand that?"

Another silence.

"We're trying," Lady Blue sighs. "We are trying, Doctor Lorimer. Of course we enjoy your inventions and we do appreciate your evolutionary role. But you must see there's a problem. As I understand it, what you protected people from was largely other males, wasn't it? We've just had an extraordinary demonstration. You have brought history to life for us." Her wrinkled brown eyes smile at him; a small, tea-colored matron holding an obsolete artifact.

"But the fighting is long over. It ended when you did, I believe. We can hardly turn you loose on Earth, and we simply have no facilities for people with your emotional problems."

"Besides, we don't think you'd be very happy," Judy Dakar adds earnestly.

"We could clone them," says Connie. "I know there's people who would volunteer to mother. The young ones might be all right, we could try."

"We've been *over* all that." Judy Paris is drinking from the water tank. She rinses and spits into the soil bed, looking worriedly at Lorimer. "We ought to take care of that leak now, we can talk tomorrow. And tomorrow and tomorrow." She smiles at him, unselfconsciously rubbing her crotch. "I'm sure a lot of people will want to meet you."

"Put us on an island," Lorimer says wearily. "On three islands." That look; he knows that look of preoccupied compassion. His mother and sister had looked just like that the time the diseased kitten came in the yard. They had comforted it and fed it and tenderly taken it to the vet to be gassed.

An acute, complex longing for the women he has known grips him. Ginny ... dear god. His sister Amy. Poor Amy, she was good to him when they were kids. His mouth twists.

"Your problem is," he says, "if you take the risk of giving us equal rights, what could we possibly contribute?"

"Precisely," says Lady Blue. They all smile at him relievedly, not understanding that he isn't.

"I think I'll have that antidote now," he says.

Connie floats toward him, a big, warm-hearted, utterly alien woman. "I thought you'd like yours in a bulb." She smiles kindly.

"Thank you." He takes the small, pink bulb. "Just tell me," he says to Lady Blue, who is looking at the bullet gashes, "what do you call yourselves? Women's World? Liberation? Amazonia?"

"Why, we call ourselves human beings." Her eyes twinkle absently at him, go back to the bullet marks. "Humanity, mankind." She shrugs. "The human race."

The drink tastes cool going down, something like peace and freedom, he thinks. Or death.

I SEE YOU

by Damon Knight

*In his series of anthologies, Orbit, Damon Knight has
gained a reputation for being a prime literary exponent
of avant-garde writing and experimental construction in
the "science fiction" short story. We put that term in
quotes because, to us, many of Orbit's contents do not
strike us as sf at all. However Knight himself seems to
eschew that sort of thing in his own writing. He has not
produced many tales of his own lately, but, as in the following, they have been clear, concise, and strikingly
original. He should write more himself and edit less of
the other.*

You are five, hiding in a place only you know. You are
covered with bark dust, scratched by twigs, sweaty and hot.
A wind sighs in the aspen leaves. A faint steady hiss comes
from the viewer you hold in your hands; then a voice: "Lorie, I see you—under the barn, eating an apple!" A silence.
"Lorie, come on out, I see you." Another voice. "That's right,
she's in there." After a moment, sulkily: "Oh, okay."

You squirm around, raising the viewer to aim it down the
hill. As you turn the knob with your thumb, the bright image
races toward you, trees hurling themselves into red darkness
and vanishing, then the houses in the compound; and now
you see Bruce standing beside the corral, looking into his
viewer, slowly turning. His back is to you; you know you are
safe, and you sit up. A jay passes with a whir of wings,
settles on a branch. With your own eyes now you can see

268

Bruce, only a dot of blue beyond the gray shake walls of the houses. In the viewer, he is turning toward you, and you duck again. Another voice: "Children, come in and get washed for dinner now." "Aw, Aunt Ellie!" "Mom, we're playing hide and seek. Can't we just stay fifteen minutes more?" "Please, Aunt Ellie!" "No, come on in now—you'll have plenty of time after dinner." And Bruce: "Aw, okay. All out's in free." And once more they have not found you; your secret place is yours alone.

Call him Smith. He was the president of a company that bore his name and which held more than a hundred patents in the scientific instrument field. He was sixty, a widower. His only daughter and her husband had been killed in a plane crash in 1978. He had a partner who handled the business operations now; Smith spent most of his time in his own lab. In the spring of 1990 he was working on an image intensification device that was puzzling because it was too good. He had it on his bench now, aimed at a deep shadow box across the room; at the back of the box was a card ruled with black, green, red and blue lines. The only source of illumination was a single ten-watt bulb hung behind the shadow box; the light reflected from the card did not even register on his meter, and yet the image in the screen of his device was sharp and bright. When he varied the inputs to the components in a certain way, the bright image vanished and was replaced by shadows, like the ghost of another image. He had monitored every television channel, had shielded the device against radio frequencies, and the ghosts remained. Increasing the illumination did not make them clearer. They were vaguely rectilinear shapes without any coherent pattern. Occasionally a moving blur traveled slowly across them.

Smith made a disgusted sound. He opened the clamps that held the device and picked it up, reaching for the power switch with his other hand. He never touched it. As he moved the device, the ghost images had shifted; they were dancing now with the faint movements of his hand. Smith stared at them without breathing for a moment. Holding the cord, he turned slowly. The ghost images whirled, vanished, reappeared. He turned the other way; they whirled back.

Smith set the device down on the bench with care. His hands were shaking. He had the thing clamped down on the bench all the time until now. "Christ almighty, how dumb can one man get?" he asked the empty room.

You are six, almost seven, and you are being allowed to use the big viewer for the first time. You are perched on a cushion in the leather chair at the console; your brother, who has been showing you the controls with a bored and superior air, has just left the room, saying, "All right, if you know so much, do it yourself."

In fact, the controls on this machine are unfamiliar; the little viewers you have used all your life have only one knob, for nearer or farther—to move up/down, or left/right, you just point the viewer where you want to see. This machine has dials and little windows with numbers in them, and switches and pushbuttons, most of which you don't understand, but you know they are for special purposes and don't matter. The main control is a metal rod, right in front of you, with a gray plastic knob on the top. The knob is dull from years of handling; it feels warm and a little greasy in your hand. The console has a funny electric smell, but the big screen, taller than you are, is silent and dark. You can feel your heart beating against your breastbone. You grip the knob harder, push it forward just a little. The screen lights, and you are drifting across the next room as if on huge silent wheels, chairs and end tables turning into reddish silhouettes that shrink, twist and disappear as you pass through them, and for a moment you feel dizzy because when you notice the red numbers jumping in the console to your left, it is as if the whole house were passing massively and vertiginously through itself; then you are floating out the window with the same slow and steady motion, on across the sunlit pasture where two saddle horses stand with their heads up, sniffing the wind; then a stubbled field, dropping away; and now, below you, the co-op road shines like a silver-gray stream. You press the knob down to get closer, and drop with a giddy swoop; now you are rushing along the road, overtaking and passing a yellow truck, turning the knob to steer. At first you blunder into the dark trees on either side, and once the earth surges up over you in a chaos of writhing red shapes, but now you are learning, and you soar down past the crossroads, up the farther hill, and now, now you are on the big road, flying eastward, passing all the cars, rushing toward the great world where you long to be.

It took Smith six weeks to increase the efficiency of the image intensifier enough to bring up the ghost pictures clearly. When he succeeded, the image on the screen was instantly recognizable. It was a view of Jack McCranie's office; the picture was still dim, but sharp enough that Smith could see the expression on Jack's face. He was leaning back in his chair, hands behind his head. Beside him stood Peg Spatola in a purple dress, with her hand on an open folder. She was talking, and McCranie was listening. That was wrong, because Peg was not supposed to be back from Cleveland until next week.

Smith reached for the phone and punched McCranie's number.

"Yes, Tom?"

"Jack, is Peg in there?"

"Why, no—she's in Cleveland, Tom."

"Oh, yes."

McCranie sounded puzzled. "Is anything the matter?" In the screen, he had swiveled his chair and was talking to Peg, gesturing with short, choppy motions of his arm.

"No, nothing," said Smith. "That's all right, Jack, thank you." He broke the connection. After a moment he turned to the breadboard controls of the device and changed one setting slightly. In the screen, Peg turned and walked backward out of the office. When he turned the knob the other way, she repeated these actions in reverse. Smith tinkered with the other controls until he got a view of the calendar on Jack's desk. It was Friday, June 15th—last week.

Smith locked up the device and all his notes, went home and spent the rest of the day thinking.

By the end of July he had refined and miniaturized the device and had extended its sensitivity range into the infrared. He spent most of August, when he should have been on vacation, trying various methods of detecting sound through the device. By focusing on the interior of a speaker's larynx and using infrared, he was able to convert the visible vibrations of the vocal cords into sound of fair quality, but that did not satisfy him. He worked for a while on vibrations picked up from panes of glass in windows and on framed pictures, and he experimented briefly with the diaphragms in speaker systems, intercoms and telephones. He kept on into October without stopping and finally achieved a system that would give tinny but recognizable sound from any vibrating surface—a wall, a floor, even the speaker's own cheek or forehead.

He redesigned the whole device, built a prototype and tested it, tore it down, redesigned, built another. It was Christmas before he was done. Once more he locked up the device and all his plans, drawings and notes.

At home he spent the holidays experimenting with commercial adhesives in various strengths. He applied these to coated paper, let them dry, and cut the paper into rectangles. He numbered these rectangles, pasted them onto letter envelopes, some of which he stacked loose; others he bundled together and secured with rubber bands. He opened the stacks and bundles and examined them at regular intervals. Some of the labels curled up and detached themselves after twenty-six hours without leaving any conspicuous trace. He made up another batch of these, typed his home address on six of them. On each of six envelopes he typed his office address, then covered it with one of the labels. He stamped the envelopes and dropped them into a mailbox. All six, minus their labels, were delivered to the office three days later.

Just after New Year's, he told his partner that he wanted to sell out and retire. They discussed it in general terms.

Using an assumed name and a post office box number which was not his, Smith wrote to a commission agent in Boston with whom he had never had any previous dealings. He mailed the letter, with the agent's address covered by one of his labels on which he had typed a fictitious address. The label detached itself in transit; the letter was delivered. When the agent replied, Smith was watching and read the letter as a secretary typed it. The agent followed his instruction to mail his reply in an envelope without return address. The owner of the post office box turned it in marked "not here"; it went to the dead-letter office and was returned in due time, but meanwhile Smith had acknowledged the letter and had mailed, in the same way, a large amount of cash. In subsequent letters he instructed the agent to take bids for components, plans for which he enclosed, from electronics manufacturers, for plastic casings from another, and for assembly and shipping from still another company. Through a second commission agent in New York, to whom he wrote in the same way, he contracted for ten thousand copies of an instruction booklet in four colors.

Late in February he bought a house and an electronics

dealership in a small town in the Adirondacks. In March he signed over his interest in the company to his partner, cleaned out his lab and left. He sold his co-op apartment in Manhattan and his summer house in Connecticut, moved to his new home and became anonymous.

You are thirteen, chasing a fox with the big kids for the first time. They have put you in the north field, the worst place, but you know better than to leave it.

"He's in the glen."

"I see him, he's in the brook, going upstream."

You turn the viewer, racing forward through dappled shade, a brilliance of leaves: there is the glen, and now you see the fox, trotting through the shallows, blossoms of bright water at its feet.

"Ken and Nell, you come down ahead of him by the springhouse. Wanda, you and Tim and Jean stay where you are. Everybody else come upstream, but stay back till I tell you."

That's Leigh, the oldest. You turn the viewer, catch a glimpse of Bobby running downhill through the woods, his long hair flying. Then back to the glen: the fox is gone.

"He's heading up past the corncrib!"

"Okay, keep spread out on both sides everybody. Jim, can you and Edie head him off before he gets to the woods?"

"We'll try. There he is!"

And the chase is going away from you, as you knew it would, but soon you will be older, as old as Nell and Jim; then you will be in the middle of things, and your life will begin.

By trial and error, Smith has found the settings for Dallas, November 22, 1963: Dealey Plaza, 12:25 p.m. He sees the presidential motorcade making the turn onto Elm Street. Kennedy slumps forward, raising his hands to his throat. Smith presses a button to hold the moment in time. He scans behind the motorcade, finds the sixth floor of the Book Depository Building, finds the window. There is no one behind the barricade of cartons; the room is empty. He scans the nearby rooms, finds nothing. He tries the floor below. At an open window a man kneels, holding a high-powered rifle. Smith photographs him. He returns to the motorcade, watches as the second shot strikes the President. He freezes time again, scans the surrounding buildings, finds a second marksman on a roof, photographs him. Back to the motorcade. A third and fourth shot, the last blowing off the side of the President's head. Smith freezes the action again, finds two gunmen on the grassy knoll, one aiming across the top of a station wagon, one kneeling in the shrubbery. He photographs them. He turns off the power, sits for a moment, then goes to the washroom, kneels beside the toilet and vomits.

The viewer is your babysitter, your television, your telephone (the telephone lines are still up, but they are used only as signaling devices; when you know that somebody wants to talk to you, you focus your viewer on him), your library, your school. Before puberty you watch other people having sex, but even then your curiosity is easily satisfied; after an older cousin initiates you at fourteen, you are much more interested in doing it yourself. The co-op teacher monitors your studies, sometimes makes suggestions, but more and more, as you grow older, leaves you to your own devices. You are intensely interested in African prehistory, in the European theater, and in the anti-civilization of Epsilon Eridani IV. Soon you will have to choose.

New York Harbor, November 4, 1872—a cold, blustery day. A two-masted ship rides at anchor; on her stern is lettered: MARY CELESTE. Smith advances the time control. A flicker of darkness, light again, and the ship is gone. He turns back again until he finds it standing out under light canvas past Sandy Hook. Manipulating time and space controls at once, he follows it eastward through a flickering of storm and sun—loses it, finds it again, counting days as he goes. The farther eastward, the more he has to tilt the device downward, while the image of the ship tilts correspondingly away from him. Because of the angle, he can no longer keep the ship in view from a distance but must track it closely. November 21 and 22, violent storms: the ship is dashed upward by waves, falls again, visible only intermittently; it takes him five hours to pass through two days of real time. The 23rd is calmer, but on the 24th another storm blows up. Smith rubs his eyes, loses the ship, finds it again after a ten minute search.

The gale blows itself out on the morning of the 26th. The sun is bright, the sea almost dead calm. Smith is able to catch glimpses of figures on deck, tilted above dark cross-sections of the hull. A sailor is splicing a rope in the stern, two others lowering a triangular sail between the foremast and the bowsprit, and a fourth is at the helm. A little group stands leaning on the starboard rail; one of them is a woman. The next glimpse is that of a running figure who advances into the screen and disappears. Now the men are lowering a boat over the side; the rail has been removed and lies on the deck. The men drop into the boat and row away. He hears them shouting to each other but cannot make out the words.

Smith turns to the ship again: the deck is empty. He dips below to look at the hold, filled with casks, then the cabin, then the forecastle. There is no sign of anything wrong—no explosion, no fire, no trace of violence. When he looks up again, he sees the sails flapping, then bellying out full. The sea is rising. He looks for the boat, but now too much time has passed and he cannot find it. He returns to the ship and now reverses the time control, tracks it backward until the men are again in their places on deck. He looks again at the group standing at the rail; now he sees that the woman has a child in her arms. The child struggles, drops over the rail. Smith hears the woman shriek. In a moment she too is over the rail and falling into the sea.

He watches the men running, sees them launch the boat. As they pull away, he is able to keep the focus near enough to see and hear them. One calls, "My God, who's at the helm?" Another, a bearded man with a face gone tallow-pale, replies, "Never mind—row!" They are staring down into the sea. After a moment one looks up, then another. The *Mary Celeste*, with three of the four sails on her foremast set, is gliding away, slowly, now faster; now she is gone.

Smith does not run through the scene again to watch the child and her mother drown, but others do.

The production model was ready for shipping in September. It was a simplified version of the prototype, with only two controls, one for space, one for time. The range of the device was limited to one thousand miles. Nowhere on the casing of the device or in the instruction booklet was a patent number or a pending patent mentioned. Smith had called the device Ozo, perhaps because he thought it sounded vaguely Japanese. The booklet described the device as a distant viewer and gave clear, simple instructions for its use. One sentence read cryptically: "Keep Time Control set at zero." It was like "Wet Paint—Do Not Touch."

During the week of September 23, seven thousand Ozos were shipped to domestic and Canadian addresses supplied by Smith: five hundred to electronics manufacturers and suppliers, six thousand, thirty to a carton, marked "On Consignment," to TV outlets in major cities, and the rest to private citizens chosen at random. The instruction booklets were in sealed envelopes packed with each device. Three thousand more went to Europe, South and Central America, and the Middle East.

A few of the outlets which received the cartons opened them the same day, tried the devices out, and put them on sale at prices ranging from $49.95 to $125. By the following day the word was beginning to spread, and by the close of business on the third day every store was sold out. Most people who got them, either through the mail or by purchase, used them to spy on their neighbors and on people in hotels.

— In a house in Cleveland, a man watches his brother-in-law in the next room, who is watching his wife getting out of a taxi. She goes into the lobby of an apartment building. The husband watches as she gets into the elevator, rides to the fourth floor. She rings the bell beside the door marked 410. The door opens; a dark-haired man takes her in his arms; they kiss.

The brother-in-law meets him in the hall. "Don't do it, Charlie."

"Get out of my way."

"I'm not going to get out of your way, and I tell you, don't do it. Not now and not later."

"Why the hell shouldn't I?"

"Because if you do I'll kill you. If you want a divorce, OK get a divorce. But don't lay a hand on her or I'll find you the farthest place you can go."

Smith got his consignment of Ozos early in the week, took one home and left it to his store manager to put a price on the rest. He did not bother to use the production model but began at once to build another prototype. It had controls calibrated to one-hundredth of a second and one millimeter, and a timer that would allow him to stop a scene, or advance or regress it at any desired rate. He ordered some clockwork from an astronomical supply house.

A high-ranking officer in Army Intelligence, watching the first demonstration of the Ozo in the Pentagon, exclaimed, "My God, with this we could dismantle half the establishment—all we've got to do is launch interceptors when we see them push the button."

"It's a good thing Senator Burkhart can't hear you say that," said another officer. But by the next afternoon everybody had heard it.

A Baptist minister in Louisville led the first mob against an Ozo assembly plant. A month later, while civil and criminal suits against all the rioters were still pending, tapes showing each one of them in compromising or ludicrous activities were widely distributed in the area.

The commission agents who had handled the orders for the first Ozos were found out and had to leave town. Factories were fire-bombed, but others took their place.

The first Ozo was smuggled into the Soviet Union from West Germany by Katerina Belov, a member of a dissident group in Moscow, who used it to document illegal government actions. The device was seized on December 13 by the KGB; Belov and two other members of the group were arrested, imprisoned and tortured. By that time over forty other Ozos were in the hands of dissidents.

You are watching an old movie, *Bob and Ted and Carol and Alice*. The humor seems infantile and unimaginative to you; you are not interested in the actresses' occasional seminudity. What strikes you as hilarious is the coyness, the sidelong glances, smiles, grimaces hinting at things that will never be shown on the screen. You realize that these people have never seen anyone but their most intimate friends without clothing, have never seen any adult shit or piss, and would be embarrassed or disgusted if they did. Why did children say "pee-pee" and "poo-poo," and then giggle? You have read scholarly books about taboos on "bodily functions," but why was shitting worse than sneezing?

Cora Zickwolfe, who lived in a remote rural area of Arizona and whose husband commuted to Tucson, arranged with her nearest neighbor, Phyllis Mell, for each of them to keep an Ozo focused on the bulletin board in the other's kitchen. On the bulletin board was a note that said "OK." If there was any trouble and she couldn't get to the phone, she would take down the note, or if she had time, write another.

In April, 1992, about the time her husband usually got home, an intruder broke into the house and seized Mrs. Zickwolfe before she had time to get to the bulletin board. He dragged her into the bedroom and forced her to disrobe. The state troopers got there in fifteen minutes, and Cora never spoke to her friend Phyllis again.

Between 1992 and 2002 more than six hundred improvements and supplements to the Ozo were recorded. The most important of these was the power system created by focusing the Ozo at a narrow aperture on the interior of the Sun. Others included the system of satellite slave units in stationary orbits and a computerized tracer device which would keep the Ozo focused on any subject.

Using the tracer, an entomologist in Mexico City is following the ancestral line of a honey bee. The images bloom and expire, ten every second: the tracer is following each queen back to the egg, then the egg to the queen that laid it, then that queen to the egg. Tens of thousands of generations have passed; in two thousand hours, beginning with a Paleocene bee, he has traveled back into the Cretaceous. He stops at intervals to follow the bee in real time, then accelerates again. The hive is growing smaller, more primitive. Now it is only a cluster of round cells, and the bee is different, more like a wasp. His year's labor is coming to fruition. He watches, forgetting to eat, almost to breathe.

In your mother's study after she dies you find an elaborate chart of her ancestors and your father's. You retrieve the program for it, punch it in, and idly watch a random sampling, back into time, first the female line, then the male . . . a teacher of biology in Boston, a suffragette, a corn merchant, a singer, a Dutch farmer in New York, a British sailor, a German musician. Their faces glow in the screen, bright-eyes, cheeks flushed with life. Someday you too will be only a series of images in a screen.

Smith is watching the planet Mars. The clockwork which turns the Ozo to follow the planet, even when it is below the horizon, makes it possible for him to focus instantly on the surface, but he never does this. He takes up his position hundreds of thousands of miles away, then slowly approaches, in order to see the red spark grow to a disk, then to a yellow sunlit ball hanging in darkness. Now he can make out the surface features: Syrtis Major and Thoth-Nepenthes leading in a long gooseneck to Utopia and the frostcap.

The image as it swells hypnotically toward him is clear and sharp, without tremor or atmospheric distortion. It is summer in the northern hemisphere: Utopia is wide and dark. The planet fills the screen, and now he turns northward, over the cratered desert still hundreds of miles distant. A dust storm, like a yellow veil, obscures the curved neck of Thoth-Nepenthes; then he is beyond it, drifting down to the edge of the frostcap. The limb of the planet reappears; he floats like a glider over the dark surface tinted with rose and violet-gray; now he can see its nubbly texture; now he can make out individual plants. He is drifting among their gnarled gray stems, their leaves of violet horn; he sees the curious misshapen growths that may be air bladders or some grotesque analogue of blossoms. Now, at the edge of the screen, something black and spindling leaps. He follows it instantly, finds it, brings it hugely magnified into the center of the screen: a thing like a hairy beetle, its body covered with thick black hairs or spines; it stands on six jointed legs, waving its antennae, its mouth parts busy. And its four bright eyes stare into his, across forty million miles.

Smith's hair got whiter and thinner. Before the 1992 Crash, he made heavy contributions to the International Red Cross and to volunteer organizations in Europe, Asia and Africa. He got drunk periodically, but always alone. From 1993 to 1996 he stopped reading the newspapers.

He wrote down the coordinates for the plane crash in which his daughter and her husband had died, but never used them.

At intervals while dressing or looking into the bathroom mirror, he stared as if into an invisible camera and raised one finger. In his last years he wrote some poems.

We know his name. Patient researchers, using advanced scanning techniques, followed his letters back through the postal system and found him, but by that time he was safely dead.

The whole world has been at peace for more than a generation. Crime is almost unheard of. Free energy has made the world rich, but the population is stable, even though early detection has wiped out most diseases. Everyone can do whatever he likes, providing his neighbors would not disapprove, and after all, their views are the same as his own.

You are forty, a respected scholar, taking a few days out to review your life, as many people do at your age. You have watched your mother and father coupling on the night they conceived you, watched yourself growing in her womb, first a red tadpole, then a thing like an embryo chicken, then a big-headed baby kicking and squirming. You have seen yourself delivered, seen the first moment when your bloody head broke into the light. You have seen yourself staggering about the nursery in rompers, clutching a yellow plastic duck. Now you are watching yourself hiding behind the fallen tree on the hill, and you realize that there are no secret places. And beyond you in the ghostly future you know that someone is watching you as you watch; and beyond that watcher another, and beyond that another . . . Forever.